AGING IN
RURAL
AMERICA

OTHER RECENT VOLUMES IN THE SAGE FOCUS EDITIONS

AGING IN RURAL AMERICA

C. Neil Bull
editor

SAGE PUBLICATIONS
International Educational and Professional Publisher
Newbury Park   London   New Delhi

For information address:

SAGE Publications, Inc.
2455 Teller Road
Newbury Park, California 91320

SAGE Publications Ltd.
6 Bonhill Street
London EC2A 4PU
United Kingdom

SAGE Publications India Pvt. Ltd.
M-32 Market
Greater Kailash I
New Delhi 110 048 India

Printed in the United States of America

Library of Congress Cataloging-in-Publication Data

Main entry under title:

Aging in rural America / [edited by] C. Neil Bull.
     p. cm. — (Sage focus editions ; 162)
  "Published in cooperation with the Midwest Council for Social
Research in Aging."
  Includes bibliographical references and index.
  ISBN 0-8039-4885-9 (cl). — ISBN 0-8039-4886-7 (pbk.)
  1. Aged—United States—Social conditions. 2. Aged—Services for—
United States. 3. United States—Rural conditions. I. Bull, C. Neil.
HQ1064.U5A63457 1993
305.26′0973—dc20   93-25528

93 94 95 96 97 10 9 8 7 6 5 4 3 2 1

Sage Production Editor: Astrid Virding

Contents

Foreword

Aging in Rural America is further contribution to social gerontology from one of the "invisible colleges" (Crane, 1972) the Midwest Council for Social Research on Aging (MCSRA). The council, now in its 30-somethingth year, forms a network of over 184 scholars and former pre- as well as postdoctoral students from many Midwestern and neighboring universities and research centers. MCSRA's Inter-University Training program was funded by several private and federal agencies, thanks to the efforts of Warren Peterson, originally with the Institute for Community Studies in Kansas City. Funds for numerous program activities have come from collaborative MCSRA efforts of editors and writers, as witnessed by *Aging in Rural America*. The royalties from this book, as from previous ones, will go to this invisible college, guided by an official board of elected officers.

What makes MCSRA an invisible college, in Crane's terms, is the fact that although each of us has an academic home base, scattered among several states in America and Canada, together we form a separate, independent unit of scholars that engages in cooperative research, mutual education, and research training in social gerontology. The faculty served as preceptors for the fellows of the council who were located in our schools whenever we had training funds (over 25 years of our existence). Some of us doubled as directors of training under Warren Peterson's overall directorship. Others participated as visiting scholars. Fellowships were awarded on both the pre- and the postdoctoral levels. All the participants, often with several hats as time went on, the directors, members of the faculty development program, preceptors, visitors, and fellows, met several times a year and presented work in progress (the "predocs" developments on their dissertations, the "postdocs" and faculty work on their own projects). Visiting scholars offered the newest theory and methods in social gerontology and then stayed around to discuss issues, to provide suggestions as to our studies and simply to socialize on a more informal level. We came from several different disciplines, including architecture. We talked, we helped each other with references, methods, and techniques as well as ideas, and we thoroughly critiqued everything.

Our predoc fellows finished their degrees at their home universities with the help of the council, and all of us benefited, as evidenced by numerous publications. We are a productive lot! In fact, we gained not only individually, as attested by each curriculum vitae, but also collectively.

As Robert K. Merton (1973), Diane Crane (1972), Harriet Zuckerman (Zuckerman & Merton, 1973), and other sociologists of science point out, contributions to knowledge in any discipline are dependent on the invisible networks of scholars, "informal clusters of scientists collaborating at newly developing research frontiers" (see Storer, 1973).

In fact, collaboration within MCSRA has produced several major contributions to social gerontology and sociology. This includes *Older People and their Social World*, edited by Arnold Rose and Warren Peterson; *Research Instruments in Social Gerontology*, Volumes 1, 2, and 3, edited by David Mangen and Warren Peterson; *Social Bonds in Later Life*, edited by Warren Peterson and Jill Quadagno (Sage, 1985); and *The Legacy of Longevity: Health and Health Care in Later Life*, edited by Sydney Stahl (Sage, 1990). Neil Bull's *Aging in Rural America* is the next, but definitely not the last, in this series. The editors and chapter authors of these books have assigned the royalties to MCSRA, which has helped this university to continue its work even in the absence of governmental or foundations grants.

Neil Bull joined the council in 1971 as a postdoc, after arriving at the University of Missouri, Kansas City, with a PhD from the University of Oregon. He now has several titles at UMKC, including Interim Associate Dean, College of Arts and Sciences; Professor of Sociology; and Director, National Resource Center for Rural Elderly. This has not kept him from continuing creative endeavors—*The Elderly Volunteer: An*

Annotated Bibliography is scheduled to appear at the same time as this book.

Aging in Rural America is a major contribution by a number of prominent scholars to the growing and increasingly important field of social gerontology. This scientific discipline is relatively new and was severely short of interested scholars and of both theoretical and empirical content when the Midwest Council for Social Research on Aging was created. Without MCSRA, many of us from a variety of fields would not have developed an interest in gerontology or contributed to its pool of researchers and teachers. All of us who have been part of this university without walls have benefited, and it is with great pleasure that I write this foreword for the latest cooperative effort, which focuses on rural America, under the editorship of C. Neil Bull.

HELENA Z. LOPATA
Past President, MCSRA

Introduction

Since the publication in the mid-1980s of two excellent books on the rural elderly (Coward & Lee, 1985; Krout, 1986), social gerontologists have devoted increasing attention to the very special needs and attributes of rural older persons. The major focus of these two books was to start to answer the question, "How does the social and physical context in which rural elders live impact them in their daily lives?" I felt that it was now time to pull together in one volume some of the growing yet diverse research that updates and answers this question.

As we enter the 21st century, the need to provide services to the increasing number of elderly will become more and more acute. This book offers a review of recent findings and, when applicable, up-to-date research results. It does not include works that have as their focus the practice or service delivery aspects of rural aging because a second book, edited by John Krout (forthcoming from Sage), will bring together this information on community-based services from both researchers and practitioners.

Before reading over the individual contributions in this book, the reader should be aware that there is disagreement in the field as to just how many rural elderly there are and what constitutes "rural." First, and more easily dealt with, is the numbers of rural elderly. Approximately 1 in 4 older persons lives in a small town or rural community, or a total of just over 8 million are nonmetropolitan elders (as outlined by Clifford & Lilley in Chapter 1).

The problem of what constitutes "rural" is much more difficult. The search for a single definition of *rural* has been in progress for so long that many academics and practitioners have almost given up hoping that there will ever be a definition usable to all. Two major definitions are most commonly used. The Census Bureau defines as *rural* communities with less than 2,500 in population—this rural-urban distinction has been used in many research projects. The other distinction compares metropolitan with nonmetropolitan areas, defining nonmetropolitan areas as everything outside of *Metropolitan Statistical Areas* (MSAs). We can no longer rely on these rather simple dichotomies mainly because there is growing evidence that on some variables there is more variation within the category of *rural* (e.g., between farm and non-farm populations) than between the categories of *rural* versus *urban*.

We now need to look on the concept *rural* as a continuum rather than a dichotomy. At one end of the continuum would be our large cities, such as Los Angeles and New York, and at the other end small towns, villages, and the sparsely populated open country. There is a slow movement, especially in rural health research, toward using a continuum even though the researcher is now faced with defining a greater number of cutting points. When reading the contributions in this book, the reader must be aware what *each* author means by *rural* and what measure he or she uses.

To reach the goal of updating in a single volume the various fields that deal with the rural elderly, leading scholars were invited to contribute only original works. Each author was asked to show what is known in her or his field and relate this knowledge to either the author's ongoing research or to suggestions on what might be the next set of actions necessary for the understanding of the impact that a rural context has on the lives of older Americans. I had hoped to be able to include 24 contributions from the well over 40 outlines I received for review and thus to ensure a wide coverage of the topics pertinent to rural elders. However, page limitations forced me to reduce both the number of chapters and the size of each of the contributions.

Aging in Rural America is organized into four parts covering some of the major aspects of rural aging. The choice of which chapter belongs in which part is mine, but careful reading shows the links between many of the topics covered and I do not intend to make clear distinctions between each section.

Part I, "Characteristics of Rural Elderly", sets the background for many of the following chapters by presenting the general population statistics used to define and categorize both the numbers of rural elderly and their major characteristics and how subpopulations are looked at.

The opening chapter by William Clifford and Stephen Lilley, titled "Rural Elderly: Their Demographic Characteristics," defines what is meant by the term *rural* and then describes the characteristics of non-metropolitan persons aged 65 and over. It also examines the trends in both the numbers and the proportions of the elderly with respect to age, gender, and race. This analysis is followed by reports on marital, family, educational, poverty, and income statuses. The chapter ends with a description of the impacts of mortality and migration on the rural elderly.

Taking the theme of migration further, the second chapter by Charles Longino and William Haas, "Migration and the Rural Elderly," dispels the myth that the rural elderly are a stable population. Rather, the authors show that the elderly can be used as a bellwether of migration trends, and they demonstrate their effect on community development and return migration patterns. Such movement changes the characteristics of communities and influences the number, levels, and types of needed services.

The last chapter in this section, by Lucy Rose Fischer, "The Oldest-Old in Rural Minnesota," covers a subpopulation that is of growing importance—that of the rural elderly over the age of 85. This fastest growing segment of our population tends to be poorer and less educated as well as having less access to services. Fischer outlines a profile of the oldest-old, their important needs, resources, and activities. Even though the needs of this population are painfully obvious, there are substantial numbers who are very active and are able to live with their chronic illnesses.

Part II, "Resource Development", contains chapters that have as their emphasis the community in which rural elders find themselves—how they fit into community development, define community needs, and use the community infrastructure.

Chapter 4 by Marvin Kaiser and Henry Camp, "The Rural Aged," is the most general and shows the roles elderly play in both producing as well as using community services. The authors make the case that the elderly are not just passive recipients of services. In many rural communities, they are a substantial proportion of the population and many of them can contribute through both service and work. The authors stress that attention must be paid to ways that the elderly can make such contributions both to policy and to community development.

John McClain, J. Michael Leibowitz, Stephen Plumer, and Karin Lunt continue this theme in Chapter 5, "The Senior Center as a Community Focal Point." The authors study four senior centers as they tried to become community focal points serving the elderly and look to see how these organizations aid in community development.

Joseph Belden, in his chapter "Housing for America's Rural Elderly," covers the need for housing for the growing number of rural elderly, the present housing characteristics, and the public programs available for rural areas. He gives special emphasis to the needs of persons with lower incomes while at the same time providing urban and rural comparisons.

Another specific part of the rural infrastructure, transportation is the subject covered by Mary Kihl in Chapter 7, "The Need for Transportation Alternatives for the Rural Elderly." Kihl outlines a study of transportation needs, travel patterns, and travel preferences in a nine-county area on the Iowa-Missouri border.

Part III, "Physical and Mental Health," contains chapters covering one of the more well researched subjects with respect to rural elders. It is not surprising that attention has focused on this area as the elderly use health services so heavily and costs have increased so rapidly.

Suzanne Ortega, Martha Metroka, and David Johnson in their chapter "In Sickness and in Health" explore the paradox that rural residents and the elderly, groups with relatively poor physical health, do not appear to exhibit high rates of mental health problems as measured by depression. The authors explore the relationships between place of residence, age, physical health, and social support as they impact on depression.

Next, Margaret Penning and Neena Chappell look at rural and urban differences in "Health Promotion and Disadvantaged Elderly." This chapter examines if there are rural-urban differences in the effectiveness of a health promotion program in two Canadian provinces. Using longitudinal data, the authors focus on the economically disadvantaged elderly between the ages of 55 and 74.

The third chapter in this part, "The Rural Aged, Social Value, and Health Care" by James Thorson and F. C. Powell, also uses both rural and urban data to explain the paradox of high levels of satisfaction among the rural elderly in the face of less than adequate health services.

In her chapter "Rural Geriatric Mental Health Care," Eloise Rathbone-McCuan reviews the major issues contributing to a lack of adequate mental health services for the rural elderly. She also makes several suggestions concerning the necessary steps needed to overcome some of the critical shortages that are documented.

This third part of the book ends with a chapter by Novella Perrin, "Elder Abuse: A Rural Perspective." The author first looks at definitions of elder abuse, the incidence of abuse, theories of abuse, and assessment of this behavior. Rural-urban differences are then outlined and problems of service availability addressed.

Part IV, "Social Supports," focuses on both the formal and informal support networks. The first chapter by Betty Havens and Beverly Kyle, "Formal Long-Term Care," takes a "system approach" by examining organizations that can play the role of a single locus of responsibility by examining all available options along the continuum of care. In this manner the right mix of services to keep the elderly functioning at the most independent level possible should be chosen.

The next chapter by Gary Nelson and Mary Anne Salmon, "The Rural Factor in Developing State and Local Systems of Home and Community Care," looks at the continuum of long-term care and explores community capacity factors that influence the availability of both home and community care systems. The authors present a series of recommendations involving home and community care networks.

The third chapter in this section, by Vira Kivett, "Informal Supports Among Older Rural Minorities," focuses on minority populations that have for too long been overlooked because of a lack of sensitivity to racial and ethnic values. The author writes specific sections on African Americans, Hispanic Americans, Native Americans, and Asian Americans.

The final chapter, by Raymond Coward, Gary Lee, and Jeffrey Dwyer, "The Family Relations of Rural Elders," looks at the informal system focusing on the family as the primary support role in determining the quality of life and well-being of rural elders. The authors look at the effect residential differences have on the availability of family members, the interaction between parents and adult children, and the patterns of caregiving supplied by different family members.

I regret that certain areas were not covered in this book. Certainly much could and should be written covering the whole area of policy formation and policy implementation. Also sorely missing is more good empirical data on minority populations. This latter omission makes it very difficult to interpret national rural trends when large areas of the country, especially the South and Southwest, are dominated by minority populations whose elderly are growing in importance. Although covered briefly in several chapters here, there is also a need for more information on the sources of income of rural elders. Last, there are some specific areas that need to be updated—church and religion, crime, drug use and drug abuse, and the contributions and use of older volunteers.

I would like to thank the National Resource Center for Rural Elderly (NRCRE), funded by the Administration on Aging and situated at the University of Missouri-Kansas City, for the help they supplied through their many contacts in the rural network. It was from my helping with their preparation of a bibliography in 1990 (revised in 1991) as well as my being one of the major organizers of a conference, "The National Conference on Rural Elderly" held in Kansas City in October 1990, and again my organization of the national symposium titled "The Future of Aging in Rural America" held in Kansas City in June 1991, that allowed me to see the need for this book. The many papers presented at both of these forums led me to the outline of the areas that need greatest attention. Share Bane, the NRCRE's director, and Sandy Custard, our research assistant, provided much expertise in the early days of the project. Also, the Publication Committee of the Midwest Council for Social Research on Aging contributed guidance and suggested authors to contact. Special thanks must go to Sid Stahl for listening and guiding me through the process based on his knowledge from a previous MCSRA publication. Finally, I would like to thank the authors for their patience and the time they spent to cut their original manuscripts to meet our tight page limit.

C. NEIL BULL
University of Missouri–Kansas City

PART I

Characteristics of Rural Elderly

1

Rural Elderly
Their Demographic Characteristics

WILLIAM B. CLIFFORD
STEPHEN C. LILLEY

This chapter has as its focus the demographic characteristics of people 65 years of age and over who live in the nonmetropolitan areas of the contemporary United States. First we define *rural* and *nonmetropolitan*. Then we examine trends in the numbers and proportions of elderly across rural America and discuss age, race, and gender composition among this group. Third, we report on the marital, family, educational, poverty, and income statuses of the rural elderly. Finally, we describe the mortality and migration experiences of this population.

Rural and Nonmetropolitan

As a way of complementing the conventional rural-urban distinction, which is based on population density and size of place, the U.S. Bureau of the Census uses the designation of *Metropolitan Statistical Area (MSA)*. MSAs consist of counties (or townships in New England) that have either a city with a population of at least 50,000 or a Bureau of the Census urbanized area of at least 50,000 and a total metropolitan statistical area population of at least 100,000. People living in MSAs are the "metropolitan" population; those living outside an MSA constitute the "nonmetropolitan" population. Both metropolitan and nonmetropolitan areas contain rural and urban populations, indicating substantial heterogeneity within each category. Nevertheless, this

3

distinction probably reflects differences in settlement more accurately than the rural-urban dichotomy (Clifford, Heaton, Voss, & Fuguitt, 1985; Glasgow, 1988). This chapter uses the metropolitan-nonmetropolitan distinction as the primary unit of analysis. One major advantage is that a richer variety of data are readily available than with the conventional urban-rural distinction. Moreover, up-to-date information using the urban-rural categories are simply not available until the full release of the 1990 census.

How Many Nonmetropolitan Elderly

Of the 31 million people aged 65 and over in 1990, 8 million or 26% lived in nonmetropolitan areas and 23 million lived in metropolitan areas (Table 1.1). The percentage of elderly in nonmetropolitan areas in 1980 was 29%, indicating that the nonmetropolitan elderly are a declining proportion of the total elderly population. (Note that absolute numbers are presented in this table in order to reduce the need for additional tables. The percentages discussed in the text are derived from these numbers.) The elderly accounted for a larger proportion of the total population in nonmetropolitan counties than in metropolitan counties—15% compared to 12%. Both figures reflect increases from 1980, when the elderly made up 13% of the nonmetropolitan population and 11% of the metropolitan population (Glasgow, 1988). There were similar increases in each of the age categories above 65 years.

During the turnaround period of the 1970s, nonmetropolitan areas experienced faster growth than in the 1980s, probably associated with in-migration of the elderly into rural counties, aging-in-place, and out-migration of young persons (Lichter, Fuguitt, Heaton, & Clifford, 1981). In that decade the elderly population in metropolitan areas grew by 28% compared to 27% in nonmetropolitan areas. The decline in relative change in nonmetropolitan areas suggests a reversal of that turnaround.

The rate of population growth among the elderly exceeds that of the total population. The total national population increased from 227 million to 249 million (10%) over the decade of the 1980s, and the elderly population increased from 26 million to 31 million (19%) during this same period. In metropolitan areas, the total population increased 14% (169 million to 193 million) and the elderly 27% (18 million to 23 million). During the same period, the total nonmetropolitan population

Table 1.1 Population of the United States by Age, Race, and Gender for Metropolitan and Nonmetropolitan Areas: 1990 (in thousands)

Area, Race, and Sex	All Ages	65 and Over	65-69	70-74	75-79	80-84	85 and Over
Metropolitan							
Total	192,726	23,004	7,558	5,893	4,464	2,855	2,234
Male	93,823	9,161	3,363	2,491	1,726	972	609
Female	98,902	13,843	4,196	3,402	2,737	1,883	1,625
White	150,863	20,270	6,553	5,188	3,960	2,559	2,009
African American	25,122	1,984	705	510	373	223	173
American Indian, Eskimo, and Aleut	1,002	54	21	14	10	5	4
Other	15,738	696	280	181	121	67	47
Hispanic	20,205	1,029	388	254	188	115	83
Nonmetropolitan							
Total	55,984	8,238	2,553	2,102	1,658	1,078	847
Male	27,415	3,404	1,170	918	673	394	249
Female	28,569	4,833	1,384	1,184	984	684	598
White	48,823	7,582	2,347	1,938	1,525	994	779
African American	4,864	525	159	131	108	70	57
American Indian, Eskimo, and Aleut	956	61	22	15	12	7	5
Other	1.341	70	26	18	13	8	6
Hispanic	2,149	132	48	33	25	16	11
Total	248,710	31,342	10,112	7,995	6,121	3,934	3,080

SOURCE: U.S. Bureau of the Census, 1990 Census of Population.
NOTE: Subtotals may not add to totals because of rounding.

declined by 2% (57 million to 56 million), and the elderly grew by 11% (7 million to 8 million). The decline in the total population in nonmetropolitan areas again signals the end of the turnaround, at least for the population under 65 years of age.

It is generally true that as size of place and proximity to urban areas increases, the concentration of elderly decreases (Clifford et al., 1985). In 1980, a gradient by size of largest place ranged from 12% elderly for counties not adjacent to metropolitan areas in which the largest place was 10,000 or more persons to 15% for those counties in which the largest place was less than 2,500. Glasgow (1988) reports the percentage of elderly in nonmetropolitan areas generally is highest in villages with fewer than 2,500 inhabitants and lowest in large towns and the open countryside. The greater concentration of elderly in rural villages and small towns is largely a result of younger persons' seeking job opportunities in large urban centers leaving older populations behind (Clifford, Heaton, Lichter, & Fuguitt, 1983). Also, farmers may move into town after they retire, reducing the farm population while swelling village and small town populations with older persons (Glasgow, 1988).

The concentrations of elderly vary from region to region. However, Krout (1986) reports that in 1980 the higher proportion of population aged 65 and over found in nonmetropolitan areas existed for every census region, every census division except the Pacific, and all but 11 states (Arizona, Colorado, Florida, Louisiana, Maryland, Nevada, Oregon, Rhode Island, Tennessee, Vermont, and West Virginia). Clifford et al. (1985) indicated that in the 1970 to 1980 decade the South had the highest rate of growth in the elderly population (41%) followed by the West (39%), Northeast (29%), and North Central regions (22%). It is important *not* to assume that the highest percentages and the highest rates of growth are synonymous with the greatest numbers of the aged, especially given the varying and changing patterns of distribution. The primary concentration of older Americans *is* in cities and towns.

Age Composition

The largest number (23 million) and proportion (74%) of the elderly population resides in metropolitan areas. We find this same pattern within each age group of the elderly. There is a tendency for the percentage living in metropolitan areas to decrease with an increase in age, so that at age 85 and over the proportion living in metropolitan areas has dropped to 72.5%. Whether this is due to differentials in survivorship, to migration, or to a combination of the two is difficult to determine.

Within the elderly population the great majority are concentrated close to age 65 (58% 65-74 years of age); those aged 85 and over are a relatively small minority (10%), though they are increasing. These percentages represent less concentration at the lower end of the 65 and over scale than in the past. Zopf (1986) reports that in 1900, 71% of the elderly were between 65 and 74 and only 4% were 85 and older. In the year 2050, it is projected that 46% of the elderly will be 65-69 and 22% 85 and over. The heavy concentrations of the elderly in the "younger" group exist in both the metropolitan and nonmetropolitan populations. However, there is a slight tendency for greater proportions of the elderly in the upper age categories to live in nonmetropolitan areas than in metropolitan areas. If these patterns of distribution continue into the future, we will see greater concentrations of the "old-old" in nonmetropolitan areas.

Race Composition

Elderly African American persons have higher proportions in the ages near 65 than do white persons, and they are less represented in the older ages. Fourteen percent of the white population is 65 and over as contrasted with only 8% of the African American population (Table 1.1). The smaller relative number of African Americans to whites occurs in both metropolitan and nonmetropolitan areas. And the percentage of white and African American elderly is greater in nonmetropolitan than in metropolitan areas (16% and 13%). Higher birth and death rates contribute most to lower proportions of elderly in the African American population.

The large majority of both white and African American elderly reside in metropolitan areas with elderly African Americans much more likely than whites to live in the central cities of metropolitan areas (Krout, 1986). However, a greater percentage of white than African American elderly reside in nonmetropolitan areas (27% for whites, 21% for African Americans). Further, most of the African American nonmetropolitan elderly live in the South, and most nonmetropolitan areas outside the South have very small numbers of African American elderly (Parks, 1988).

Some general observations can be made about the Hispanic and Native American elderly. First, in 1990, 11% of the nation's 1,161,283 Hispanics lived in nonmetropolitan areas—a low percentage compared to whites or African Americans. Second, in both metropolitan and nonmetropolitan areas the relative number of elderly Hispanics is small, 5% and 6%, respectively. These low percentages of elderly are due to high fertility rates and high levels of immigration by younger Hispanics. Third, in the case of Native Americans, 53% of the 114,453 Native American (American Indian, Eskimo, and Aleut) elderly live in nonmetropolitan areas. Due to high levels of fertility in this group, the relative number of elderly for the total Native American population is small in both metropolitan and nonmetropolitan areas, 5% and 6%, respectively.

Gender Composition

Females have a greater survival potential than males at all ages because of lower death rates. As a result, men in the older ages are more likely than women to be concentrated near age 65, whereas women are distributed more evenly among the age ranges. In 1990, for instance, 36% of the nation's older men, but 46% of the women, were aged 75 and older. In contrast, 36% of the elderly males and 30% of the elderly females were 65-69 years of age (Table 1.1). A similar pattern prevails in both metropolitan and nonmetropolitan areas, with the relative number of males and females in the upper age category in the nonmetropolitan areas exceeding the relative numbers in metropolitan areas.

In 1990, 6 of every 10 older persons in the United States were female, and females outnumbered males by 6 million. A statistic often used to measure the relationship between males and females in a population is the sex ratio—the number of males per 100 females. A sex ratio indicating more females than males is found in each residence category: 67 for the total elderly population, 66 for metropolitan areas, and 70 for nonmetropolitan areas. These ratios indicate that women are more likely to reside in metropolitan areas than are males. The data also show that males make up a larger percentage of the nonmetropolitan elderly than of the metropolitan elderly. Krout (1986) suggests that this difference is largely a consequence of sex-specific migration patterns in which elderly widows often move from small towns and villages to metropolitan areas, whereas elderly widowers are more likely to remain in the rural areas. The differences in sex ratios have important and predictable influences on the marital status and living arrangements of the elderly living in nonmetropolitan and metropolitan areas.

Marital and Family Status

Current Population Survey results provide the latest data on marital and family status. For both residence categories, most men 65 and over were married and lived with their spouses; few lived alone (Table 1.2). In contrast, elderly women were much more likely to be widowed than

Table 1.2 Percentage Distribution of Persons 65 Years and Over by Marital Status for Metropolitan and Nonmetropolitan Areas—1990

	Percentages					
	Total		*Metropolitan*		*Nonmetropolitan*	
	Male	*Female*	*Male*	*Female*	*Male*	*Female*
Never married	4.2	4.9	4.5	5.3	3.4	3.9
Married, spouse present	74.3	39.7	72.8	38.8	78.3	42.4
Married, spouse absent	2.3	1.7	2.4	1.9	2.2	1.3
Separated	1.5	1.0	1.6	1.2	1.3	.6
Other	.8	.7	.8	.7	.9	.8
Widowed	14.2	48.6	15.1	48.6	11.7	48.5
Divorced	5.0	5.1	5.2	5.5	4.4	3.8

SOURCE: U.S. Bureau of the Census (1991), *Marital status and living arrangements: March 1990*, Current Population Reports, Series P-20, No. 450. Washington, DC: U.S. Government Printing Office.

married. More of the elderly of both sexes were married and fewer widowed in nonmetropolitan than in metropolitan areas, although the differences between metropolitan and nonmetropolitan widowed females were negligible.

Although very few of the current cohort of elders of either gender were divorced or separated, men were more likely than women to report these statuses. Divorce and separation occurred least frequently in the nonmetropolitan areas for both males and females. Likewise, the proportions of elderly that were never married were quite small for both sexes. Females were more likely than males to have remained single, with females in metropolitan areas having the largest proportion and nonmetropolitan males the smallest.

The family statuses of males and females differ sharply, as we might expect, based on the sex ratio and marital status data discussed above. A much greater proportion of older men were living in a family setting than were older women, regardless of residence category (Table 1.3). For the majority of these men this family included a spouse, but significantly fewer women were living in families that included a spouse. Females lived alone (about 4 out of 10) more often than did males. It is also apparent that "husband-wife families," for both elderly men and women, were more prevalent in nonmetropolitan areas than in metropolitan areas.

Some of the residential differences in marital and family statuses between males and females are due to the tendency of married women

Table 1.3 Percentage Distribution of Persons 65 Years and Over by Family
Status and Gender for Metropolitan and Nonmetropolitan Areas—
1990

	Metropolitan	Nonmetropolitan
Male		
In family groups	81	84
Husband-wife family	73	78
Other	8	6
Not in family groups	19	16
Nonfamily householder	17	15
Other	2	1
Female		
In family groups	56	54
Husband-wife family	38	42
Other	18	12
Not in family groups	44	46
Nonfamily householder	42	45
Other	2	1

SOURCE: U.S. Bureau of the Census (1990), *Household and family characteristics: March 1990 and 1989*, Current Population Reports, Series P-20, No. 447. Washington, DC: U.S. Government Printing Office.

to outlive their spouses and the lower probability of older women re-
marrying. However, migration is an important factor (Clifford, Heaton,
& Fuguitt, 1982). These researchers reported higher proportions of
people in dependent-type households moving from nonmetropolitan to
metropolitan areas. In contrast, there were relatively more independent
households among those elderly who migrated from metropolitan to
nonmetropolitan areas. They suggest that this selective migration is
likely to increase the social and economic impact of elderly residential
mobility in both metropolitan and nonmetropolitan areas.

Educational Status

The data in Table 1.4 show striking differences in years of schooling
completed among elderly living in metropolitan and nonmetropolitan
areas of the nation. A significantly higher proportion of the elderly
living in metropolitan areas (58%) completed 12 years or more of

Table 1.4 Percentage Distribution of the Elderly Population by Years of School Completed for Metropolitan and Nonmetropolitan Areas—1989

Years of school	Metropolitan	Nonmetropolitan
0-4	5.3	7.1
5-7	9.0	11.3
8	12.3	18.1
1-3 years of high school	15.6	17.0
4 years of high school	34.3	30.2
1-3 years of college	11.2	8.8
4 years of college	7.2	4.0
5 or more years	5.2	3.4

SOURCE: U.S. Bureau of the Census (1991), *Educational attainment in the U.S.: March 1989 and 1988*, Current Population Reports, Series P-20, No. 451. Washington, DC: U.S. Government Printing Office.

schooling than did the elderly in nonmetropolitan areas (46%). Over half of the elderly residing in nonmetropolitan areas have less than a 12th-grade education. In fact, 36% of the nonmetropolitan elderly completed 8 years or less compared to 27% in metropolitan areas.

Of course, the educational attainment of elderly Americans has been rising rapidly, just as it has been in the general population. This is due partly to younger people with more education aging into the 65 and over category and partly to the older ones with less education dying (U.S. Bureau of the Census, 1983). Serow and Sly (1988) report that persons aged 55-59 and 60-64, the "young-old," reported educational experiences in 1980 that were generally similar in duration to those of all segments of the population younger than themselves but that were substantially greater than those of all segments older than themselves. They suggest that this cohort and all successive cohorts who will become part of the elderly population through the year 2015 will have, at the midpoint, completed high school and will have some post-secondary education. This change in educational attainment should have some impact on tastes and expectations and the nature and type of services demanded by these older persons.

Poverty and Income

Although poverty rates decreased by nearly one half among the elderly in the period from 1970 to 1986, some significant age and

12   Demographic Characteristics

Table 1.5 Percentage of the Elderly Population in Poverty for Metropolitan and Nonmetropolitan Areas—1989

	Metropolitan		Nonmetropolitan	
Age Group	Census Definition[a]	Relative Poverty[b]	Census Definition	Relative Poverty
65-74	7.8	17.9	11.7	27.2
75-84	12.8	28.6	19.8	40.8
85+	16.0	32.8	24.6	43.8
65+	10.0	22.3	15.4	33.0
All ages	12.1	18.9	15.9	26.6

SOURCE: McLaughlin & Jensen, 1991.
[a]Census definition: Based on family money income and poverty thresholds that are determined by an "economy" food plan for families of various sizes.
[b]Relative poverty: Income-to-poverty threshold ratio that is less than one half the median family-income-to-needs ratio for the nation.

residence variations exist. The elderly in nonmetropolitan areas are more likely to be poor than their metropolitan counterparts. Moreover, the gap between them tends to increase with age, as shown in Table 1.5. Relative poverty, which is an income to needs ratio, shows much higher levels overall than the Census Bureau definition and much higher rates in nonmetropolitan areas than in metropolitan areas. For the old-old in nonmetropolitan areas, 44% report family incomes below one half of the median income to needs ratio for the rest of the population. In contrast, only 21% of the entire population have incomes below this level. McLaughlin and Jensen (1991) report that even after controlling for age, gender, race, marital status, and living arrangements, the nonmetropolitan elderly are more likely to be poor than the metropolitan elderly.

Generally, lower incomes are found among families in which the householder is 65 years of age or older. The average income of the nonpoor elderly in metropolitan areas was $30,624 compared to $22,768 for the nonmetropolitan group. In the case of the elderly poor, those in nonmetropolitan areas tended to fare slightly better than those in metropolitan areas. These slightly higher income levels among the nonmetropolitan poor ($5,258 versus $4,958) may be related to patterns of income receipt. Higher proportions of the elderly poor in nonmetropolitan areas have income from earnings, Social Security, supplemental security income, and interest income (McLaughlin & Jensen, 1991).

Table 1.6 Death Rates for Persons 65 Years and Over by Race and Gender for Metropolitan and Nonmetropolitan Areas—1970 and 1989 (rates per 1000)

	1970			1989		
	65-74	75-85	85+	65-74	75-84	85+
Metropolitan	35.9	79.6	173.0	26.0	58.3	146.3
White						
Male	48.4	101.0	200.6	33.5	76.2	176.2
Female	24.8	66.7	165.9	19.4	48.3	139.6
All other						
Male	56.1	90.3	134.9	38.0	72.3	133.3
Female	36.9	64.0	114.9	22.4	48.2	112.1
Nonmetropolitan	35.1	79.9	179.4	28.3	62.9	154.2
White						
Male	46.4	99.1	209.2	37.1	83.2	185.7
Female	23.9	66.4	169.3	19.9	49.6	143.8
All other						
Male	53.8	91.9	141.6	47.1	83.6	154.7
Female	36.8	64.4	121.1	27.0	54.6	122.6

SOURCE: U.S. Department of Health, Education and Welfare (1974 and 1992), *Vital statistics of the United States, 1970, Vol. 2—Mortality, Part B*, HRA 74-1102. Rockville, MD: Author. National Institutes of Health (mimeographed), 1992.
NOTE: The 1970 rates are based on metropolitan status as of 1973 and the 1989 rates are based on metropolitan status as of 1983.

Mortality

One distinctive feature of nonmetropolitan America has been its health status. The idea has been that rural areas are decidedly disadvantaged in terms of health status. One way to assess this idea is to examine mortality differentials between metropolitan and nonmetropolitan America. As shown in Table 1.6, the rates are consistently higher in nonmetropolitan areas than in metropolitan areas across all racial and gender categories. The data also show dramatic reductions in mortality over the period of time covered, with the greatest decline favoring the elderly in metropolitan areas. Much of this decline in the rates of mortality is associated with reduced deaths from cardiovascular diseases.

Throughout this century, African Americans have experienced higher death rates than whites, and this differential continues to persist. However, if African Americans survive until age 75 or 80, their survival potential is somewhat better than that of whites. This "crossover" effect exists for males and females and in both metropolitan and nonmetropolitan areas. In fact, the differences are more dramatic in the nonmetropolitan areas. As a whole, these findings tend to support the idea that nonmetropolitan areas are at a disadvantage in terms of health status. However, more detailed analyses would be required to describe fully the apparent differences in mortality between metropolitan and nonmetropolitan areas.

Migration

One of the notable shifts in the pattern of migration over the last two decades was the "turnaround" in the 1970s. The United States witnessed a new pattern of migration marked by deconcentration in large metropolitan areas and corresponding growth in nonmetropolitan areas. The elderly were an important part of this movement, and their movement to nonmetropolitan areas preceded that of the general population (Fuguitt & Tordella, 1980; Longino, 1982).

This pattern of migration continued into the 1980s. However, toward the end of the decade signs were appearing that the turnaround was a short-lived trend (Engels & Forstall, 1985; Long & DeAre, 1988). The data presented in Table 1.7 show that at the beginning and the end of the decade, there was a net positive exchange of elderly persons into nonmetropolitan areas from metropolitan areas. In the case of the younger population a net out-migration from metropolitan areas was evident at the beginning of the decade, but at the end of the decade it appears that younger persons were once again moving from nonmetropolitan areas to metropolitan areas. These data also indicate that the elderly migrating from nonmetropolitan areas to metropolitan areas do not favor the central cities of the metropolitan areas and that those elderly leaving metropolitan areas tend to be from the balance of metropolitan areas rather than from the central cities.

The March 1990 *Current Population Survey* also provides some insights into characteristics of movers during 1989-1990. Elderly migrants from nonmetropolitan to metropolitan areas tend to have completed more years of school than metropolitan to nonmetropolitan elderly migrants (60% versus 45% have completed high school or more). In contrast, metropolitan to nonmetropolitan migrants tend to have greater incomes than nonmetropolitan to metropolitan migrants. Also, metropolitan to nonmetropolitan migration tends to be more selective of

Table 1.7 Mobility to and from Nonmetropolitan Areas for Persons 65 Years and Over—1980-1981, 1987-1988, and 1989-1990 (in thousands)

	1980-1981		1987-1988		1989-1990	
	Under 65	65+	Under 65	65+	Under 65	65+
From outside MSAs to MSAs	2065	91	1778	42	1873	58
To central cities	851	29	779	17	804	21
To balance of MSAs	1214	62	998	26	1069	37
From MSAs to outside MSAs	2245	105	1553	98	1715	88
From central cities	1116	41	647	40	798	42
From balance of MSAs	1128	265	6547	240	6210	303
Outside MSAs at both dates	9006	265	6547	240	6210	303

SOURCE: U.S Bureau of the Census (1983 and 1991), *Geographical mobility: March 1980 to March 1981*, Current Population Reports, Series P-20, No. 377 (1983); and *Geographical mobility: March 1987 to March 1990*, Current Population Reports, Series P-20, No. 456 (1991). Washington, DC: U.S. Government Printing Office.

intact households than the opposite stream. These differentials are similar to those reported by other researchers (Clifford et al., 1982; Heaton, Clifford, & Fuguitt, 1984; Longino, 1990).

It is important to note that the elderly as a group have lower rates of mobility than other age groups and that they generally move for different reasons than the younger population. The reasons are often associated with retirement, other changes in the life cycle, a desire to be near relatives, and improved amenities. This is reflected in the fact that post-1980 change in nonmetropolitan population shows retirement counties growing four times faster than other nonmetropolitan counties (Glasgow, 1990; Glasgow & Reeder, 1990). For a more detailed discussion of migration and the rural elderly, see Chapter 2 in this book by Longino and Haas.

Conclusions

This overview of the rural elderly population in the United States has highlighted a number of demographic issues. The United States is an urban/metropolitan society, with most of its young and old populations living in metropolitan areas and with the elderly widely distributed throughout the country, although nonmetropolitan areas generally have higher proportions of population 65 and over. The absolute number of older persons increased in both residential categories, but the nonmetro-politan elderly are a declining proportion of the total elderly population. The elderly continue to experience a net migration gain in nonmetro-politan areas and, although the absolute numbers of elderly migrants are small in comparison to young migrants, nonmetropolitan areas tend to benefit from this exchange in regard to higher economic and social statuses. African Americans and other races have lower proportions of the elderly, women have higher proportions, and both are more concen-trated in metropolitan areas. The nonmetropolitan elderly have lower incomes and experience higher levels of poverty than their metropolitan counterparts. And finally, mortality rates tend to be higher in nonmetro-politan areas than in metropolitan areas.

We have considered some of the demographic characteristics of the elderly as a whole, but future work needs to give more attention to subgroups of the elderly population. Limited data restricted coverage in this analysis. Much greater attention needs to focus on the variations within the aged population. Anticipated increases in the old-old demand attention, especially given the fact that they represent such a relatively large and increasing number of the nonmetropolitan elderly.

What are the impacts of these trends and differentials? This is one of the most important gaps in our knowledge. It may be that issues such as ease of access to services or low density service provision are more critical when considering the nonmetropolitan elderly than focusing on small differences in residence at the national level. These relatively small differences may mask larger variations at the substate level. Local communities have faced differing patterns of growth in the elderly population. Set within the context of shifting patterns of population redistribution and the recent changes in the demographic components that create growth in the elderly population, a systematic analysis of the social and economic consequences of demographic changes in the elderly is needed.

Finally, the analysis points to the dilemma in discussing *nonmetro-politan* America or *the* nonmetropolitan situation. There is no homoge-neous nonmetropolitan population and there is no one nonmetropolitan situation. Instead, there are many different nonmetropolitan populations defined in different ways and made up of different subgroups. The heavy concentrations of older populations in nonmetropolitan areas call atten-tion to the special needs of this growing population. Clearly, any broad-based policy for nonmetropolitan areas should consider the spe-cial needs of the elderly.

2

Migration and the Rural Elderly

CHARLES F. LONGINO, Jr.
WILLIAM H. HAAS III

The rural elderly are often viewed as a residentially stable population. This is not true. Although city dwellers do tend to move more frequently during their lives than rural residents, long-term mobility trends stand in the background of the current demographic composition of the rural elderly population. The gradual movement of young people out of rural areas to larger population concentrations is a very old pattern. Population movement in the United States has responded to many economic and political pressures. Declining economic opportunities and weakening place ties may stimulate out-migration, whereas expanding economic opportunities tend to spur in-migration. Not surprisingly, rural communities with high birthrates and regions with limited opportunities are areas of high out-migration, whereas urban, industrial regions and communities with expanding opportunities tend to have high in-migration (Longino, 1992a; Prehn, 1986). Before 1920, a majority of U.S. citizens lived in rural areas; but since that time, the proportion in urban areas has inched up every decade, so that by 1990, 75.2% did so (U.S. Bureau of the Census, 1991).

Metropolitan deconcentration (the movement out of the big cities to smaller, but not necessarily rural, places) is another macro-level process that affects geographic mobility in our time. Many nonmetropolitan counties in the United States experienced a slowing of population decline in the 1960s; in the 1970s, their net migration rates climbed above the break-even point, signaling a genuine and widespread "metropolitan-nonmetropolitan turnaround." Older people seem to have been in the *vanguard* of migration to nonmetropolitan counties; the turnaround for them happened in the 1960s rather than the 1970s. This reversal of a long-term trend of nonmetro-to-metro migration has been of great interest to demographers. Mounting evidence now indicates that although deconcentration continues in nonmetropolitan America for the population as a whole, by the late 1980s metropolitan counties were outgrowing nonmetropolitan ones (Long & DeAre, 1980). Nonetheless, some older persons move into rural areas, and some leave them every year.

"Who Moved Among the Elderly?" is the title of the first comprehensive census analysis of the population characteristics of older movers (Biggar, 1980). At the time that Biggar wrote, a wealth of demographic literature had established that migrants are rarely a replica of the larger population from which they are drawn (Bogue, 1969). Further, the focus of migration research on labor market factors had defined migration for family, health, amenities, and other reasons as "epiphenomenal"—those migrants for whom economic selectivity principles had little application (Peterson, 1975). In this research environment, Biggar's article made a strong statement. She was able to show that elderly movers of different distances (nonmovers, local movers, intrastate migrants, and interstate migrants) had distinctive profiles. Local movers were generally not economically and socially as well off as nonmovers, and intra- and interstate migrants were more so. On average, interstate migrants had the most positive characteristics. This being the case, the geographic mobility of the elderly can make a difference to the local areas into which they move. It is not just a matter of more or fewer older residents, but what kinds of people are moving in or out and the impact that their presence or absence can have on the rural community.

It is important to understand the nature and impact of migration of the elderly in rural America for three reasons. First, many of the retirees who move to rural areas in response to the development of planned retirement communities in scenic locations tend to have strikingly different characteristics than those of the older rural population aging in place around them. Second, there is a slow depletion of the most frail elderly persons out of the rural areas into larger communities. This retreat is nearly invisible because it resembles a phased exit. And third, there is the flow of retirees to rural areas who moved from these same or nearby communities to the cities in the region when they were young and in search of greater economic opportunities. Their return changes the composite characteristics of the elderly in some interesting ways. Because of their roots and family ties, these migrants are also nearly invisible.

Metropolitan/Nonmetropolitan Elderly Migration Patterns

The Elderly as a Bellwether of Migration Trends

Older migrants are not motivated by the same constellation of pushes and pulls as younger migrants who must connect with jobs and with schools for their children. Older migrants can move to be near relatives or to engage in recreational life-styles favored by climate and geography. For this reason, older migrants are not as constrained in their choices as are others. Because they are more flexible in destination choices, they are sometimes ahead of certain migration trends.

A redistribution of the U.S. population by age occurred for several decades, largely unnoticed until the 1970s. The outlines of this change are sketched by Heaton (1981) as follows:

> Core counties of large metropolitan areas have continuously experienced net out-migration of the elderly at least since 1950, while fringe counties and smaller SMSAs have gained migrants in the same period. In the 1960s and 1970s, the out-migration from core counties has more than offset in-migration to other SMSA counties producing metropolitan net out-migration. (p. 2)

In addition, Fuguitt and Tordella (1980) demonstrate that many nonmetropolitan counties in the United States experienced a slowing of population decline in the 1960s, and in the 1970s their net migration rate climbed above the break-even point, signaling a genuine and widespread rural-urban turnaround. Older people migrate at roughly half the rate as the general population and certainly do not account for the reversal of this major, long-term trend by themselves. However, they seem to have been in the vanguard of migration to nonmetropolitan counties, showing earlier net migration increases in such places, especially those high in climatic and recreational amenities. Much of the literature posits the 1970s as the time for the turnaround. For the elderly, the 1960s seem to be the period in which it began. Other researchers have commented on the general population shifts, especially those by the aged (Golant, Rudzitis, & Daiches, 1978; Lichter, Fuguitt, Heaton, & Clifford, 1981; Long & DeAre, 1980). These observations were based entirely on reports of net migration rates, which may not reflect important volumes of change. For example, if a rural county with few older people gains a few more through in-migration, its net migration rate dramatically increases. A metropolitan county, however, would have to lose many more people to reduce its rate perceptibly. Thus, net migration stacks the deck in favor of growth in the least populated areas.

Longino (1982) sought to further document the "forerunner of change" finding of Fuguitt and Tordella (1980) using 1960 and 1970 1-in-100 samples of census microdata. The metropolitan and nonmetropolitan origins and destinations of elderly migrants in those two censuses were examined, and a matrix of "streams" between these types of environments was created.

About half the migrants were moving from one metropolitan environment to another. A much smaller proportion, from one tenth to nearly one quarter, were moving about outside metropolitan areas, thus exchanging similar nonmetropolitan environments. Among the minority (about one third) of migrants who were moving between environmental types, evidence for the metropolitan-nonmetropolitan turnaround was compelling.

In a three-decade analysis of the same trends, Longino, Wiseman, Biggar, and Flynn (1984) found that the metropolitan-to-nonmetropolitan turnaround identified earlier apparently continued in 1980. The turnaround continued not because the flow to the nonmetropolitan regions increased, as it did in 1970, but because the flow of migrants into the cities from smaller places continued to decline.

Distance of the Move as an Important Variable

Beyond the verification of the turnaround, however, the 1970 and 1980 census data also point to the importance of long-distance migrants in the process. First, although the turnaround appeared to occur both among interstate and intrastate migrants, only among the interstate migrants was there an actual increase in the percentage of those who moved out of the large cities into small communities. A decline in movement *into* metropolitan settings during the period under study accounts for the appearance of a turnaround among intrastate migrants.

The proportion who left metropolitan areas for other types of settings did not increase at all. Proportionately, then, older interstate migrants came to dominate the metropolitan-to-nonmetropolitan stream during the period under study. The implication of this finding could be of great importance to those for whom older people are either clients or a market. If long- and short-distance migrants tend to move for different reasons or differ greatly in their economic and social characteristics, then the shift that has been identified in this analysis could imply other unmeasured characteristics of new arrivals in a county (Biggar et al., 1980), such as differences in health and social service need.

Amenity Migration and Rural Economic Development

The reasons for relocation of older migrants are complex and have to do with the attraction of amenities, friendship network maintenance (Wiseman, 1980; Wiseman & Roseman, 1979), and the ability to make a psychic move of identity from one place to another (Cuba, 1984; Longino, 1992b). During early retirement, kinship functions can be managed over considerable distances. At least the support needs of the recently retired migrant (although such proximity is usually considered desirable) do not *require* the nearness of kin. Typical of migrants at this life course stage, perhaps, are those moving to retirement communities in the Sunbelt region or to nonmetropolitan small town settings. Such migrants tend to be younger, healthier, wealthier, and more often have intact marriages than other migrants. The poorer retirees often cannot afford to make such a move for the sake of amenities and life-style considerations (Litwak & Longino, 1987; Longino, 1992b).

Several studies reporting on the characteristics of older migrants showed that metropolitan-to-nonmetropolitan migrants, especially those moving longer distances, tend to have more income, to be married, and to live in their own homes. Life-style concerns, therefore, may motivate moving to areas of smaller scale more than they would encourage moves to the city (Glasgow & Beale, 1985). Sofranko, Fliegel, and Glasgow (1983) demonstrated that older metropolitan-origin newcomers living in the rural countryside have less access to goods and services than in-town newcomers but that they are more satisfied and more likely to perceive a net improvement over their former residence.

For several decades, economic development in small cities and towns has tended to emphasize only one strategy: bringing in industrial plants from larger places. Economically struggling industries, always on the lookout for pools of accessible, nonunionized labor, were willing to be courted by these communities. Unfortunately, many of these communities are not able to compete favorably with urban areas for the plants that relocate because they simply do not have the infrastructure; and because agriculture alone is not providing the necessary diversification needed to sustain economic growth in these communities, they experience economic decline.

In this context, coaxing amenity migrants into these communities seems like an ideal answer to their economic development needs. Amenity migration is a clean industry and one that boosts the local economy largely through consumerism. When retirees move across state lines, their incomes boost the local economies at their destinations. On a statewide basis these annual sums can be quite large (Glasgow, 1990; Longino & Crown, 1989, 1990).

More important, below the state level, significant economic resources are transferred to the host communities by the amenity retirement migrants. Local commerce gains new, more affluent customers. Real estate and the home construction trades benefit from the upscale tastes of the retirees. Financial institutions obtain new depositors. Local governments receive additional revenue from property and sales taxes.

A growing body of research evidence documents the positive effect of amenity migration. The Western North Carolina Retirement Migration Impact Study, for example, obtained detailed 1989 spending and financial data from 630 in-migrating retirees in the predominantly rural mountainous area (Serow & Haas, 1992). The host communities' commerce captured 87% of the in-migrants' purchases, or over $20,000 per household in 1989. This figure did not include the average $13,299 spent on a vehicle by 38% of the households in the previous year. Construction and real estate industries benefited from home purchases averaging $108,884 per purchase. These items along with utilities, insurance, and health care averaged $35,975 in expenditures during the year. Similar expenditure patterns have been documented among the migrant retirees to the New Jersey shore (Heintz, 1976) and rural areas along the southeastern U.S. coast of the Atlantic Ocean (Bennett, 1990).

The direct purchases are only the visible part of the economic impact. Multiplier effects applied to the retirees' expenditures in western North

Carolina revealed that the economic impact was double the initial amount due to the money's circulation in the local economy. As a result, the average retirement migrant household's overall impact on the local economy was $71,600. Measured by employment, each household's expenditures create 1.5 jobs at an average income of $14,900. Beyond spending, retirees to rural western North Carolina had additional inputs into the local economy. Retirees produced capital for local development by average deposits in local financial institutions of $22,719 per household. The minority (7%) had invested in local business ventures. Their investments averaged $45,921. Finally, retirees paid averages of $2,213 and $1,136 for state and local taxes. On both the state and local levels, these amounts are equal to the cost of the services the older migrants may require. In other words, they pay their way.

Numerous rural counties who have provided access to local recreational amenities have developed strong vacation industries and have later become, without much thought or effort, the location of a growing community of retired amenity migrants, many of whom had vacationed there for years. Recently, other rural areas have begun actively courting potential retired migrants. For example, North Carolina and South Carolina produce magazines for the express purpose of attracting retirees. In addition, there are now two manuals for attracting retirees for "fun and profit" (Fagan, 1988; Severinghaus, 1989).

There are good reasons for sounding a note of caution, however. Rural counties that are just now considering retirement migration as a mechanism for economic development will need to invest heavily in vigorous marketing. The demographic evidence shows that for the next 15 years there will be smaller birth cohorts coming to retirement age because of the fertility dip during the Great Depression of the 1930s. The potential supply of amenity migrants may stop growing and even shrink slightly. At the same time, an increasing number of rural counties have "discovered" retirement migration as a development strategy. Hence, competition to attract these migrants will increase just as their supply is leveling off.

There is always a conservative voice in rural communities that opposes attracting older migrants, which might be said to have a "gray peril" mentality (Longino, 1988a). Three objections are typically raised in these quarters. First, they argue, the retirees' demands will burden the health care system. In fact, what often happens is that supply follows demand. That is, amenity migrants with their Medicare cards and medigap insurance can easily purchase medical services; and, in turn, their consumption power attracts physicians to these normally underserved rural counties (Haas & Crandall, 1988).

Second, opponents suggest that retirees will vote against school bond initiatives because they have no children or grandchildren in local schools. The Western North Carolina Retirement Migration Impact Study (Serow & Haas, 1992) addressed this issue. It found that 82% of the retirees who had a chance to vote on school bond issues voted in the affirmative. Heintz (1976) reported similar findings in New Jersey.

Finally, opponents express some anxiety about whether the development of an amenity retirement economy will interfere with other types of economic growth. The retirees often are attracted by scenic amenities. Will amenity migrants work against attracting smokestack industry into their scenic paradise, thereby thwarting other economic development strategies? This possibility is a reasonable concern, as amenity migrants tend to be on the side of the environmentalists (Aday & Miles, 1982; Haas, 1980). The western North Carolina study found that almost 70% of the employment opportunities created by the retirees were in retail sales and services, a sector of the economy with lower wages and often few benefits.

Dependency Migration and the Staged Rural Exit

The major expansion of job opportunities in the first half of this century occurred within metropolitan areas, whereas the greatest decline occurred in rural areas and small towns. As a result, when the young enter the job market, they are pushed out of the nonmetropolitan areas and are attracted into the metropolitan ones by higher standards of living and greater economic opportunities. Their parents, by contrast, have fewer incentives to leave the less urban areas and small towns because, through seniority, they hold whatever jobs are available. In turn, when these older people become disabled and need household help, some may find themselves moving to their children in the city.

When older people develop chronic disabilities that make it difficult to carry out everyday household tasks such as shopping, cooking, cleaning, and emergency first aid, they experience a push to change their living environment (Jackson, Longino, Zimmerman, & Bradsher, 1991; Longino, Jackson, Zimmerman, & Bradsher, 1991). The disability is typically compounded when deficits from widowhood are added because the spouse who provides help and motivation for performing these tasks is no longer present (Bradsher, Longino, Jackson, & Zimmerman, 1992). In this situation, if older people live at a distance from their children's homes, they may have to move in order to get the services they need. If home-delivered services are readily available or if family and friends are nearby and eager to help, then a move may be forestalled. Census studies have shown that older persons moving out of non-metropolitan areas indicate higher levels of dependency than those moving into these types of locations. A higher proportion, for example, were widowed and living dependently, especially with their children, at their destination (Clifford, Heaton, & Fuguitt, 1982; Glasgow, 1980; Longino, 1980; Longino et al., 1984). These patterns are consistent across three census decades, from 1960 to 1980 (Longino, 1990). Moving to larger-scale places, therefore, may often be motivated by health and economic concerns, especially for the old-old and the widowed. The family caretaking component of these moves cannot be studied in a very focused way using census data. As we have seen, however, the national pattern clearly points to a larger dependent older population moving up the metropolitan hierarchy than those moving in the opposite direction, and more of them are living with children or in institutions, implying a higher level of need for care. The particular microprocesses by which this interplay of family caregiving and residential mobility occurs, however, must be studied at the local level.

Rowles (1983) describes this process in West Virginia as moving through a sequence of six stages. First, the children relocate. This is followed by a number of accommodation strategies so that loss of social and other support from children is compensated by shifts in support within the house and the surrounding community. The third stage features seasonal migration, when the parents visit their children's homes. In Rowles's sequence, a crisis requires the parents to relocate in the fourth stage, generally with or near to the child. After the crisis situation has stabilized, the fifth stage finds the parents holding on to their home and returning for visits to maintain it and to keep up network ties in the community. The sixth stage is severance, when the parents (or parent) no longer return. Older persons who have no children or younger relatives who live nearby may turn earlier to institutional help, and some may move to a metropolitan area where resources are superior.

Would severely disabled older persons leave nonmetropolitan areas if services were more readily available locally? The family is the basic caretaker of the elderly, and institutions tend to become involved only after the physical and emotional resources and commitment of the family are exhausted (Litwak, 1985). The scattering of the family geographically across generations, therefore, makes the residential relocation of the severely disabled segment of the older population nearly inevitable, especially in nonmetropolitan areas.

Where are the older people who do not interact very much with their adult children? According to Lee (1988), at least in Washington state, they are found more often among rural nonfarm residents than elsewhere. Those on farms and in urban places tend to be somewhat less isolated from their kin. One would expect, therefore, to find the migration solution more often used among rural nonfarm residents, particularly after widowhood, than among those in other residency categories. Greene (1984) points out that in the absence of family support, the rural elderly end up in nursing homes when they are younger and less disabled than urban persons with similar health conditions. Everyday experience confirms the more common choice of the migration option to early institutionalization. It is not unusual when asking a real estate agent in a small town about a well-kept but unoccupied house, for example, to be told that "Mrs. Smith has gone to live near her daughter in the city. She could no longer take care of herself, and she was lonely." Residential mobility is often related to family caregiving and old age, and rural nonfarm residence seems to amplify the issue.

Rural Return Migration

Nonmetropolitan communities stand out in their ability to attract interstate migrants back to their state of birth. These persons are referred to in the demography literature as *return migrants*. The Retirement Migration Project (Longino et al., 1984) found that over one quarter (26.9%) of interstate migrants who were changing from metropolitan to nonmetropolitan locations were return migrants as opposed to just over one tenth (11.8%) of those going in the opposite direction. As mentioned earlier, most migrants, regardless of their age, are not returning; those who return have some special qualities that may illuminate migration to rural America.

Longino and Serow (1992) have argued that there are two distinctive types of return migration in the United States: provincial and counterstream return migration. The hypothesis of migration for a job when one is young, ultimately followed by a return to one's roots after retirement, has appealed to theorists (Wiseman & Roseman, 1979; Wiseman &

Virden, 1977). The advantages are obvious: the retiree gains a lower cost of living (Serow, Charity, Fournier, & Rasmussen, 1986) in a location where the world-wise experience and greater retirement income give the retiree a higher status than relatives who never left. This pattern, described by French geographer Françoise Cribier (1980) as "provincial return migration," is one prototype. Research has consistently confirmed that the characteristics of migrants over age 60, on the whole, are positive, indicating a relatively high level of residential and financial independence. Collectively, these migrants are younger, married homeowners; they are more likely to be amenity migrants (Rogers & Watkins, 1987). Consequently they tend to rejuvenate and enrich the older populations in areas to which they move.

The perception that provincial return migration is a variety of amenity migration, however, contradicts the national studies that have examined the characteristics of older return migrants (Longino, 1979; Serow & Charity, 1988). These studies demonstrate that return migrants, in aggregate, are slightly more dependent, economically and socially, than nonreturn migrants of the same age. This approach, the counterstream return migration pattern, interprets elderly return migration as part of a cyclical migration process after retirement. Thus, consistent with life course theories of elderly migration, return migrants should have higher mean ages than nonreturn migrants; but this is not the case. Neither the provincial return nor the counterstream return migration model consistently explains the findings of earlier studies of migrant characteristics.

Longino and Serow hypothesized that the strong regional character of return migration offered a clue to this puzzle. Regional differences in return migration patterns were first detected by Serow (1978) and Longino (1979) when they discovered that the proportion of older migrants returning to their states of birth varied greatly between regions, a point confirmed later by Rogers (1990). In several Southern states, for example, nearly half of their older migrants were returning home. Longino and Serow expected that the aggregate characteristics of return migrants to the South and West, the two less urbanized regions, would be consistent with the profile of provincial return migrants. Conversely, counterstream return migration, consistent with the Litwak-Longino model of elderly migration, was expected to be found in counterstreams from major amenity destination states to the original states from which older migrants tend to come. Consistent with these expectations, they found return migrants to the South and West were, in the aggregate, younger and more often married and living independently, and those to the Northeast and Midwest had aggregate characteristics differing from the norm in the opposite direction. Return migrants across regions moving into the Sunbelt are more like amenity migrants, and those moving out of the Sunbelt are more like counter-stream migrants.

In studies of ethnicity and retirement migration, regional preferences are also pronounced, and return migration is much higher into states containing enduring Hispanic enclaves, primarily the South and West (Biafora & Longino, 1990). In a similar vein, Longino and Smith (1991) found that there is a high rate of interregional return migration among older African-American migrants, especially among those returning to the South. Although none of these studies explicitly separated out the return migrants and examined their unique characteristics, the inference drawn from them is that provincial return migration may largely account for the differences in region-specific characteristics of older return migrants. The South is the major regional recipient of return migrants and, in this region, interregional migrants are even more like provincial return migrants. The fact that nearly one quarter of these cross-regional migrants are not white throws an interesting light on Southern return migration (Longino, 1990). The expectation generated by these findings that interstate return migration of retirees to *nonmetropolitan regions*, particularly in the South and West, will fit the profile of provincial regional migration remains to be finally tested with 1990 census data.

Conclusions

Rowles and Watkins (1991) sum up these concerns in their recent study of the impact of elderly migration in Appalachia:

> Recent trends in Appalachia's elderly population led to a variety of concerns. How do we provide appropriate health care and service delivery to an increasingly diverse elderly population? Will relationships with local family and a supportive community sustain them? Or has social and economic change in Appalachia since World War II undermined the very existence of mecha-nisms of informal support that conditioned their expectations? Will increasing numbers of lifelong elderly Appalachians be forced to join their children in cities on the border of the region? Will it be possible to provide needed assistance to back-to-the-land and return migrants who, socialized to the services available in urban communities outside the region, may have high

expectations regarding the availability of support when they become vulnerable? And, finally, when the current cohort of amenity migrants, so warmly welcomed in the resort areas where they have invested their retirement savings, eventually ages and develops the need for extensive supportive services, will such services be available? Developing a perspective on the appropriate provision of services for such a diverse population presents a challenge to scholars and to practitioners. (p. 12)

Migration is a complicating issue in planning for a rural elderly population because it adds to the population's diversity. When local planners think of the elderly part of their population, they do not think about the "imports"—those who have moved to rural areas in response to the development of planned retirement communities in scenic locations. They may have strikingly different population characteristics than those of the older rural population aging in place around them. Yet they show up in the population statistics with which planning and program funds are justified. Second, planning for the most frail among the elderly population often assumes that they will all remain in the community, and this may not be a good planning assumption. The retreat of the most frail is nearly invisible because, as we have seen, it resembles a multi-staged exit. And third, the provincial return migrants to rural areas who moved yet may not seem like outsiders at all but simply relatives finally returning home from cities where they have worked. It is easy to forget that they are migrants. Their return, however, changes the composite population characteristics of the elderly in local areas.

3

The Oldest-Old in Rural Minnesota

LUCY ROSE FISCHER

The aging of our population is both miracle and debacle. The oldest-old—people age 85+—constitute the fastest growing segment of the population. The size of the oldest-old population is a testimony to the success of modern medicine. People are increasingly likely to survive into very old age both because of significant advances in the treatment of acute diseases and also because of accessible health care, through Medicare and Medicaid. Even so, the likelihood of suffering from an accumulation of chronic conditions rises precipitously with age. As our society ages, ever-growing numbers of people need assistance with activities of daily living and require expensive long-term care. Almost daily, newspaper reports decry the perilous rise in the cost of health care, including long-term care.

The rise in the numbers of oldest-old poses particular problems for small towns and rural communities. Rural elderly tend to be poorer and less educated and have access to fewer services, such as housing, social services, transportation services, and medical care. The lack of access is particularly a problem for health care services. To some degree, there

AUTHOR'S NOTE: The Minnesota Senior Study received funding from the Mardag Foundation; Blandin Foundation; Amherst H. Wilder Foundation; F. R. Bigelow Foundation; Minnesota Board on Aging; the Metropolitan Area Agency on Aging—Metropolitan Council; The Saint Paul Foundation; Thirteen Area Agencies on Aging in Minnesota; Hennepin County; and the Center for Urban and Regional Affairs, University of Minnesota. I would like to thank Philip W. Cooper, who did all the computer data analysis for this study, other staff at Wilder Research Center, members of the Minnesota Senior Study Advisory Committee, and the seniors who were interviewed for this project.

is more neighboring in small towns—more involvement with informal helpers, that is, relatives, friends, and neighbors. But older persons in rural areas are also more likely to live far from all their adult children, who tend to move to urban centers in search of jobs (see Fischer, Mueller, Cooper, & Chase, 1989; Newhouse & McCauley, 1987; Scott & Roberto, 1987; Zopf, 1986).

This chapter provides a profile of the oldest-old in rural Minnesota, with data from the Minnesota Senior Study. What are the characteristics of this population? What are their most important needs? What are their resources and their activities?

The Minnesota Senior Study

The Minnesota Senior Study, the first statewide survey in nearly 20 years, is based on telephone surveys in 1988-1989 with a representative statewide sample of about 3,000 non-institutionalized Minnesotans age 60 and older (see Fischer et al., 1989; Fischer, Mueller, Lossness, & Cooper,1990; Fischer, Mueller, & Cooper, 1991). The population of Minnesota is divided about equally between the Twin Cities metropolitan area, which is largely urban and suburban, and Greater Minnesota, which is comprised primarily of rural areas and small communities. The data reported here are from Greater Minnesota (about 2,400 respondents). About 6% of the sample are age 85+ (161 respondents). For much of the analysis, data on the 85+ population (the oldest-old) are compared with older persons aged 60 to 84 (the young-old). The questionnaire covered a broad range of topics: demographic characteristics; housing; transportation; health and daily functioning; social supports; employment; and participation in volunteer work.[1]

The sample is drawn from non-institutionalized elderly. Minnesota has a relatively high rate of institutionalization for the elderly, particularly at older ages. Approximately 37% of persons age 85+ live in long-term-care institutions, compared to about 24% of the oldest-old in the United States (see Longino, 1988b). The exclusion of the institutionalized elderly means that the most frail and the most needy are systematically left out of the sample.

Greater Minnesota

A disproportionate number of elderly live in Greater Minnesota: about three fifths of elderly, compared to about half of the general population, live in out-state regions. Although there are a few cities in Greater Minnesota, much of the state is very rural. Over two thirds of the sample of oldest-old live in areas with populations under 10,000. Although the older population has been growing in Greater Minnesota, the economic uncertainty of the last decade has made it increasingly difficult for small communities to provide services to the elderly, such as long-term care, transportation, and other health and social services. The recession of 1980-1982 accelerated the trend toward reduced employment in agriculture. Approximately 70,000 jobs were lost throughout Minnesota during this period of recession, with 70% of the losses occurring in Greater Minnesota. Then, during the farm crises of 1985-1986, large numbers of farms went bankrupt.

One issue of rising concern to both older and younger populations, especially in rural communities, is accessibility to and availability of medical services. Reimbursement rates are much lower in rural than in metropolitan areas, and small communities are finding it increasingly difficult to keep and recruit physicians. An article in the *Mankato Free Press* noted that

> the small-town or country doctor is becoming an endangered species, disappearing through the flight to urban centers and retirement. The flow is creating a physician shortage that is forcing small communities into hot competition for medical services. (Gersten, 1990)

Rural elderly often live very far from clinics and hospitals. For certain specialized health services, they have to travel even farther—to the Twin Cities or to the Mayo Clinic, in Rochester.

Minnesota is different from many other regions of the United States in that it is more rural and its population is relatively homogeneous. The percentage of racial minorities is small, and a large percentage of the population is Lutheran, of Scandinavian or German origins. Older Minnesotans, perhaps in part because of their ethnic and cultural heritage, are more likely to live in institutions and less likely to live with their children than elderly in other regions of the country.

Cohort Versus Age

As Table 3.1 shows (see next section), the oldest-old are strikingly different from the young-old in Greater Minnesota. A higher percentage

Table 3.1 Profile of the Oldest-Old in Greater Minnesota: Characteristics of Persons Age 85+ versus 60-84

	Age 85+	Age 60-84
Gender		
Male	25%	38%
Female	75%	62%
Marital Status		
Married	25%	70%
Widowed	69%	23%
Other	7%	7%
Education		
Less than high school	66%	42%
High school graduate	8%	34%
At least some college	26%	24%
Living Arrangement		
Alone	64%	25%
With spouse	23%	70%
With others, not spouse	13%	5%
Housing Tenure		
Own home	67%	87%
Rent unsubsidized	11%	6%
Rent subsidized	17%	5%
Other	6%	2%
Housing for Seniors		
Living in senior housing	18%	5%
Income and Poverty Status		
Per capita income	$4,956	$9,000
Below poverty	45%	13%
Below 125% of poverty	61%	23%
Veteran Status		
Men who are veterans	15%	56%
Health and Daily Functioning		
Hospitalized in last year	26%	15%
Problem eating solid food[a]	17%	7%
Vision problem[b]	38%	15%
Hearing problem[c]	20%	8%
Problems with personal care	21%	4%
Problems with preparing meals	18%	4%
Problems grocery shopping	31%	8%
Problems with light housework	14%	4%
Problems with heavy housework	67%	30%
Problems getting outside	18%	4%
At least one functional problem[d]	40%	11%

(Continued)

Table 3.1 (Continued)

	Age 85+	Age 60-84
Transportation problems		
Lack of transportation is a problem	19%	5%
Not a driver or spouse of driver	62%	11%
Deficits in Social Support System		
Have *no* living children	22%	10%
Have *no* local children	48%	41%
See friends *less* than weekly	24%	13%
No one to care if sick	26%	13%
Helping and Volunteering		
Help to families	18%	60%
Volunteer for organizations	29%	58%
Services to individuals	22%	47%
Total Unweighted Sample[e]	(161)	(2,239)
Total Weighted Sample[f]	(191)	(3,291)

NOTE: All reported differences are significant at $p<.01$.
[a]Respondents were asked: "Do you ever have difficulty eating solid food because of problems with your mouth or teeth?"
[b]Respondents were asked: "Even with glasses, do you have a vision problem that interferes with daily activities, such as reading?"
[c]Respondents were included as having a hearing problem if they could not "hear most things people say" without a hearing aid.
[d]Includes problems with personal care, preparing meals, light housework, shopping for groceries, and/or getting outside.
[e]These data are based on Phase I and Phase II of the Minnesota Senior Study, the statewide and regional samples.
[f]Data are weighted twice—by size of region and by number of persons age 60+ in the household, so that the sample represents persons age 60-84 and age 85+ living in Greater Minnesota.

are women—they are much more likely to be widowed and living alone; they have less formal education; they are much poorer; they are much more likely to have problems in daily functioning; and they tend to have fewer social involvements. There are really two reasons for these differences between the young-old and the oldest-old: the effects of aging and the impact of birth cohort. Members of a birth cohort grow up and grow old together, and their lives are affected by the same historical events.

Some of the differences between the oldest-old and the young-old clearly reflect a cohort factor. For example, a very high proportion of recently retired men are veterans. Men age 60 to 84 are almost 4 times more likely to be veterans than men age 85+. Elderly men who are currently young-old are the generation that experienced massive conscription for World War II. Conversely, most of the oldest-old were too young to fight in World War I and too old to fight in either World War II or the Korean War. Another cohort difference is educational attainment. Two-thirds of the oldest-old did not complete high school (compared to about two fifths of the young-old). A recent study of the oldest-old notes:

> This very low level of education is important in understanding the oldest old's difficulty in performing certain tasks, such as managing money. Also those with low educational levels are not likely to be sophisticated users of social services and often need extra help in making it through the bureaucratic maze. (Bould, Sanborn, & Reif, 1989, p. 43)

Other differences between the oldest-old and the young-old, however, are associated with the effects of aging. The 85+ population has a much higher percentage of women, because more women survive into very old age. Similarly, the oldest-old are much more likely to be widowed and living alone, having survived the death of their spouses. In fact, the oldest-old are survivors in another sense. Only about 1 in 10 persons in their cohort has lived to age 85. That is, they have outlived 90% of their age-peers! But among these survivors, even among the noninstitutionalized elderly, there are high levels of health and functional problems. The risk of health problems rises precipitously in very old age.

Some differences between the oldest-old and other elderly may be either age-related or cohort-related, or from some combination. The oldest-old are much more likely to be poor. This may be, in part, a cohort effect. People who are now the oldest-old were born around the turn of the century. They were in their 30s or 40s during the Great Depression, an experience that limited their accumulated wealth. Moreover, they retired 20 or more years ago, so that their income-at-retirement (except for Social Security) has been steadily devalued by inflation. But aging, as well as inflation, has eaten away at their incomes, because they have had 20 or more years to use up their income and savings.

The oldest-old are twice as likely to have no living children. This is likely to be in part because they had fewer children, since they were in their childbearing years during the Depression, a time of substantially lowered fertility rates. But aging is also a factor, since some of their children have died.

Needs of the Oldest-Old

Bette Davis put it well: "Old age is not for sissies." The profile, in Table 3.1, suggests that the oldest-old constitute an extraordinarily needy population. The oldest-old in rural Minnesota tend to have very low incomes. A substantial majority of the oldest-old are living in poverty (three fifths have incomes below 125% of the poverty level). Compared to the young-old, they are less likely to be living in their own homes and much more likely to live in senior housing, especially in housing that is government-subsidized.

Despite the fact that this sample excludes the most frail elderly, who reside in institutions, a large percentage—two fifths—have one or more functional deficits and need help with personal care, preparing meals, light housework, shopping, and/or getting outside. All of the differences between the oldest-old and the young-old in health and daily functioning, as shown in Table 3.1, are substantial.

The most common health problems in very old age are chronic conditions and functional deficits (see Bould et al., 1989). For example, nearly two fifths of this sample report having vision problems—that is, even with glasses they have a vision problem that interferes with daily activities such as reading. Many of the functional needs of the oldest-old relate to frailty and a loss of energy: not being able to do heavy housework, or even light housework; not being able to manage one's own grocery shopping or make meals; or not having sufficient strength to get outdoors without help.

A very large percentage of the oldest-old—three-fifths—do not drive a car or have a spouse who drives. The inability to drive is largely a function of health declines, including vision problems, although the sample undoubtedly includes some elderly widowed women who never learned to drive and who had depended on their spouses.

Interestingly, there is *not* a significant difference in self-reported health. A similar proportion—about two thirds—of the young-old and oldest-old report their health as good or excellent. One possible explanation for the lack of an expected age difference is that persons with acute health problems tend not to survive into very old age and/or they cannot continue to live outside of institutions.

What all of this suggests is that the oldest-old living in rural areas of Minnesota have many needs for services: income supports, housing that is subsidized and specially designed for seniors, transportation services, medical services, and long-term care. There are about 41,000 persons aged 85 and over in Greater Minnesota, living both in the community and in institutions. About half to three fifths of this population (or 21,000 to 25,000 people) require long-term care services. And about half of those with care needs are in nursing homes or other institutions. The rest are living at home with help from their families, neighbors, or formal service providers (such as public health nurses or home delivered meals programs).

Providing services to the elderly in rural areas and small towns presents special challenges. In some regions of the state, the populations are very dispersed, with densities of only 10 to 20 people per square mile. The per-person cost of transportation services, home delivered meals, home health care, and many other services is much higher for dispersed populations than for urban areas. Moreover, elderly living in remote areas often have very limited access to clinics, hospitals, and other service providers. If two fifths of the oldest-old living in these communities need help with their functional activities of daily living, what resources do they have to support them?

Social Resources

As we have noted from Table 3.1, most of the oldest-old in Greater Minnesota live alone, whereas most of the young-old live with a spouse. The oldest-old are also more likely to live with someone else, not a spouse. The someone else can include children, siblings, friends, or roommates. For widowed elderly, moving into the home of children or other relatives offers a support system: people in the household can provide personal assistance and help with household chores, meals, transportation, and companionship. But for many American elderly, living with and being dependent on children is undesirable (see Streib, 1965). The oldest-old in Minnesota are *less* likely to live with their children or other relatives than are elderly in other parts of the United States (Longino, 1988b). This may reflect the German and Scandinavian heritage of much of this population, with its strong emphasis on independence from family (Woehrer, 1978).

Nearly half of the oldest-old in Greater Minnesota have no children living nearby. Some have never had children; their children may have pre-deceased them; some have moved away from their children, often to live in lakeside retirement communities in Greater Minnesota; and for most, their children have moved away. Whatever the reason, having no children living nearby is a serious social deficit. After spouses, adult children are the most dependable caregivers for the elderly (see Fischer with Hoffman, 1984; Shanas, 1980). In fact, the oldest-old with health and functioning problems have a lot of contact with their children, *if* they have children living nearby. The great majority (nearly three quarters) of those with functional problems and with children living nearby see their children almost daily. Conversely, a large proportion of the oldest-old in rural Minnesota lack primary support-givers: they have neither spouses nor children nearby.

It is apparent, from Table 3.1, that many of the oldest-old have deficits in their social support systems. The oldest-old not only have more needs for help but they also are much more likely to lack support-givers than the young-old. Many of the oldest-old are quite isolated; almost a quarter see friends only rarely—that is, less than weekly. Similarly, about a quarter say that they would have no one to care for them if they were to become sick or disabled. The oldest-old are about twice as likely as the young-old to lack potential caregivers. For people without social supports, the line between living independently and moving to institutional care is often slim and slippery.

To get a better understanding of social resources, it is useful to look at support systems for persons with functional problems. As noted above, 40% of the oldest-old have one or more functional deficits. What are the living arrangements for very old persons with functional problems? About two thirds live alone. In fact, there is no difference in living arrangement—that is, whom they live with—between those with and without functional deficits. However, some of those living alone are in senior housing. In fact, the oldest-old who have functional deficits and who live alone are twice as likely to live in senior housing as those without functional problems. Although few senior housing facilities around Greater Minnesota offer extensive services for their residents, supportive services tend to be more available to residents of senior housing than to elderly living in their own homes. Virtually all senior housing projects have some special design features to accommodate the needs of frail seniors and persons with disabilities—such as hand railings on bathtubs, bathrooms that are wide enough so that wheelchairs can slide through, and buzzers to call for help. It is also easier for public health nurses and other service providers to reach seniors in housing projects, where they are likely to have several clients, than elderly living in their own homes, spread all around the countryside. Furthermore, there are often peer support systems in senior housing facilities, so that residents check on and help one another (Hochschild, 1973).

All together, 42% of the oldest-old in Greater Minnesota with functional deficits live alone outside of senior housing. When we make a projection to the population, we find that, in rural areas and small communities around Minnesota, there are about 4,000 very old persons who are living on their own with fairly substantial functional impairments. This figure is, however, an underestimate of the number of oldest-old who have critical needs for help and whose support systems are shaky. According to other studies, many very old couples serve as mutual caregivers, where both members of the couple are impaired and they manage with great difficulty and sometimes with help to keep living in the community (see Bould et al., 1989; Fischer & Eustis, in press).

Social Activities and Involvement

Table 3.1 includes only variables for which there are statistically significant differences between the oldest-old and the young-old in Greater Minnesota. Not shown, therefore, are the ways in which persons age 85 and older are similar to the young-old. Both the oldest-old and the young-old are similar in these respects:

- 40% see their children at least several times a week (that is, if they have living children)
- 40% talk to their children on the telephone at least several times a week (also, if they have living children)
- 62% talk on the telephone to friends at least several times a week
- 87% say they have someone to confide in

This suggests both that many of the oldest-old are *not* socially isolated and also that, in some ways, the oldest-old are *very similar to the young-old in their social involvements.*

Furthermore, it appears that the oldest-old are at least as active in senior centers as the young-old. About a third of the oldest-old say that they participate in activities at senior centers. About one quarter of the young-old participate in senior centers. The difference between the young-old and the oldest-old is not statistically significant (at $p < .01$).

It is also clear, nonetheless, that there are some important differences in levels of social activities. Table 3.1 shows that the oldest-old tend to be substantially *less* involved in helping and volunteering (see Fischer et al., 1991). They are much less likely to help their families. This includes baby-sitting for grandchildren, providing services to adult children, and caregiving. The oldest-old may give less help to their children and grandchildren, in part, because less help is needed. The children of people age 85 and older are at least in their middle years and are often seniors themselves; it would be very rare for these children to be the parents of immature children who would need babysitting. They are also well past the early years of their marriages, when they might have relied on their parents for help with setting up their households. It is also likely, however, that the oldest-old may be excused from much family helping. Even when they have great grandchildren, their relatives probably assume that they do not have the energy and strength to baby-sit for young children.

The oldest-old are about half as likely as the young-old to do formal volunteer work (help to or through organizations) or to provide informal voluntary services to neighbors and friends (help with transportation, visiting, bringing meals, and so forth). How much of the apparent decline in volunteering comes from age per se and how much is associated with problems in functioning? Even with no functional limitations, the oldest-old are less likely to volunteer, formally or informally, than the young-old. Nonetheless, older people age 85 and older *without* problems in daily functioning are much more similar to younger elderly. The implication is that *a lot of the reduced rate in formal and informal volunteering is explained by problems in functional health.*

The most common kind of informal voluntary service is help with transportation. Among the oldest-old who are able to drive (or have a spouse who drives), the rate of informal volunteering is almost as high as for the young-old. Of course, a minority of the oldest-old continue to drive (fewer than two fifths of those still living in the community are either drivers or spouses of drivers). For those who do drive, however, it appears that they also continue to help others by offering transportation—especially driving other elderly to church, grocery shopping, and so forth.

Another factor is the amount of time contributed by older volunteers. According to data from the Minnesota Senior Study, for those who volunteer, there is no significant difference by age. This finding clearly suggests that the difference in voluntary participation between the oldest-old and young-old is largely a matter of health and frailty—not age per se. The oldest-old who make a commitment to volunteer are just as involved in voluntary activities as the young-old. In other words, those who are healthy and functionally able are very similar in their activities to the young-old.

Implications

The portrait of the oldest-old in rural areas of Minnesota is both strikingly negative and positive. On the one hand, the needs of the oldest-old are painfully evident. A very high proportion are living in poverty. One might argue that living costs are not as high in small towns and rural communities as in metropolitan areas or that retirees do not have high living expenses. But the income levels for the oldest-old in these regions are extremely low. Trying to live on less than $5,000 a year has to be tough—no matter where or what the living circumstances. Whether this poverty is caused by cohort or aging factors does not matter much to the current generation of oldest-old. It is possible— although not inevitable—that future generations of elderly may be somewhat better off—but *only if* they begin their retirement years with more accumulated resources and future rates of inflation are substantially lower.

On the other hand, the portrait here also offers an argument for optimism. It is important to make a clear distinction between health problems and age. The chronic conditions that impair functioning for the oldest-old are related to diseases (Bould et al., 1989). The risk of health problems is much higher for the oldest-old than for people at younger ages, but disease and frailty are *not* inevitable for the oldest-old. Substantial numbers of very old people are very active. In fact, one of the most striking findings from this study is that the oldest-old who are functionally able are similar in most ways to the young-old. They are active in senior centers, maintain ties with friends, and help others in their community through formal and informal volunteering. Policy planners, service providers, volunteer coordinators, and others need to understand not only the needs of this population but also this positive side of the picture. The oldest-old, if they are in reasonable health, can lead active and productive lives and continue to be a resource to their communities.

Note

1. The data for this chapter are taken from Phases I and II of the Minnesota Senior Study. Phase I was the statewide survey, with approximately 1,500 interviews. Phase II provided separate reports for each of the 12 regions of Greater Minnesota. For Phase II, an additional 1,500 interviews were conducted to increase the sample to 200 in each region. The Greater Minnesota sample, therefore, is a stratified sample. For this chapter, the data have been weighted twice. The first weighting factor multiplies the sample by regional proportions. The second factor adjusts for the number of persons age 60+ in the household. A telephone survey contacts households. For this study, a weighting procedure was needed, because persons in households with two or more older persons were under-represented in the sample.

PART II

Resource Development

4

The Rural Aged

Beneficiaries and Contributors to Rural Community and Economic Development

MARVIN A. KAISER
HENRY J. CAMP

> When considering rural economic development, most people do not per-
> ceive older adults as a significant factor. Yet the two concepts are integrally
> related.
>
> *Aging and Rural Economic Development* (1989, p. 2)

Introduction: Defining the Issue

The United States, and the rest of the world, is in the midst of a major
demographic revolution, the aging of the population, that promises to
have significant effects on all parts of our society (Pifer & Bronte,
1986). Nowhere is this demographic revolution more evident than in the
rural areas of the United States. It is no secret that much of rural America
is becoming "gray America." Between 1 in 3 to 1 in 4 of all older persons
in this country reside in rural places. In the more rural states of the
Midwest the percentage of the aged living in rural areas is considerably
higher. In Kansas, for example, 61% of all older persons live in small
towns and rural areas. In addition, many of the small town and rural

45

aged, as are their communities, are victims of economic distress and isolation. In Kansas, 31% of the aged have annual incomes below $10,000 and 11% live in poverty. Thirty-eight percent of older Kansas women and 9% of older Kansas men live alone.

This picture of the aged, including the rural aged, appears to lend credence to the notion that to be elderly is to be dependent and in need of care. Thus, policies and programs focusing on older persons have placed major emphasis on creating systems of care and pensions that treat the aged as disengaged and passive rather than as active and contributing individuals.

Indeed, the provision of health and social services, as well as economic support, for the frail and functionally dependent aged is essential. But, is that the only or even most appropriate strategy to addressing population aging? Clearly, there are other paths. For example, the Vienna International Plan of Action on Aging (1982) declared that aging policy and programming throughout the world ought to work to develop a *balanced* view of aging, that is, to concern itself with both the humanitarian and the developmental aspects of aging. Thus, recognizing and providing for the physical, emotional, and financial needs of the aged are important. However, that is an insufficient response. The aged also have a role to play in the maintenance and development of the family, the community, and the market. Recognition and support for that role must be present. Older persons are not just "another problem" to be addressed by society. They are a resource, provided that they are given the opportunity to be such.

The provision of such opportunities and the recognition of the positive developmental role that older persons play in the life of the family and community are in keeping with the tradition of older persons themselves. We cannot ignore the fact that it was these same individuals who built our communities and our country. It is these individuals, now "old," who built and maintained our transportation and communication systems, our farms, and our health care and educational institutions. They struggled through the Depression and fought our wars. Although the manner in which their contributions were made may shift with age, their resourcefulness does not, if opportunities continue to be present.

How does one go about creating this "balanced view," this provision of opportunities for the aged to be a resource, to be productive contributors to community and economic development in rural communities? To address this question we must first have a better understanding of the rural aged and the rural context in which the aged live.

Defining the Issue for Rural Places

The 1980s was a decade of economic crises throughout much of rural America. As noted in a recent U.S. Congress report, "Rural America is at the proverbial crossroads. Many rural communities show signs that raise concern for their future: loss of economic vitality, a relative decline in income, high unemployment, low workforce participation, and an exodus of talent" (Gibbons, 1991, p. 2). During the years 1979-1986, 48% of rural counties remained stable or declined in employment. And although some rural counties improved their job situation during the later 1980s, farm-dependent counties of mid-America continued to experience high rates of employment decline (*Rural Conditions and Trends*, 1990, p. 6). These economic changes had negative consequences on the lives and well-being of rural Americans and their communities. Atash (1990) notes: "The adverse effects of the farm financial crisis were reflected by losses in employment and income, high rates of farm loan delinquencies, farm foreclosures and bankruptcies, increased incidences of suicides, poverty, and the out-migration of educated young adults" (p. 44).

A number of alternatives have been proposed as responses to these deepening problems faced by rural communities, including the Poppers' (1987) call for a return of the plains to the pre-white conditions by returning the land to a great commons and Daniels and Lapping's (1987) settlement policy of concentrating public economic resources to stimulate growth centers in rural areas. While not debating the merits and/or drawbacks of these approaches, we point out that additional opportunities and resources are available to assist in addressing rural concerns, some of which have been insufficiently articulated and explored. One among these is the role of the elderly in rural community and economic development. Currently, the growing elderly population often signals a call for increased services for that elderly population. As users of services within the "acquiescent functionalist" perspective, the elderly are seen as a further drain of scarce resources and are viewed as passive recipients. As noted above, a more balanced approach to population aging suggests that the aged can also play a significant role in rural development. With active participation of the elderly, rural communities may be in a stronger position, not only to survive but to thrive.

Alternative Paradigms of Aging

As noted above, the aging of the world's population has elicited a response that tends to focus on the needs and problems of the aged. In this framework, health and social service policies and programs are expanded to meet the needs of the aged who are frail and dependent. Income security programs are developed to provide an income floor to protect the aged against destitution. As Townsend (1981) noted, within this model the aged tend to take on the assigned role of a dependent and passive population. They easily become another societal problem, a real or potential burden in need of society's care. An alternative or parallel way of looking at the aged is through the "developmental" or "productive" lens. In this context, population aging is addressed through policy and program development as it impacts on production, consumption, savings, and general economic and social conditions in the society. This model suggests that the aged are an asset who can and do make significant contributors to family, community, and economic systems. Conceptually, there are at least three roles that this developmental or productive view of aging suggests as it relates to rural communities: older persons as workers, older persons as volunteers, and older persons as consumers (Kerschner, 1991).

Older Workers

Through the work of the American Association of International Aging (AAIA), the notion of older person as worker has become much clearer. Beginning in 1986 with a grant from the U.S. Department of Health and Human Services, the AAIA undertook an action research project to assemble data on senior enterprise development trends worldwide (Ficke & Kerschner, 1990). This project identified that successful senior income-generating projects were present in numerous developing countries but that the idea had received little attention in the United States. What the AAIA discovered at both the international and domestic levels was exciting:

- A senior citizens service agency organized a child-care center that provides day care for children aged 6 weeks to kindergarten. All direct care staff are 55 and older.

- A self-service laundromat was sponsored by a home for the destitute elderly. The laundry has the dual purpose of providing financial support for services provided by the home as well as providing jobs for the elderly who live in the home.
- A group of volunteers initiated an elder crafts shop to serve as a marketing arm for crafts produced by older people and home-based older workers throughout the country. The shop draws from more than 1,000 crafters on a regional basis who must be at least 60 years of age. The artisans receive 60% of the retail price of the item and the remaining 40% covers marketing and administrative expenses (Kerschner & Ficke, 1990).

Although some older persons may not desire to continue or return to paid employment, evidence suggests that many would if opportunities were present and structured appropriately (Cohen-Mansfield, 1989; Skoglund, 1979). A recent study by the National Center for Policy Analysis (1990) estimated that 700,000 persons receiving Social Security throughout the United Stated would return to work in the formal sector if laws were altered so that they would not be penalized for their employment earnings. The National Council on Aging (Commonwealth Fund, 1990) reported that 1.9 million persons aged 50-64 are ready and able to go back to work. It is also clear that jobs, whether paid or volunteer, that are aimed at the elderly should be flexible in terms of part-time possibilities and accessibility. The AAIA research found that it is possible to stimulate the local economic environment to generate income-producing jobs for and by the aged, either through senior entrepreneurship or by providing opportunities for older persons to be employees. Aside from the increased income that many older workers experienced, the jobs provided older people with an opportunity to socialize and remain active, brought in additional funds to support community economic development and social service activities, and helped communities and businesses to begin to view their older citizens as valuable resources for locally based economic and community development.

Senior Volunteers

It is also clear that the aged can be a resource and contribute to community and economic development through a wide range of volunteer activities. More than 400,000 older persons participate in the Retired Senior Volunteer program, the Foster Grandparent program, and the Senior Companion program. Twenty percent of VISTA and 12% of the Peace Corps are older volunteers. The American Association of Retired Persons (1985) reported that 40% to 45% of the those 55 years of age and older volunteer an average of 15 hours per month in formal volunteer activities. In addition, the AARP study found that only 8% of those surveyed expressed a lack of interest in volunteering and 31% of those not currently in a volunteer program would be interested in volunteering *if asked*.

Senior Consumers

The role of the older person as consumer has received extensive coverage in the past few years. The "Mature Market" has moved from being a market that was largely ignored to become the target of a massive redirection of marketing strategies. Cook (1989) points out the following:

- The 50+ market is enormous—more than 60 million people.
- The 50+ market is the growth market of the next couple of decades.
- The 50+ market has money—almost $900 million. Although the Mature Market comprises only about ¼ of the country's population, 50+ households control more than ¾ of the country's total financial assets.
- The 50+ market not only has money, it spends money.
- The 50+ market demands quality in what it buys and courteous, efficient, informed service when it buys. (pp. 1-2)

If one looks for an interrelation between population aging and those interested in economic development, this issue of the mature market has garnered the most attention. A number of states, including Arkansas and Nebraska, have set about detailing the economic impact of older citizens on their state's economy. In each of these cases the aged were important contributors to the economic vitality of the state both through the direct impact and the multiplier effect of their income and expenditures.

Pennsylvania, through its Department on Aging, is moving to structure public/private sector partnerships that will recognize and utilize the resource of older persons, both as consumers and as workers through a system of retiree-based economic development. The Department of Aging determined that older persons spend in excess of $24 billion annually, representing 23% of all consumer expenditures in Pennsylvania. The major expenditures were in the areas of housing, food, and transportation. Other states, including Alabama, Colorado, Kansas,

Michigan, and Texas, have identified productive aging as important subjects for research, special innovative projects, and advocacy.

Rural Community Development and Productive Aging

There is evidence of the increased recognition that older Americans are a crucial cog in rural economic development efforts. The *Kansas Governor's Task Force on the Future of Rural Communities* (1988) states: "The older citizens of Kansas represent significant resources. The talents, time and economic resources should be recognized, and utilized by rural communities desiring to improve their situation" (p. 1). However, what is left unsaid is how communities go about recognizing and utilizing the significant human resource that the aged represent in rural places.

Effective rural community and economic development occurs as the result of a partnership between those most affected by the issue in the community and those outside the community. The stage is set when extra-community groups provide models, personpower, and resources to supplement those of the community. However, the community remains the key as it provides the commitment, the sense of purpose, and the leadership necessary for sustaining the development process.

Development efforts work best when they are undertaken and supported at the community level, that is, from the bottom up. Effective leadership comes from the people who are affected by the problem. Top down approaches to development can be effective through the availability of financial resources. However, when the dollars are gone, the community's ability or commitment to sustain the efforts are limited and often fail (Luke, Ventriss, Reed, & Reed, 1988).

How do communities with limited expertise, leadership, manpower, and resources become involved in development, particularly when it involves venturing into an issue such as productive aging? Three issues serve as inhibitors to community development success. The first is the lack of a game plan, that is, the availability of models or creative problem-solving techniques. The second is the lack of personpower, namely, persons with the time, energy, and creativity to see a new project through. The third is the inability of communities to prime the pump with the availability of financial resources to get a project started.

For purposes of this chapter, two current efforts involving the aged in rural community and economic development, one international and one domestic, are described. The international effort focuses on work in the Dominican Republic, in which most of the effort is on enhancing the employment opportunities for older persons. The domestic project, undertaken in Kansas, is an effort to introduce and develop productive aging demonstration projects as viable additions to rural community economic development strategic planning and action.

International Projects

The Dominican Republic is a developing country of 7 million people. It has a small but rapidly growing population of persons 60 years of age and older. In 1980, 249,000 persons were 60 years of age and older (4.5% of the population). By the year 2020, it is estimated that 1,144,000 (10% of the population) will be in that age group. It is estimated that only 4% to 8% of older persons have some type of pension and that health and social services are very limited.

Beginning in 1989, a strategy for a countrywide activity to expand economic, social, and cultural opportunities for the aged was undertaken. The purpose of the action strategy was to tap into the experience of a broad range of existing national and community-level organizations in order to introduce these organizations to the concept and practice of productive aging. The primary objectives of the strategy were these:

1. To encourage interest and involvement of organizations, including those in agriculture, microenterprise, urban and rural development, environment, aging health, and social service, in practical research and action to promote productive aging, particularly activities that helped older persons generate income.
2. To facilitate practical, community-based projects that demonstrate the capabilities of older people and enhance their economic and social contributions to themselves, their communities, and the country at large.
3. To initiate mechanisms for linking the individual initiatives into an integrated countrywide effort to support productive aging.
4. To identify methods for including aging in the policy and program agendas of the social and economic development organizations of the country.

To implement this strategy a number of practical projects were undertaken. One set of activities focused on age-segregated institutions. The first of such projects was the establishment of a self-service laundromat in a home for the aged run by a group of Roman Catholic nuns.

With financial assistance from HelpAge International and the Welfare Foundation of the United States and with technical assistance from the American Association for International Aging, the project was undertaken and completed. In its 3 years of operation, the self-service laundromat, which serves the entire community, has provided a substantial profit, as well as "in kind" service and support for the old-age home. A second project focused on the development of microenterprises, including chicken farms and a small winery, which are run by, and provide financial support for, groups of older persons in three different parts of the country. These projects have been developed by the Dominican Republic affiliate of HelpAge International.

A second set of activities focused on integrating the aged into the developmental activities of several age-neutral international and national development agencies that had no special aging agenda or focus. The first of these integrated activities was sponsored by the United Nations Development Program (UNDP). The UNDP had undertaken a successful hydroponic gardening program for low-income persons and families in two areas of the country. In visiting an urban hydroponic gardening site, it was discovered that nearly one third of the participant families were headed by individuals 60 years of age and older. In each case, the older family member was a very active participant in the actual working of the hydroponic garden, generating both financial resources and food. This realization lead the UNDP to expand its hydroponic gardening activities to other groups of aged in other parts of the country.

A second institutionally based, age-integrated activity was developed in consultation with the Asociación para el Desarrollo de Microempresas, Inc. (ADEMI), a microenterprise bank founded in 1983. In 1990, approximately 14,000 ADEMI small loans were made to individuals. Approximately 15% to 20% of the 1990 loans were made to persons 50 years of age and older. The ADEMI currently actively seeks and supports microenterprise loans to older persons and is developing a special loan portfolio for such individuals.

A third institutionally based, age-integrated activity was the development of a loan program for older women to purchase cows. In 1990, the Fundación para el Desarrollo Comunitario, Inc. (FUDECO), the Dominican Republic Save the Children affiliate, discovered that poor health, poor economic situations, and hunger were the major worries for the aged in a rural part of the country that they served. With financial assistance from a religious community in the United States, the loan program was organized for older women to purchase cows in order for these women to have both income from the calves and milk for themselves and their families. The major outcome of the project, beyond the first time ownership of anything on the part of many of these older women and the nutrition from the milk, has been the sense of power and control the women now feel they have over their lives.

These activities, although originally isolated from one another, have created a momentum and consciousness about the potential resources that the aged represent in the Dominican Republic. This consciousness resulted in the convening of a countrywide meeting on productive aging in the spring of 1991. The meeting had 50 participants, representing a broad range of national and international development organizations, national and local education, health and social service agencies and organizations, and private sector businesses. The purpose of the meeting was to provide a mechanism for participants to discuss the problems and opportunities associated with productive aging, share examples of productive aging, and promote strategies for expanding productive aging throughout the country. At the conclusion of the meeting, a national task force on productive aging was formed to support and monitor productive aging activities and to encourage additional agencies and organizations, both age-integrated and age-segregated, to become involved in aging projects. This strategy has produced a number of outcomes. They include the following:

1. A country-based leadership and international support network for productive aging are being developed through the establishment of a national productive aging task force.
2. Productive aging activities are being encouraged and are occurring throughout the country in both urban and rural settings.
3. Existing private and public organizations, including age-neutral organizations, have integrated productive aging activities into their programs.
4. A network of individuals, interested in and committed to the concept of productive aging, has been set in place.
5. Opportunities for some of the aged, and especially the poorest of that population, to expand their income and independence have been established.

Domestic Projects

Based on the experiences and lessons learned from the international projects and funded in part by a grant from the U.S. Department of

Commerce's Economic Development Administration (EDA), Kansas State University's Community Service Program (CSP) undertook productive aging demonstration projects in four nonmetro western Kansas counties. The two most rural counties were experiencing "aging in place." Preliminary 1990 census data indicated that the proportion of the aged 65+ was above 20% in each county. The previous decade was a period of economic hardship for both counties. They experienced substantial losses in employment, services, and the out-migration of younger citizens. The two larger counties had smaller proportions of the aged and fared better economically, primarily as a result of an expanding meat packing industry in the area. All four counties had developed active community- and countywide economic development associations and were deeply concerned about the future of their communities.

Beginning in 1989 and continuing through 1991, CSP teams worked within each county to generate awareness and support for the role productive aging could play in community development efforts. To do this, CSP teams pursued three specific objectives: (1) to generate interest and support for potential local productive aging projects, (2) to identify projects matching community needs with the resource potential of the aged in the community, and (3) to solidify community ownership of productive aging. What follows is a brief overview of some of the practical outcomes from the demonstration projects. One set of activities focused on volunteerism on the part of the aged. Although some of the aged had served as volunteers in the community prior to the demonstration projects, we found that rural communities tended to have a few elderly highly active and many elderly inactive. We further found that most of the communities were too small to have coordinated volunteer centers, such as a local RSVP program. One of the projects that emerged was the creation of a volunteer center, which created an identity whereby volunteers and those needing volunteers could report. One volunteer center was housed in the community's senior center. In this case, the center continued to perform its more traditional senior service roles *and* contributed to the volunteer needs of the community. As it turned out, this was a direct demonstration of the more balanced view of the roles played by the aged in rural community life.

Another set of activities focused on income-generating opportunities for the aged. One community developed a companion care program, providing training and placement for more than 60 persons aged 65 and older. That community also developed a temporary employment program for persons 65 and older, successfully placing over 100 people in income-generating opportunities. Both of these programs were housed within the community's senior center.

The volunteer and income-generating projects contributed to the needs of the community as well as the needs of individuals. Further, these productive aging projects demonstrated to the community and community leaders ways in which the aged can be seen as valuable contributors to community life.

Lessons Learned

As a result of these international and domestic aging and development efforts, several lessons have been learned. These lessons provide clues toward the requirements for a broader implementation of rural productive aging activities.

1. *The Presence of Key Leaders.* The availability and participation of key leaders is vital. These leaders, one or more of whom must be local—that is, from the community or area—must have the commitment, knowledge, and energy to initiate and carry the strategy through its implementation.

2. *The Involvement of Key Organizations.* The experience in both domestic and international settings suggests that while age-segregated organizations are important, age-integrated, community-development-oriented organizations are vital to the success of productive aging projects. Historically, most age-segregated organizations address the humanitarian needs of the aged, as recipients, through the provision of health and social services. The transition, although possible, to promote the aged as contributors to community and economic development, is often beyond the perceived mission of health and social service organizations. Age-integrated, community development organizations, while focusing on the productive potential of individuals, also bring the institutional base and the financial and human resources necessary for the sustainable growth of productive aging activities.

3. *The Availability of Resources.* As noted above, the aged in rural places and the rural environment itself are often victims of scarce resources, financial and human. The availability of financial support as seed money for project development has been an important ingredient for success. At a second level, the availability of human resources, including external community human resources, has been equally important for two reasons. First, given the paradigm or conceptual shift needed to promote productive aging activities, it is important that

resources be available to provide the leadership and insights necessary for the community to see the aged as a valued community development resource. As Mattson and Burke (1989) note, small towns tend to undergo socioeconomic transformation due to exogenous forces. Second, human resources can also play a vital technical assistance role in the development and implementation of productive aging activities that respond to the needs and capacities of the aged.

4. *The Development of Community-Based Ownership.* Throughout the projects described above, a basic strategic planning approach was used to support the involvement and ownership by the individuals and organizations that were the targets of the projects. As noted, key persons and organizations were brought into the process from the beginning to give leadership, direction, coordination, and support to the projects. These individuals and organizations represented the aged themselves, health and social service organizations traditionally serving the aged, and age-integrated, community-development-oriented organizations and individuals. In each case, data gathering focused on the needs, circumstances, and activities of the aged, as well as the needs and opportunities present in the community. Each project began by presenting local individuals and community organizations visions about the productive roles of the aged in community activities. Next, a set of action steps or strategies was developed and implemented. Finally, the local leadership assumed responsibility for evaluative feedback for the project to the coordinating body.

Conclusion

In addressing the aging of the population in rural places, we have argued for a balanced approach. As noted by the Vienna International Plan of Action on Aging, "the problem of aging today is not just one of providing protection and care, but of the involvement and participation of the elderly and the aging" (1982, p. 23). To be sure, the health, social, and economic needs of the rural aged must be addressed in a manner that assures they get at least equity of access to the services provided their urban counterparts. However, it is also apparent that the rural aged are more than passive recipients of services. They represent a significant development opportunity for rural places, as well. Given the fact that large numbers of the rural elderly are capable and desirous of continued contributions through service and work for themselves, their families, and their communities, it is important to recognize those contributions and to provide an environment for continued productivity in accord with their desires and capabilities.

Throughout this discussion, the development of a conceptual and policy approach to the aged has been encouraged that sees them as assets and resources for their self-support, for their families and for their communities. Such an approach serves both the aged and the places in which they live. For the aged this means (1) movement from marginal to key status in the community, (2) movement from being viewed as another problem to being part of the solution, (3) expansion of opportunities for their continued active participation in the social, cultural, and economic life of the community, and (4) the provision of income for those aged who are in need. For the community, this means (1) the aged become a resource and even a special opportunity to promote community and economic development, (2) the aged move from being a burden to being a valued part of the community, and (3) the aging of the community becomes an asset rather than a liability.

Ultimately, development—that is, the expansion of choices and opportunities—as well as increased wealth occurs in an environment where the resources and talents of all citizens are available and utilized to contribute to the good of the community. In Third World countries, with a limited network of services and opportunities, it is apparent that development, to be meaningful, must involve and have a positive impact on all its citizens. In the so-called developed countries, it is also becoming more clear that community and economic development depends on the active participation of all members of the community, including the aged. For the individual, this active participation means the opportunity for fulfillment of human potential, regardless of age. For the community, it means an expansion of the energy, resources, and options for development. To expand opportunities for, and emphasize the importance of, the aged in rural places for community and economic development is to recognize that finding fulfillment through participation in every stage of one's life is the ultimate destiny of each person living in a community.

5

The Senior Center
as a Community Focal Point

A Strategy for Rural Community Development

JOHN W. McCLAIN, Jr.
J. MICHAEL LEIBOWITZ
STEPHEN B. PLUMER
KARIN S. LUNT

Rural senior centers throughout the nation may increasingly find themselves in positions of influence and stature in their local communities
and, in many instances, may evolve into key participants in the mainstream of community planning and development. A major impetus for
this phenomenon appears to be the evolutionary process of becoming a
community focal point. The evolutionary process may, in part, be driven
by the implementation of systematic networking strategies that can
simultaneously heighten community awareness of the concerns of older
citizens and their families while bringing together traditional and nontraditional service providers in often historical collaborations.

This chapter reports on community focal point development at four
senior centers in rural Nebraska. The authors suggest that the organizational strategy employed in this effort, although requiring further study,
may lead to a means of improving services to older rural residents
through the revitalization of the participating senior center and to

improved communication, coordination, and planning by community leaders, the business community, service providers, and older residents. Improvements that have resulted from this process include the following:

• Increased community awareness about the senior center and the varied needs of older residents
• Access to an expanded pool of volunteers
• Cooperative arrangements between service providers, the senior center, and the business community
• Location of services at the senior center site by cooperating service providers
• Joint planning and programming among service providers and other community organizations and the business community
• Joint staff and volunteer training
• Improved outreach to the unserved and underserved older residents
• Expanded and more effective information and referral services
• Access to an expanded population of older persons, including the frail and the young-old

The project emerged from the historical concern (Krout, 1991) that too little was known about senior centers in rural areas and, more specifically, about the processes that would enhance their capacity to evolve into community focal points. Rural senior centers as a collective are seen as less able to expand their programming in the manner that urban senior centers can (Krout, 1989, 1991). However, their unique role in a less resource-rich rural environment might provide the impetus for successful focal point development. The purpose of the 2-year modelling effort was to test the assumption that rural senior centers have the unique capacity to engage in focal point development using innovative community development strategies. The authors believe that such an effort to mobilize rural resources is supported by the growing national/regional commitment to rural resource revitalization (Bull, Howard, & DeCroix, 1991; Heartland Center for Leadership Development, 1990). Given this revitalization, the community climate may support a senior center/community focal point's emergence as a strategic participant in the mainstream of community development.

The Concept of a Community Focal Point

The concept of a *community focal point* was first formally articulated within the national Aging Network through the 1973 amendments to the

Older Americans Act of 1965. Title V of the amendments authorized funds to develop multipurpose senior center facilities to "provide a focal point in communities for the development and delivery of social services and nutritional services designed primarily for older persons."

The 1978 amendments to the act stated: "Area Agencies should designate, where feasible, a focal point for comprehensive service delivery in each community, giving special consideration to designating multipurpose senior centers as such focal points" (Sec306[a][3]PL89-73). In 1991, the U.S. Administration on Aging published a handbook presenting a precise definition of a community focal point and projecting its impact on the community that it serves. According to the Administration on Aging (AoA) (1991), a focal point has the following characteristics:

1. It is a highly visible facility where anyone in a community can obtain information and access to services.
2. It does not serve a single or limited function but rather assures access to a broad and comprehensive array of services and opportunities for older people, either on-site or through referral.
3. It is proactive in finding out about new resources, creating linkages with other organizations, and assuring that the information given out is accurate and up-to-date.
4. It publicizes available services and opportunities for older people and reaches out to the community's older residents and caregivers, especially those who are more vulnerable.

The articulated expectations surrounding the establishment of community focal points were that the Aging Network in each state could ensure that services to older citizens and their families were well-known and maximally utilized, that the focal point could stimulate the expansion of programs and services in a time of limited funding, and that the interagency communication fostered by a community focal point would serve to minimize fragmentation and duplication of service efforts. The criteria for the designation of community focal points, according to the Administration on Aging, was to be determined by Area Agencies on Aging and was viewed as variable dependent on local considerations.

Although there are few definitive studies that support the ultimate feasibility of utilizing senior centers as community focal points (in part because of a lack of clearly defined and uniform organizational procedures and programmatic outcomes), there are compelling arguments raised by Krout (1986, 1989) and others that suggest that the broad membership of many senior centers (i.e., socioeconomic, health status), their varied programming, their efforts to serve frail senior citizens, and their relative visibility in the local aging network of services place them in a more strategic position to evolve into community focal points. To date, there has been no systematic investigation of the organizational processes and the programmatic outcomes associated with the transformation of rural senior centers into community focal points. We do know that rural senior centers are perceived to have characteristics that may prove beneficial to community focal point development.

Rural Senior Centers

It has long been determined that programs in rural areas provide fewer resources for all residents, particularly those who are elderly (Kim, 1981; Krout, 1987; Nelson, 1980; Schneider, Chapman, & Voth, 1985; Taietz, 1973). The findings of several key national/community studies of rural senior center service delivery (Krout, 1983a; Leanse & Wagner, 1975; Schneider et al., 1985) suggest the following:

1. Rural senior centers have less programmatic space than urban senior centers.
2. Rural senior centers report smaller budgets as well as a smaller number of total activities and services than urban senior centers.
3. Rural senior centers are less likely to be part of multi-site organizations.
4. Rural senior centers are significantly less likely to report an increase in paid staff than urban senior centers and more likely to report an increase of volunteer staff.
5. Rural senior centers are not necessarily serving more high-risk or frail older citizens than urban centers but more frequently provide in-home services to residents in the community.
6. Rural senior center participants are more likely to be participants in other community activities.

Although comparisons of rural senior centers with urban senior centers generally demonstrate a wide disparity in the range and scope of resources, we must remind ourselves that urban areas tend to be more resource-rich in general. The relative abundance of resources, competing organizational coalitions, and urban political realities may indeed negatively impact on the potential of urban senior centers to evolve into the "ideal type" of an influential community focal point (Krout, 1986). Senior centers in rural areas may be the dominant, central point of service delivery and a primary source for information/referral (Krout, 1989). Indeed many senior centers in rural areas report growth in resources and staff (Krout, 1991). In order to enhance their evolution into a community focal point (and potentially into the mainstream of community service planning for the elderly and other underserved populations), organizational strategies must be devised that overcome the deficits of a scarcity of staff and program resources and a tenuous organizational stature in the broad community (Krout, 1986; 1989). Such organizational strategies were piloted with four rural Nebraska senior centers and may have implications for community focal point development in other rural communities in the nation.

Case Study—Nebraska

In 1989, the Nebraska Department on Aging (NDoA) received a 2-year grant from the federal Administration on Aging to launch an initiative to evolve four rural senior centers into community focal points. The communities of Chadron, Madison, Kimball, and O'Neill, Nebraska were chosen by two collaborating Area Agencies on Aging (the Northeast Nebraska Area Agency on Aging and the Aging Office of Western Nebraska) based on their significant proportions of senior citizens. Other project collaborators were the University of Nebraska and the National Council on Aging.

The broad goal of the project was to stimulate a state-level and community-level consciousness that the rural senior center, through its evolution into a community focal point, could emerge as a primary advocate for older persons while simultaneously generating a greater public awareness of the interdependence between elderly residents and all age groups residing in a rural community. Optimally, it was felt that the process of becoming a community focal point could potentially elevate community perceptions of older residents and professionals who advocate for older residents as valuable resources, radically departing from often historical perceptions of them as impediments to maintaining community vitality.

The four communities (Kimball, 37%; Chadron, 24%; Madison, 36%; and O'Neill, 35%) have significant populations of citizens who are aged

60 or older. Indeed, the proportion of older persons in each of the four communities is as large as that to be expected into the 21st century based on current national aging population projections. The Chadron Senior Citizen Center and the Kimball Friendship Senior Center (located in the northwestern and southwestern portions of the state, respectively) are within the region of the Aging Office of Western Nebraska. The Northside Community Center (located in the town of Madison in the northeast portion of the state) and The Golden Age Center (in the north central portion of the state) are within the region of the Northeast Nebraska Area Agency on Aging. All four rural agricultural communities have experienced either significant population losses throughout the years or the residents have "aged in place." Although each of the senior centers is located in its respective county seat, none of the county seats are resource-rich; therefore, location provided no strategic advantage to the senior centers.

As a result of a battery of surveys conducted in the spring of 1990 among service providers and a representative sample of seniors in the four communities served by the senior centers, a profile emerges of the perceptions of these programs in the broader environment. Each of the four senior centers served as meal sites and also provided home-delivered meals on a daily basis. Beyond a variable menu of recreational programs (i.e., piano, billiards, television, cards, quilting), the senior centers offered medical screening, information and referral services, and legal services. Most community residents (who were randomly surveyed) had heard of the community center and those who participated were satisfied with the programs, a finding consistent with those in other rural communities (Schneider et al., 1985). Consistent with national surveys, nonparticipants primarily indicated that they were "too busy" or "still employed" (Leanse & Wagner, 1975).

The four senior centers, in general, had good working relationships with many of the service providers in their communities (Table 5.1). Although few contractual relationships were established (i.e., by memorandum of agreement or contracts), community providers collaborated with the senior centers in educational programming, referrals, and staff training. Irrespective of the informal networking of service providers and the generally positive perceptions of senior citizens of each senior center, until community focal point development was initiated, there was no formal mechanism for comprehensively addressing the needs of senior citizens, citizens who in many instances represented approximately 25%-40% of each community's population.

Table 5.1 Service Provider Survey—1990

	Chadron Senior Center N = 12	Northside Center N = 21	Golden Age Center N = 17	Friendship Center N = 16
Percentage who worked with local senior center	83%	86%	59%	88%
Frequency:				
Daily	9%	5%	0%	0%
Weekly	27%	44%	21%	46%
Monthly	46%	39%	58%	39%
Annually	18%	11%	21%	15%
Percentage satisfied with working relationship	100%	86%	100%	100%

Organizational Strategy—Focal Point Development

In order to optimally position the four rural senior centers for evolving into community focal points, several key strategies were employed. A Statewide Resource Council (SRC) was established as well as four Community Resource Councils (CRC), one for each model community. In addition, the two Area Agencies on Aging hired full-time community focal point developers as well as provided part-time programmatic support in order to free the senior center directors to become more involved in the modelling effort. As characteristic of a modelling period, resources were available that may be scarce or nonexistent in "real life." However, the data and training materials resulting from the modelling effort provided guidelines for transforming rural senior centers into community focal points in the absence of abundant resources.

Statewide Resource Council

The purpose of the Statewide Resource Council (SRC) was to advise the Nebraska Department on Aging on strategies that might facilitate community focal point development in the four model communities and to serve as the statewide nucleus of a broad coalition of public and private agencies sharing a common perception of the needs of older citizens. The short-range goal of the SRC was to insure that local

Table 5.2 Membership of the Nebraska Resource Council for Older Individuals

Nebraska Hospital Association	Nebraska Public Power District
Health Care Provider	Area Agency of Aging Representative
Nebraska Department of Roads	Nebraska Department of Social Services
Nebraska Policy Research Office	Nebraska Technical Community College
Nebraska Department of Labor	Association
Nebraska Department of Public Instruction	Nebraska Bar Association
Interchurch Ministries of Nebraska, Inc	Nebraska Indian Commission
Nebraska Association of County Officials	Nebraska Energy Department
Nebraska Department of Economic	Librarian
Development	Educator
University of Nebraska-Lincoln Cooperative	
Extension Service	

providers (often funded by or themselves local representatives of state-wide bureaucracies) were made aware of and remained committed to the modelling effort in each rural community. The community focal point developers often utilized the SRC as a "sounding board" when local issues required an objective analysis. The long-range goal of the SRC (perhaps the most ambitious) was to "de-compartmentalize" the needs of older citizens by cultivating a recognition that only a broad governmental network could comprehensively address the multiple needs of senior citizens in the state and that the Nebraska Department on Aging, although a primary advocate, should not be viewed as the sole advocate for older Nebraskans (Table 5.2).

Community Resource Councils

Community Resource Councils (CRCs) were established as adjunct organizational entities for each of the four rural senior centers. Each CRC, which served as a link between the senior center board of directors and the larger community of service providers, was organized by the community focal point developers and senior center directors. The CRCs were viewed as critical to the evolutionary process that would transform rural senior centers into focal points because the CRC membership represented a coalition of prominent community agencies and groups (some historically viewing themselves as providers of services for older residents and others viewing themselves as advocates for older persons for the first time). The CRC not only increased the visibility of the senior center in each community, it added stature—which has been determined to be essential to broad community service programming involvement (Krout, 1989). Senior center directors were, in turn, invited to join such mainstream community development organizations as the local chambers of commerce because of the CRC connection. Irrespective of the level of networking undertaken by each senior center director and/or board of directors prior to the installation of the CRC, its incorporation in every instance formalized communitywide planning for older citizens for the first time in the history of the particular community (McClain, Leibowitz, Lunt, Thorson, & Foster, 1992).

Typically, CRCs represented an array of traditional and nontraditional agencies and groups and its membership was unique for each community (Table 5.3). Issues addressed by CRCs ranged from service duplication to the problems of latchkey children and the roles that elders could play in this emerging family situation. CRCs stimulated Community Resource Fairs and resource pooling and in one instance established a study group to explore ways of attracting private developers for the purpose of building low-cost apartments for older persons in the community. Senior center board of directors, responding to the local surveys undertaken by the CRCs, designed and implemented marketing strategies aimed at attracting younger seniors, for example, providing evening meals at the center for young seniors coming home from their jobs. Entrepreneurial activities such as attracting elder tourists to the community were enhanced by CRC support.

Community Focal Point Developers

The organization of the CRCs could not have occurred during the modelling period without the aggressive leadership/coordination of the community focal point developers (CFPDs). Hired by the Area Agencies on Aging, the two CFPDs each assumed responsibility for working with two rural senior centers (Madison/O'Neill; Kimball/Chadron). The community focal point developers, in partnership with the senior center directors, performed the critical tasks of (1) marketing the focal point concept to the senior center boards of directors and to prospective members of the CRCs, (2) establishing lines of communication between senior center board members and CRC members and (3) assisting the CRC in shaping its programmatic agenda (McClain et al.,

Table 5.3 Community Resource Council Memberships

Chadron	
Social Services	Home Health Services
Physical Therapist	Community Action
Home Extension	Senior Center Board
Attorney	Senior Citizen
R.S.V.P.	Religious Organization
Chamber of Commerce	Bank
State College	
Kimball	
Chamber of Commerce	Senior Center
Sheriff	Bank
Mayor	Insurance Company
Nursing Home	County Agent
Hospital	Home Extension
Social Services	Religious Organization
Madison	
Nursing Home	City Administrator
Religious Organization	Senior Citizen
Social Services	Senior Center Board Member
County Extension	Construction Company
Legal Assistance	Bank Vice President
Public Power District	Pharmacist
Community College	League of Human Dignity
O'Neill	
Social Services	Green Thumb
Nebraska Public Power	County Extension
Attorney	City Council Representative
County Supervisor	North Park Homes
Chamber of Commerce	Senior Center Board President
Community Services	Senior Citizen

1992). In addition, through the provision of trainers contracted by the Nebraska Department on Aging, the community focal point developer and the senior center director organized training programs for the board of directors of each senior center.

As was the original intent of the project, the community focal point developers departed at the conclusion of the modelling period leaving a legacy of community organization strategies that are key elements of the community focal point training manual (NDoA, 1991a). At the conclusion of the modelling period, there are strong indications that the organizational activities at both the state and community levels have generated a permanent commitment to senior center focal point development in rural areas of the State of Nebraska. On the state level, the Statewide Resource Council has evolved into the Nebraska Resource Council for Older Individuals (NRCOI) with the following mission statement (NDoA, 1991b):

> We recognize that older Nebraskans are a diverse group of individuals representing a broad spectrum of ages, interests, abilities, and needs; and that the common denominator these Nebraskans share is a desire for dignity, independence, and freedom of choice. Recognizing this diversity, the NRCOI is dedicated to encouraging the recognition of older individuals as full participants in our society. We are committed to collaborating and cooperating at all levels of state and local organization to facilitate a better quality of life for older individuals.

A major thrust of the NRCOI is the stimulation of community focal points in rural senior centers throughout the state utilizing the Community Resource Council organizational strategy. Most notably, the NRCOI is participating in the National Eldercare Campaign spearheaded by the Administration on Aging. The Nebraska Eldercare initiative will spawn community coalitions in predominantly rural areas led by AAAs and senior centers. Beyond focal point development, the NRCOI will "seek, and remove barriers to intergovernmental and intercommunity cooperation and assistance" (NDoA, 1991b).

Summary and Conclusions

In each of the communities of Chadron, Kimball, Madison, and O'Neill, Nebraska, the senior center has emerged as a leader in the local network of service provision to older citizens. Further, members of the senior center boards of directors and senior center professional staff are now formally represented on numerous community boards and councils. The Community Resource Councils are still operational and in the case of one rural senior center have been incorporated into the center's bylaws. Although no formal process currently exists for determining community focal point status in the State of Nebraska, the four rural senior centers in the modelling effort fundamentally satisfy most of the nationally recognized criteria (AoA, 1991).

A major project of the Nebraska rural community focal point demonstration project is a manual for focal point development produced by the Nebraska Department on Aging with major consultation from the

National Council on the Aging and assistance from the University of Nebraska. The manual and promotional videotape entitled "Building a Focal Point in Your Rural Community" (NDoA, 1991a) provides a step-by-step guide for organizing a focal point in a rural community, with an emphasis on the senior center serving as the organizational base. Though the demonstration project had the benefit of resources beyond those generally available to a rural senior center, the manual provides guidelines for implementing cost-effective community organization strategies. It is hoped that the manual will be of major benefit to rural senior centers throughout the nation as they initiate the process of community focal point transformation.

The project has provided a preliminary indication that rural senior centers in Nebraska can assume a more prominent role in broad community planning while simultaneously evolving into community focal points. Although rural senior centers in Nebraska may not possess the breadth and depth of resources available to many urban senior centers, the scarcity of local competing resources and existing informal relations seem to provide a sound foundation for formal organizational networking. Another factor may be the communitywide recognition that a significant proportion of the local population are either users or potential users of the center's services and that older persons represent a powerful constituency whose needs can influence local resource allocation decisions. These combinations of factors may have given the senior centers in the modelling effort a stature unattainable in larger communities and may have contributed to the vigor of focal point development and the "mainstreaming" of the senior center into broad community planning efforts.

In rural communities with aging populations and decreasing resources, community focal point development undertaken by the senior center may be the impetus for establishing coalitions of traditional and nontraditional providers of services to older people. Given the national heightened awareness of the rural economic crisis and the need to seek new coalitions and new approaches to stimulating local growth (Heartland Center for Leadership Development, 1990; NRCRE, 1991), leadership by older citizens and/or their representatives may contribute substantially to local problem-solving efforts. The rural senior center with its visibility, its access to local decision makers, and its credibility with a significant proportion of the local citizenry can play a major role in broad community development.

6

Housing for
America's Rural Elderly

JOSEPH N. BELDEN

This chapter covers housing for the nonmetropolitan and rural elderly.[1] There are two main areas of focus: (1) housing characteristics and need, including comparisons to urban conditions, and (2) public programs that provide housing for the rural elderly, particularly those of lower incomes.

Clearly, many of the biggest American cities have grinding inner-city poverty and all the accompanying problems of blighted lives and neighborhoods. But there is also severe poverty and suffering in rural America, even within a few miles of the big metropolitan areas. Hidden off the highway in those scenic places are the rural poor. A presidential commission in 1967 called them "the people left behind" (President's National Advisory Commission, 1967). A quarter-century later, the issues raised by that commission are still mostly ignored, especially those concerning the rural elderly.

Socioeconomic Conditions of the Rural Elderly

In 1990, for the first time, there were fewer elderly poor households in nonmetropolitan areas than in the central cities—1,322,000 elderly

AUTHOR'S NOTE: This chapter is drawn in part from the author's *Housing Programs and Services for Elders in Rural America*, published in 1992 by the National Resource Center for Rural Elderly.

poor people in the inner cities and 1,267,000 such persons in nonmetropolitan areas. But the poverty rate for the elderly was noticeably higher in nonmetro areas—16.1% versus 14.6% in central cities and 8.1% in the suburbs (U.S. Department of Commerce [USDC], 1991). Although minorities in inner cities are often thought of as the poorest Americans, minorities in nonmetropolitan areas have higher poverty rates, particularly for the elderly. For example, almost one half of African-American elderly people living in nonmetro places are below the official poverty line. Not as many African-American elderly poor live in nonmetro areas as in the central cities—266,000 versus 470,000—but an older African American or Hispanic is much more likely to be poor if he or she lives in a nonmetropolitan area. For some smaller groups within minority populations, poverty is even higher. An example is the plight of African-American elderly women living alone in nonmetro areas. They had a poverty rate of 67.9% in 1990 and 70.5% in 1989. For the same group in central cities, the poverty rate was 57.8% in 1990 and 56.8% in 1989. This figure for nonmetro areas of nearly 70% is among the highest poverty rates recorded by the Census Bureau for any population subgroup.

The nation's 1,267,000 elderly nonmetro poor people are mostly found in the South and the Midwest (764,000 older citizens in the South, 323,000 in the Midwest, 113,000 in the West, and only 66,000 in the Northeast). One might assume that the Southern elderly poor are largely African American, but this is not the case. The Southern total of 764,000 includes 500,000 whites, 258,000 African Americans, and 18,000 Hispanics. The total of whites, African-Americans, and Hispanics adds to more than 764,000 because Hispanics, as counted by the census, are an ethnic group and may be of any race.

Housing Conditions and Need Among the Nonmetropolitan Elderly

For the nonmetropolitan elderly, housing conditions are often much worse than in the suburbs and inner cities. There also is a metro-nonmetro gap between generations. It is not commonly known that, relatively, the metro elderly live in better and the nonmetro elderly in poorer quality housing. In metropolitan areas, senior citizens live in better quality housing than those households headed by someone under age 65, but in nonmetro areas the situation is the opposite. Older people are more likely than the nonelderly to live in substandard housing (those units with moderate or severe physical problems). The American Housing Survey, a biannual study by the Census Bureau and HUD, has a detailed definition of *moderate or severe physical problems* as deficiencies in plumbing, electricity, heating, upkeep, hallways, or kitchens.

In metro areas, 7.7% of housing units occupied by the elderly and 6.5% of units occupied by the non-elderly were substandard in 1989 (the latest national data available). But in nonmetropolitan America in 1989, 9.7% of housing units occupied by the elderly and 11.1% of units occupied by the non-elderly were substandard. Of all the substandard housing, 30% in nonmetro areas and 17% in metro areas are occupied by elderly households (USDC/HUD, 1991).

There may be several answers as to why this occurs. There is more homeownership in nonmetro areas than in the cities, including among the poor. Many elderly nonmetro people also may remain until a later age in sometimes crumbling homes. They may do this both out of preference and because there are relatively few alternatives in the form of apartments, congregate projects, or intermediate care facilities.

Also, a factor is the lower real estate values prevailing in most rural areas. The lower real estate worth in nonmetro areas means that there is less capacity and opportunity for older people living there to convert their equity into retirement funds by selling their homes. A sale may not yield funds to finance a move to other housing. Thus the rural elderly may linger on in a dilapidated home that will only become worse. Lower values also may mean less inducement to keep up maintenance and make improvements. Children and grandchildren of rural older people may no longer be living in the community or may lack the ability or financial resources to help keep up the older person's home.

Tenure, Location, and Type of Structure. More detailed data on the housing of the nonmetro elderly are found in Table 6.1. According to the 1989 American Housing Survey (the latest data available), there were 5,432,000 housing units in the nonmetropolitan United States occupied by elderly householders (i.e., heads of households). A significant point is that over 82% of nonmetro units with elderly householders are occupied by the owners of those homes, a much higher rate of homeownership than in the central cities. The nonmetro elderly are mostly in the South and Midwest. Those regions account for 4.1 million out of 5.4 million nonmetro units occupied by elderly households.

The *American Housing Survey* shows that, whether among the elderly or the non-elderly, housing in nonmetropolitan America is much more

Table 6.1 Occupied Housing Units With Elderly Householder, General Characteristics—1989 (in thousands)

	Metro Areas Suburbs	Metro Areas Central Cities	Nonmetro Areas
Total occupied units	8,442	6,227	5,432
Owner occupied	6,807	4,050	4,470
Percentage	80.6	65.0	82.3
Renter occupied	1,636	2,177	962
Units by region			
Northeast	2,418	1,550	654
Midwest	1,739	1,430	1,727
South	2,632	1,996	2,385
West	1,652	1,243	666

SOURCE: USDC/HUD, July 1991.

likely to consist of single-family detached homes than in the inner cities. Metro centers have more and nonmetro areas fewer apartments. Among the 5.4 million nonmetro elderly homes, 78% are one-unit detached, 9% are mobile homes, and less than 2% are in larger rental projects consisting of at least 50 apartments. Nonmetro housing occupied by the elderly tends to be older than suburban homes but not as old as central city units. Homes with two or more complete baths are much less likely to be found in nonmetropolitan areas.

Substandard Conditions. Whether occupied by the young or old, nonmetro housing is more likely than metro dwellings to be substandard. Over 11% of nonmetro units occupied by elderly households in 1989 had moderate or severe physical problems. This was a total of 603,000 units. That number contrasts with 507,000 elderly-headed families in central cities and 449,000 in the suburbs living in substandard housing units. Nonmetro areas are more likely than cities or suburbs to have both moderate and severe problems in these units.

Nonmetro elderly people are more likely than metro seniors to live in units with rats, holes in the floor or walls, exposed wiring, or rooms without electrical outlets. The nonmetro elderly have more plumbing problems than people in metro areas. Such problems include a lack of complete bathrooms, kitchens, and/or hot and cold piped water. Elderly-occupied nonmetro units are also more likely to have had a recent water supply stoppage or a recent breakdown in toilets. The home of a

Table 6.2 Occupied Housing Units With Elderly Householder, Income and Financial Characteristics—1989 (in thousands, except for medians)

| | Metro Areas | | Nonmetro Areas |
	Suburbs	Central Cities	
Total occupied units	8,442	6,227	5,432
Households below poverty	1,152	1,259	1,356
Percentage	13.6	20.2	25.0
Household median income	$16,565	$13,920	$11,979
Income of $20,000 or less	2,465	2,369	2,345
Percentage	29.2	38.0	43.2
Median monthly housing costs as percentage of income	21	24	19
No savings or investment	1,468	1,626	1,473
Percentage	17.4	26.1	27.1
Received food stamps	248	363	387
Percentage	2.9	5.8	7.1
Lived in rent-controlled units	31	196	—
Percentage	0.4	3.1	—

SOURCE: USDC/HUD, July 1991.

nonmetro elderly person is much more likely than an central-city or suburban home to lack a complete bathroom. More so than in central-city and suburban settings, the nonmetro elderly are less likely to have central air conditioning or warm air furnaces, more likely to have room heaters with flues—or room heaters without flues—as a main heating source, and more likely to use stoves as a main source of heat.

The Elderly Occupants of Nonmetro Housing

Table 6.2 shows that nonmetropolitan elderly households are much more likely than the central city and suburban elderly to be poor. Twenty-five percent of the nonmetro elderly were poor in 1989, up from 24% in 1987. Median household income among the nonmetro elderly is much less than in cities and suburbs. More than 43% of the nonmetro elderly had household incomes of less than $20,000 in 1989, compared to 38% in cities and 29% in the suburbs.

Although the nonmetro elderly have lower incomes, they also have lower monthly housing costs. For elderly households these costs are

Table 6.3 Occupied Housing Units With Elderly Householder, Characteristics of Occupants—1989 (in thousands, except for medians)

| | Metro Areas | | Nonmetro Areas |
	Suburbs	Central Cities	
Total occupied units	8,442	6,227	5,432
African-American households	343	1,094	391
Percentage	4.1	17.6	7.2
Hispanic households	241	340	79
Percentage	2.9	5.5	1.5
Median age of householder	73	74	74
Median years of school completed	12.3	12.2	11.2

SOURCE: USDC/HUD, July 1991.

19% of income in nonmetro areas and 24% in the inner cities. Suburban housing costs are only slightly higher than nonmetro, amounting to 21% of monthly income.

Proportionally more of the nonmetro than the metro elderly receive food stamps. However, essentially no nonmetro elderly households live in rent-controlled housing. Rent control is an almost entirely urban concept.

Table 6.3 shows that 8.7% of elderly-occupied nonmetro households were African-American or Hispanic in 1989. This is down from 9.1% in 1987. In center-city areas, 23.1% but in suburbs only 7% of elderly households are minority.

Also shown in Table 6.3 is the lower educational level of nonmetro elderly householders—a median of 11.2 years, compared to over 12 years in both city and suburb. These figures are for 1989; in 1987 the gap was wider. The gap narrowed as more people with higher levels of education became elderly. Still, the lower educational median means that the nonmetro elderly will probably have lower incomes and fewer economic and social choices.

Housing Finance and the Nonmetro Elderly

Home mortgages and other types of finance are harder to find in much of nonmetropolitan America for young and old alike. Table 6.4 shows

Table 6.4 Homeowner-Occupied Housing Units With Elderly Householder, Mortgage Characteristics—1989 (in thousands, except for medians)

| | Metro Areas | | Nonmetro Areas |
	Suburbs	Central Cities	
Total owner-occupied units	6,807	4,050	4,470
Owners with 1 or more mortgages	1,336	827	531
Percentage with mortgages	19.6	20.4	11.9
Type of primary mortgage			
FHA	137	137	60
VA	69	92	29
FmHA	13	5	33
Median term (years)	29	29	24
Current interest rate (percent)	8.5	8.3	8.6
Median total outstanding principal amount	$18,899	$18,542	$14,105
Median current total loan as percent of value	24.0	20.3	27.6

SOURCE: USDC/HUD, July 1991.

that only about 1 in 8 nonmetro units occupied by elderly homeowners have mortgages, versus about 1 in 5 in both central cities and suburbs. More of the rural elderly are likely to own their homes outright. But if they have or need a mortgage, conditions will be more difficult than in the cities. Mortgage credit, for example, is more costly and mortgage interest rates are slightly higher in nonmetro places.

The median term of mortgages was less generous for nonmetro elderly homeowners—24 years versus 29 years in both inner cities and suburbs. Mortgage loan balances are likely to be lower for the nonmetro elderly; however, the combination of term and interest rate may mean higher monthly costs for the rural elderly homeowner.

Table 6.4 also shows a difference between central-city, suburban, and nonmetro areas in the equity held by elderly homeowners. Nonmetropolitan elderly homeowners have mortgage loan balances representing on average about 28% of the value of their homes. But suburban and central-city seniors owe a median of 24% and 20% of the value of their homes, respectively. This leads to some difference in assets and wealth. The difference is due in part to the rapidly increasing values of homes in metro areas. Thus, despite a high incidence of homeownership, nonmetro elders face monthly mortgage payments that take a relatively bigger chunk of smaller incomes. And the elderly nonmetro home-owner's equity will probably be smaller than in the suburbs and cities.

Housing Resources for the Nonmetro Elderly

The preceding sections dealt with housing need and poverty. Programs exist to help meet these needs, although they lack the funding needed for the task. Funding in 1992 for all federal rural housing programs was only at about *one third* of the constant dollar levels of 1980.

The Farmers Home Administration (FmHA). In the world of low-income housing, the Farmers Home Administration's rural programs are something of a secret. Many urban-oriented housing experts are only dimly aware of such programs. Created in 1946, the Farmers Home Administration is part of the U.S. Department of Agriculture. FmHA has loan and grant programs for agriculture, housing, business, and rural communities. FmHA programs are restricted to places of less than 10,000 in population, or to places of 10,000 to 25,000 that are not within a Metropolitan Statistical Area. The FmHA definition of *rural* differs from the Census Bureau's nonmetropolitan and rural definitions.

Among the several FmHA rural housing programs, there are none solely for the elderly. But parts of two programs serve the elderly, and others are potentially useful to senior citizens.

The Rural Rental Housing Program. Known popularly as the "Section 515" program, the Rural Rental Housing Program supports both elderly and family rental projects. Section 515 of the Housing Act of 1949 authorizes FmHA to make loans for rural rental housing for persons with low or moderate incomes and for those age 62 and older. (*Rural* here of course means the FmHA definition as described above.) Loans may be used to build new rental projects or purchase and rehabilitate existing structures for rental purposes. Terms are very attractive and help make units affordable. Mortgage loans may be for up to 50 years, and interest rate reduction is available to subsidize low-income affordability. Eligible owners in the Section 515 program are individuals, for-profit corporations, partnerships, nonprofits, Indian tribes, and public agencies. Separate rules published in 1991 make consumer cooperatives eligible participants in the program.

A rental assistance program (Section 521) or HUD Section 8 subsidies can supplement tenants' rents. Funding was $573.9 million for Section

515 loans in 1991 and 1992. Section 521 rental assistance was an additional $308 million in 1991 and $320 million in 1992. Units produced in recent fiscal years were the following:

1988	16,489
1989	15,996
1990	16,063
1991	15,396

This is an impressive record, but it is important to note that in 1979 the program financed 37,000 and in 1980 34,000 units. (Housing Assistance Council [HAC], January 1992). An estimated 40% to 50% of Section 515 funds are used to produce elderly rental projects. The 515 program also may be used for congregate housing projects for the elderly. However, nursing or special care homes are not eligible loan purposes. FmHA Section 515 funds can support development and construction of congregate facilities but not the services that accompany and define such housing. The services and operating costs must have a separate and assured source of funding, or those costs must be affordable to the target population.

In early 1992, the Section 515 program came under investigation by Congress, the General Accounting Office, and the Inspector General of the Agriculture Department. Auditors reported abuses and fraud in the program by some private developers. However, on balance the program is sound and useful. No nonprofit developers of Section 515 projects are under investigation for or have engaged in fraud.

Home Repair Program. Under Section 504 of the Housing Act of 1949, FmHA makes loans and grants to help very low income rural homeowners with repairs, modernization, and improvements, including weatherization and removal of health or safety hazards. Section 504 grants help the very low income rural elderly (age 62 and older) make repairs and improvements. Grants are made when an applicant cannot afford to repay part or all of a loan.

Combined grants and loans are made when there is a partial ability to repay. Section 504 funds are available only for necessary repairs and improvements to make dwellings safer and more sanitary or to alleviate health and safety hazards.

An important feature providing flexibility in this program is that dwellings do not have to be brought up to standard code requirements.

Enforcing codes would make the program more expensive per unit and would mean a further dilution of already limited funds. Not all deficiencies in a home have to be removed, provided that major health and safety hazards are alleviated. Loans are repayable for terms of up to 20 years and carry an interest rate of 1%. Grants are subject to recapture if the property is sold in less than 3 years. Funding was $11.3 million for loans and $12.5 million for grants in 1991 (with all the grants going to the elderly). Loans may be for up to $15,000, whereas grants are limited to no more $5,000 each. Average loan and grant sizes are $3,000 to $4,000. During 1991, FmHA expended virtually all of the Section 504 grant and loan funds.

The program made loans to repair 2,557 units and grants to repair 3,385 units in 1991. This is impressive, but, as with the Section 515 program, there was much more activity in an earlier period. In 1980, for example, there were 6,900 Section 504 loans and 8,000 grants. States making the most extensive use of the program in 1991 were Maine, Vermont, Pennsylvania, Iowa, and the Pacific Trust Territories (HAC, January 1992).

One practical and important facet of the Section 504 program is that it does not try to achieve full rehabilitation of every low-income rural home. Making some basic repairs to remove hazards is a useful middle ground that will keep elderly people in their homes.

The Department of Housing and Urban Development (HUD). HUD is not primarily a rural housing agency, but there are programs within the agency that are used for the rural elderly. The HUD Section 202 program is the leading example. It funds rental housing for both the elderly and the disabled in metropolitan and nonmetropolitan locales. Only nonprofit organizations may be sponsors of Section 202 projects. By law, 25% of the funds allocated under this program are supposed to go to nonmetropolitan areas. Usually HUD meets this goal. In fiscal year 1992, the Section 202 program funded 8,220 rental units with an appropriation of $1,317.9 billion (HAC, February 1992).

A much smaller HUD program is congregate housing services for the elderly. Funding of $17.7 million in fiscal 1992 paid for meals and nonmedical supportive services in public housing or Section 202 elderly or handicapped projects. The aim is to prevent premature institutionalization (U.S. Department of Housing, 1984).

State Programs. There are some state housing programs for the elderly and a smaller number for rural areas. None are specifically for the rural elderly. As federal resources declined in the 1980s, many states expanded or created housing programs. Some of these resources provide home repair. For example, Connecticut has a Senior Citizens Emergency Home Repair Program of low-interest loans. Florida has an Elderly Homeowner Rehab Program and an Elderly Housing Community Loan Program, both providing loans to sponsors for repair programs benefiting the low-income elderly.

Several states have programs that promote shared living. California's Senior Citizens Shared Housing Program makes grants to local governments and nonprofits to help seniors find shared living arrangements. Connecticut and Ohio have similar programs. Connecticut and Florida support congregate housing for the elderly. The former provides grants and loans to create or rehabilitate congregate facilities. Florida's approach is different; 5,000 elderly or handicapped individuals annually receive grants to help pay for congregate room and board (Thompson & Sidor, 1991).

Private Resources. Some limited private resources exist for support of housing for the elderly rural poor. For example, the Housing Assistance Council (HAC) is a source of seed-money loans for elderly and other rural housing projects. These loans are short-term and help leverage permanent financing from such sources as the Farmers Home Administration. More information is available from HAC's Community Development Division at 1025 Vermont Avenue, NW, Suite 606, Washington, DC 20005.

Charitable foundations and churches have in recent time become increasingly involved with homelessness and low-income housing. Most of this activity remains focused on the cities, but some donors—such as the Ford, MacArthur, and Northwest Area Foundations—have supported rural housing programs.

Is Need Being Met?

Clearly there is extensive need for better nonmetro housing for the young and old alike. The nonmetro elderly in particular have higher levels of poverty and substandard housing than people of similar age in the cities and suburbs. There are programs to help meet need, yet shelter problems persist in nonmetropolitan America because of several barriers.

Lack of money in the existing programs is probably the biggest barrier. In 1992, the Section 504 repair program had $23.8 million to repair about 6,000 units. This is impressive, but it will not significantly reduce the number of substandard houses occupied by the rural elderly poor. For example, Section 504 grants repaired about 50,000 elderly-occupied units between 1980 and 1991. But in 1989 there were 243,000 elderly-occupied housing units with severe physical problems and 360,000 with moderate physical problems. Most of the households in these units were very low income. If the Section 504 program has loan and grant funds to repair only 6,000 units, it will obviously be some time before all need is met.

Another program-related problem is inflexibility and difficulty of access. The FmHA 504 program is easier to use but very small. The larger 515 program is very complicated and has a lengthy application process.

Isolation and other factors of geography are also a barrier. For the elderly poor, age, lack of education, a sense of stigma, and low incomes may mean a lack of knowledge of social programs or a reluctance to use them. Many nonmetro (and metro) seniors also prefer to remain in their own single-family homes as long as their health allows. These elderly people value their independence and may be uninterested in apartment living.

The Future of Housing for the Rural Elderly

Housing need among the nonmetro elderly may only intensify as baby boomers age and public resources diminish. Several steps may be useful. First, a better data base and more research are clearly needed. Unfortunately, the sources of data will become more limited, particularly information in the decennial Census of Population and Housing. The 1990 Census omits from the 100% sample—the questionnaire given to all households—a number of questions on housing and other items that were part of earlier censuses. To provide important data, the biannual American Housing Survey and the annual poverty reports from the Current Population Survey should be maintained at least at current levels of detail.

Research on housing for the rural elderly could clearly be expanded. Public and private research devotes little attention to nonfarm rural issues. Housing for the rural elderly is of course only a subset of these rural issues broadly and receives little attention. The U.S. Department of Agriculture, the agency with the largest housing programs for the rural elderly, disbanded its small rural housing research division in the mid-1980s and today conducts little research on that topic or on the rural elderly.

Another needed step is expansion of the existing programs. Given not just potential but actual application backlog for the programs cited, there is clearly a need for more funding. For example, the FmHA Section 515 rental program has great potential for expansion, especially in congregate housing for the elderly.

Also needed are efforts to increase general public awareness of the housing problems of the nonmetro elderly and poor. Both the informed general public and housing specialists are mostly uninformed about housing need in nonmetro areas.

Note

1. *Rural* and *nonmetropolitan* are used here interchangeably, although technically the two terms mean different things. The census defines *rural* as open country and communities of under 2,500 persons. *Nonmetropolitan* areas are counties not within Metropolitan Statistical Areas (MSAs). MSAs are central-city counties of 50,000 persons or more, plus surrounding contiguous counties that are metro in character.

7

The Need for Transportation
Alternatives for the Rural Elderly

MARY R. KIHL

Mobility is clearly a key to quality of life of the rural elderly, and most older residents equate such mobility with the automobile. For the most part, these elderly residents have aged in place, remaining on family homesteads in part by choice and in part because they are unable to find buyers for their homes at a time of a declining agricultural base. Ironically, while they stay, their small home towns continue to decline. Many small towns can no longer provide essential goods and services. Grocery stores are generally only found in larger towns with populations over 2,000, and clothing stores are even less readily available. Consequently if rural residents are to maintain even their basic quality of life they must typically travel considerable distances to the remaining service centers.

Over the years, drivers' licenses have helped define a life-style built on expectations of continued mobility, where travel distances were less significant than access to desired goods and services (Bell, 1987). Consequently, most elderly residents, especially those in rural areas,

AUTHOR'S NOTE: This chapter is based on a study funded by the University Transportation Centers Program of the U.S. Department of Transportation and the Iowa Department of Transportation. The results and views expressed are independent products of university research and are not necessarily concurred with by the funding agencies.

continue to drive even if their reflexes are no longer sharp enough to respond to critical driving cues (Carp, 1988).

In some rural areas the only alternative to the automobile is rural transit, which is primarily dedicated to medical or nutritional trips. As successful as this type of transit has been in serving the basic needs of a particular segment of the rural elderly population, it has not met the needs for discretionary trips. In general, the needs of the more mobile elderly who are reluctant drivers are not being met by human service vehicles. No type of "many-to-one" system can address the needs of a scattered population with scattered preferred destinations.

To help develop alternatives that could respond to this challenge, a study was conducted in 1989-1990 under the auspices of the Midwest Transportation Center. A number of previous studies have identified the transportation needs of clients of social service agencies. This study was much broader, attempting to reflect the interests of "the typical rural elderly resident." The data collection approach involved contacting older residents in their homes and establishing their travel patterns and preferences.

The Target Area

A nine-county area on the Iowa-Missouri border was selected as a target area because of the heavy proportion of senior residents (19%-27%), its rural character, and its relatively high proportion of low-income residents. The target area encompasses 4,755 square miles, includes 86 incorporated places ranging from a population of less than 100 up to 9,500, and is replete with the problems of declining service centers. The area is served by two active rural transit systems but has in recent years had limited access to other types of passenger service.

Study Orientation and Methodology

A combination of attitude surveys and trip logs was the most appropriate means of generating information not only on trip preferences but also on actual trip making among the elderly residents. In June 1989, a telephone screen of 600 households selected at random generated 148 respondents over age 55 who indicated that they were willing to keep track of their trips for a period of 1 week and to answer a brief written survey about their transportation needs. Ninety-eight (66.2%) of the logs and associated surveys were returned. These same respondents were sent a follow-up log in February 1990 to determine whether there were differences between their summer and winter travel patterns.

Respondent Characteristics

The age distribution of the respondents was as follows: 35 (37.2%) in the 55-64 age group, 33 (33.7%) in the 65-75 age group, and 26 (26.5%) over age 75, with 54% females in the sample. Approximately two thirds (65.3%) of the respondents lived in towns and the rest (34.75%) lived in rural areas. Similar to findings in the national literature (Rosenbloom, 1988), the overwhelming majority of these respondents (94.7%) had drivers' licenses. Only 2 (2%) of them said that they never had a license.

Travel Patterns

The average weekly trip rate reported was 8.3 in the summer and 7.7 in winter, both with a mode of 7 trips per respondent. For all those keeping logs, the mean trip distance was 13.3 miles with very little variation among age groups. As expected, most of the trips were to and within towns. Seven of the towns served as full-service communities with such essential services as a doctor, banking facilities, a grocery store, and other shops. Many trips to the doctor apparently required going outside of the nine-county target region. In fact, the average trip to the doctor was more than 19 miles long. A considerable proportion of shopping trips was also to points outside the target region.

Overall, the trip purpose mentioned most frequently was visiting (11.6% of the trips reported), with grocery shopping listed next most frequently (11.5%). Those who worked or carried out voluntary service did so daily, making the proportion for work trips high (11.2% of all reported trips). Other frequently mentioned trips were for recreation and trips to church or other organizations. Trips to the doctor were far less frequently reported (5.9%). Only .6% of the trips were to senior citizen centers. Approximately 20% of the trips reported were multipurpose.

Among the trips reported, 91.3% were made in personal automobiles, 7.8% in a friend's car, .6% in a public bus or van, and .2% in a taxi. The pattern in summer and winter was very similar. A small number used a rural transit van for grocery shopping and banking. Trips to churches or other organizations accounted for 39% of the trips taken in friends' cars.

Reluctant Drivers

Although the respondents were currently meeting travel needs, several questions on the survey, which accompanied the log, pointed to potential future needs. Over 53% of the respondents indicated multiple concerns about driving. Most of these respondents (65% of them) took trips with a family member or friend when such options were available. Three of the five respondents who did not drive took advantage of the rural transit service. What emerges is a response pattern whereby over 50% of the respondents did admit to concerns about driving and responded to transportation alternatives when they were available.

The log keepers were asked whether they would consider a variety of different types of transportation alternatives. They responded as follows: 21.7% indicated that they would consider a shared ride system; 18.3% said they would consider a car pool; as expected, a large proportion, 51.7%, would consider riding with a friend. Although these responses offer no assurance that respondents would actually take advantage of these transportation alternatives, they do offer some indication of interest in riding with others if options were available.

Assessment

Several indicators derived from the trip log survey pointed to a need for alternative transportation for the elderly. First, 10% indicated a driving disability. The majority of these individuals were over age 75 and female. Their average trip rate of 5.5 was lower than the overall average trip rate of 8.2. A second indication of the need for alternative forms of transportation was the reported reluctance to drive under various conditions (e.g., at night, in winter, on major highways, in congested areas).

The third indicator was less obvious but nonetheless real. Using one's own car was clearly the most popular mode of travel (90.8% of the 812 trips recorded). For 13% of those trips, however, the individual keeping the log did not drive himself or herself. The majority of these passenger trips were made by females (69%), generally traveling with their husbands. Over 41% of the personal automobile trips where the respondent was not the driver were made by individuals in the youngest age bracket (aged 55 to 64). Those over age 75 only accounted for 8.5% of the family automobile passenger trips. This oldest group, primarily elderly widows, now drive themselves especially for recreation (20.2%), shopping (14.9%), visiting (11.7%) trips, or for eating out (10.9%). These are the same discretionary trips that are not accommodated by current rural transportation.

A fourth indicator was the number of trips that were made in a friend's car. For all the trips recorded on the trip logs, a friend's car was the second most popular mode. About 29% of the participants used a friend's car as their mode for transportation at least once during the week. They would apparently be willingly to consider an alternative type of transportation system that would take them where and when they wanted to go. Given these findings, consideration of viable transportation options turns quickly to an automobile-based system.

Analysis of Transportation Alternatives

The predetermined objectives for an automobile-based system would be to maximize flexibility and responsiveness while at the same time striving for efficiency and minimizing costs. Given the widely scattered population in the target area and the relatively few full-service communities, any system could at most only approximate the ideal. Any new alternative system design would be regarded as augmenting rather than replacing existing rural transit systems.

The following key aspects would be considered in any type of systems design: potential demand, alternative design and relative capacity, insurance and risk management, operational alternatives, willingness to pay and subsidies, and marketing.

Potential Demand

The attempt to generate potential demand for an automobile-based flexible system in a set of counties that has no existing service of this type is most complex. A number of demand models were considered for potential applicability but most required data or techniques beyond the scope of this project. The model actually employed was one developed by Largo and Burkhardt (1980) to determine the demand for demand-responsive systems as they were being established in the late 1970s. In fact, Jon Burkhardt reaffirmed the model's relevance to this study.

The macro model for demand-responsive systems was applied, as a pilot study, to two counties in the study area—Decatur County, Iowa, and Worth County, Missouri. The data required to apply this model included the following:

1. The total vehicle miles per month for all vehicles in the system (*BMILES*).

2. The average required reservation time (in hours) before a passenger is picked up (*RESVTIME*).

3. The number of persons (expressed in hundreds) in the county who are likely users of the system (*HIPROBPOP*).

The logarithms of these variables were entered into an equation that gave the logarithm of the number of round-trip passengers per month (*RTPASS/M*) that could be expected. The equation used was this:

$$\log (RTPASS/M) = -1.879 + (1.099 \times \log BMILES) - (0.217 \times \log RESVTIME) + (0.194 \times \log HIPROBPOP)$$

With this equation, the amount of service provided (represented by the miles traveled per month) strongly influences the estimated number of riders. In using the equation the reservation time was set at 1 day (24 hours) because this appears to be the standard reservation time required on most rural demand-responsive systems. The figures used for the high probability population (HIPROBPOP) were those 65 and over according to the 1990 census.

The models indicated that despite the sizable proportion of elderly in the target area there would be an insufficient number of elderly alone to support a demand-responsive system. For example, if the vehicle ran 3,500 miles a month, it would generate a maximum of 172 round trips in Worth County, Missouri, and 215 round trips in Decatur County, Iowa. Even if the service were made available to all low-income residents, the demand figures would still be low: 235 round trips in Decatur county and 193 round trips in Worth County. To be viable the system would need to be made available to the general public. These low-demand figures support the concept of using a low-capacity vehicle (an automobile) to perform the service.

Alternative Designs and Relative Capacity

The study explored two different types of automobile systems: first, a type of rural jitney, and second, a coordinated volunteer system. Elements of the two approaches could also be incorporated into a type of hybrid system.

Rural Jitney Service

According to some rural transportation specialists, "the closest we have come so far in developing the ideal transit system is a shared taxi or jitney—an automobile based form of public transit made adaptable to low-density, dispersed settlement patterns; capable of providing random access service from anywhere to anywhere approximately door to door" (Melvin Webber, quoted in Behnke, 1985).

Initially, such a system could involve one car per county traveling largely to locations within that county, although relatively short trips across county lines would also be possible. Most small towns in the target region are within a 10-mile radius of a county seat town that does offer a full range of services. Twenty-four-hour call up would be essential to enable optimal pre-planning of routes. Additional pickups in town would, however, be possible on a space- and time-available basis.

To determine the feasibility of such an option an optimization model, Systan's Macro-Analytic Regional Transportation Model (SMART) (Canfield & Lim, 1983), was modified to relate to the travel patterns reflected in surveys returned by elderly residents in the nine-county target region. The model helps to assess the optimum number of passengers to be carried, given the average distance between stops and average speed of the vehicle. Since the SMART model was originally used to determine the optimum number of riders for a commuter car pool, several modifications were needed for this application. A factor for *dwell time* at each stop was added to reflect the amount of time the driver would need at each stop to get out of the vehicle and escort the elderly rider.

The modified formulas for travel within a rural area are as follows:

$$De = 1.67 + .74\ N\ (S/4)$$
$$T = 2(Dw \times N) + (De/MPM)$$

where De = estimated distance , N = number of stops per tour, S = length of side of zone (in this case the width of the county in miles), T = time of tour, Dw = dwell time (in minutes) per stop per passenger, and MPM = speed of vehicle in miles per minute.

Figuring driving time at 55 miles per hour or .91 miles per minute on country roads, and an average dwell time of 3 minutes (a figure confirmed by several rural demand responsive systems), the tour would be 22 minutes for 2 passengers and 32 minutes for 3 passengers. A fourth passenger would make the tour take 42 minutes, almost double the driving time. A significant part of the difference in time is in the dwell time.

A modified model for a trip between two towns builds in slower driving time in town than on the "express" trip between the two towns along with the 3-minute dwell time for boarding and unboarding each passenger. When the model is applied to trips between two small towns 15 miles apart, it is apparent that 3 people can be picked up in one town and delivered to different locations in the other in 47 minutes or 4 people in 55 minutes. This would not be an unreasonable trip time for elderly passengers.

The model was then used to consider the potential capacity for a single vehicle operating a combination of intrarural and intertown trips. In an hour, with careful scheduling, one vehicle could serve up to 4 intertown passengers traveling between towns 15 miles apart. It could also serve five to six 5-mile rural trips in an hour. Such a system would comfortably provide for 19 to 20 passengers (40 trips in a day), or 400 round trips a month, well surpassing the potential demand for 215 round trips a month estimated by using the Burkhardt model.

The more traditional van with nine passengers would be more efficient because dwell time can be reduced to 1 minute per passenger by having everyone get off at the same location. If, however, the nine passengers got off at nine different destinations in town, the time for a trip between two towns 15 miles apart would be 94.37 minutes. Such a long trip would discourage a potential rider who would note that, for example, the same intertown trip would take only 22 minutes in a personal automobile.

Volunteer Driver Systems

Because few rural transit systems have capital sufficient to buy automobiles or to pay the drivers to operate them, an increasing number of rural transit systems have begun using volunteer drivers to serve the widely scattered elderly riders in rural areas. Most such systems currently receive subsidies in terms of reimbursements for seniors transported from the Area Agency on Aging (AoA), which provides that top priority be given for medical trips, followed by nutritional trips. Where there is no grocery delivery service, trips to the grocery are also high priority. Other trips are possible after these purposes are met. A number of rural systems use volunteer driver programs to supplement their service. Vans are then available for larger group intertown trips or for picking up a group of individuals and delivering them all to one destination, for example a nutrition site.

Interviews with directors of volunteer driver systems indicate that the AoA reimbursement is usually passed along directly to the volunteer drivers. One of the systems also paid the drivers for lunch. Volunteer drivers use their own cars and are responsible for maintaining their own cars. A paid coordinator is responsible for keeping track of volunteers and scheduling. All systems contacted highly encouraged the 24 hour advanced reservations although most accommodate emergencies.

The systems interviewed relied on pools of volunteers ranging from 6 to 20 per county. All volunteer drivers were over 65 years of age. Some went through a specialized training program, but all were selected after a careful review of their driving record. Some systems engaged volunteers to encourage others to join the pool, whereas the coordinator recruited drivers in others. For all systems, however, the task of soliciting and retaining volunteers was a primary activity. The larger the pool, the less often it was necessary to go back to the same individual with requests and run the risk of burnout.

The capacity of such a volunteer system is considerably less than the shared-ride taxi alternative because each volunteer performs at most a limited number of trips a week. The driver of the rural jitney, however, would be a regular employee and would be expected to perform trips all day according to a prearranged schedule. Nevertheless, the volunteer system does allow the flexibility of operating several vehicles at one time in different towns and of providing for lengthy individual trips to the medical center. The volunteer also provides the reassurance of being picked up by a familiar person. It is tempting, however, for regular riders to call the volunteer directly rather than calling the dispatcher, thereby undermining the system.

Risk Management and Insurance

Relative risk and risk management becomes an important consideration when assessing any type of transportation alternative for the rural elderly. Given the small size of many rural operations, the relatively high operating costs per mile, and limited budgets, most rural systems have been reluctant to initiate any type of innovative service that might raise insurance rates (Abacus Technology, 1989, p. 10-1).

For rural transit agencies that involve volunteer drivers using their own cars, an umbrella policy is frequently deemed necessary because the family automobile insurance policies held by most volunteers exclude coverage when the automobile is used as "a public conveyance" and mileage payments and assigned pickups, in effect, make it "a public conveyance" (Vaughan & Elliot, 1978, p. 466). This approach does cover the potential liability claims against the volunteer and the rural transit agency itself. The rural transit system then carries an umbrella policy of up to $1 million, which would kick in on an excess liability claim or a claim not covered by the volunteers' own policy. To date, only minor claims have been placed and none of the systems contacted have had to test the operations of the umbrella policy. Fears of tort claims have been largely turned aside since the insurance crisis of the mid-1980s, but there still is a potential for such a claim, especially when volunteer drivers are responsible for escorting frail individuals to and from cars. Rural transit agencies would, therefore, be well advised to couple their umbrella policies with greater efforts at risk avoidance, including formal driver's training programs and careful monitoring of volunteers. Liability for any paid drivers would be covered under the more traditional employees' liability insurance, and their activities would necessarily be more closely supervised and monitored.

Proposed System

A comparison of the relative merits of these two types of automobile services does not produce conclusive results. The paid-driver jitney system is clearly more efficient, whereas the volunteer system can offer greater flexibility in terms of type of service because more than one driver is available at a time. The volunteer program saves some of the costs of a driver's salary but requires more costs in training sessions, system management, and start-up time. The level of exposure of the senior volunteer drivers, especially in systems with a limited pool of volunteers, leaves serious questions regarding the benefit of the system in terms of reducing the risk of accidents involving elderly drivers. What seems to be indicated is a type of system that would maximize the advantages of both of these types of systems.

Relying on a paid-driver jitney service for the backbone of the system would provide regular reliable service most efficiently. This system would operate in towns as well as in rural areas. It would be supplemented by volunteers in towns without taxis. Longer individualized trips to medical centers outside the county limits, and trips requiring escort service, would also be the province of the volunteer service. The jitney would perform intertown trips within the county for groups of two or three passengers, but for larger groups a van would clearly be more efficient. The van would also be most appropriate for group excursions to shopping centers outside the region.

Funding

As indicated above, costs for an automobile system would generally represent incremental costs for the host system. Most rural transit or paratransit systems are heavily subsidized by a number of federal, state, and local programs. Fortunately, federal assistance for rural transit has remained at a fairly stable level. Social service subsidies provide much needed supplemental funding based on the miles over which clients are transported. These funds are flexible in terms of transportation mode, but they introduce substantial requirements in terms of reporting procedures and service priorities.

With limitations in terms of capacity and the requirements associated with service priorities, most rural systems are inclined to invest available capital funds in vans or minibuses that can transport reasonably large numbers of individuals efficiently. Well-built vans also can accomplish many miles without an undue amount of maintenance. Vans are, however, inefficient in taking one or two people visiting and shopping because they have an operating cost of $.19-$.24 a mile, not including depreciation.

An automobile, in contrast, would be ideally suited to more individualized trips and could be operated with parallel operating costs (including fuel, maintenance, and insurance, but not depreciation) of only $.08 a mile. By extension, the automobile would be most appropriate for taking one or two people to medical appointments at a distance, reserving the minibus or van for a group of people going to the same destination.

Interest in flexible transportation is apparent in the use of taxis where available. In small towns where privately operating taxi systems are available, they can be and frequently are used to provide shared-ride service (Gallagher, 1978, pp. 82-83; Gilbert, 1977, pp. 32, 40). For most rural areas, however, there are no existing taxi companies. Unfortunately, few public systems are able to justify purchasing an automobile with public funds. Volunteer programs insist that drivers supply their own cars. An enterprising system however, might be able to request a donation of a car from a civic-minded automobile dealership and then only need to continue to use federal funding to help defray operating costs. Such a move would have the benefit of providing for a more flexible system and at the same time building civic pride in the system.

Because federally assisted systems are not permitted to charge a stated fare for service, most systems have a contribution box on the van or have passengers hand an envelop to a volunteer driver. Unfortunately, these subtle approaches have generated very little revenue to help defray costs. For systems to add more flexible service the passengers who are able will need to contribute an increased share of the costs.

It is reassuring that many rural residents in the target area would be willing to pay at least part of the costs of a service that would help them maintain their independence. User-side subsidies are well established in connection with demand-responsive service and with volunteer driver systems. When asked about willingness to pay, 50.7% of respondents to the survey discussed at the start of this chapter indicated a willingness to pay over $2 for a trip to the doctor and 28.8% would be willing to pay over $4. More than 50% were willing to pay $1 to $2 for a trip to the grocery and 9.3% of them would pay between $4 and $5 for such a trip. Nine percent indicated that they would pay $4 or more for a discretionary trip. Where existing systems do charge for individualized or recreational trips, they find seniors willing to pay (Wilson, 1985, p. 114). Individuals who cannot pay can be accommodated if coupon books are sold on a sliding scale, as is done with food stamps. Regardless of the method used, there should be a clear indication regarding the level of donation expected.

An alternative approach would involve selling subscriptions that would entitle purchasers to a specified number of trips. This concept has been tried effectively in Des Moines, Iowa, with C-Pals, a privately funded automobile-based system. Subscriptions are frequently paid by younger residents to insure their parents of continued mobility without relying on driving their own cars. A modification of this concept would potentially be possible. This type of system would still need partial subsidies to insure service to low-income residents, but it would be far less dependent on public funds.

Marketing

An automobile-based system would be designed to appeal to a broader array of seniors than those currently using the available rural transit system, but the nature of the appeal to potential riders is critical. Typically, independently minded rural elderly turn away from anything that appears to be associated with government programming. They do, however, respond to ideas suggested by a relatively small group of friends.

According to Moschis (1987), most older people have about 15 friends who provide companionship, support, and information. These friends not only provide information but they also sift and validate information coming from other sources. Older people do watch a considerable amount of television, but they focus on TV advertising only after they have heard about a product or service from a friend. Generally, TV spots are too brief to provide an initial appeal to the elderly. The elderly are typically avid readers of newspapers and will have time to focus more fully on a service described in the paper. However, to translate knowledge into action would again take a recommendation from a friend (Moschis, 1987, pp. 119, 157, 203).

With these ideas in mind it is possible to develop strategies that can effectively market the transportation system to a group that can be classed at best as "reluctant consumers". A key issue in developing this strategy would be to develop an appealing image for the system. Over 80% of the senior residents who participated in the 1989 Iowa-Missouri telephone survey were familiar with the existence of the current rural systems in their area, but they commented that they did not need to use them. They perceived that those systems were for those who had no other way to travel. If the augmented systems are to have broader appeal, they will need to change this image.

The automobile-based systems would have a number of elements that could be stressed in developing this expanded image. Flexibility and availability are two key aspects. They would relate to the primary importance that the elderly place on the value of "the personal touch" (Pitts & Woodside, 1984, pp. 214-215). This concept could be further enhanced by emphasizing the service qualities expected from a familiar, caring driver. Where volunteer programs have been successful, invariably the relationship with the drivers is highlighted. This close association with the driver was also clearly evident in interviews with current users of the rural transit systems in the target area. However, if the system is to appeal broadly to a variety of elderly residents, its image will also need to include the aura of professionalism. A "clubish" transportation group, although very reassuring to those involved, appears exclusive to those not regularly involved.

To be effective in marketing this new image to the rural seniors will require using a word-of-mouth approach rather than relying on media presentations. One approach, similar to that used in community development, would be to generate local enthusiasm about the augmented systems by appealing to community leaders who would then share information with potential users and form a type of coalition advisory group (*Public Transportation Coalition Building,* 1989). This would enable the communities themselves to "own the system" (Robinson & Lovelock, 1979 p. 43). Another approach, which could operate in tandem with that just described, would be to have organizations and groups that involve elderly residents directly contact their members. These marketing approaches will take considerable time and effort, but the potential for success is far greater than simply distributing fliers and featuring a ribbon cutting on television.

Conclusion

An automobile-based system would appeal to two groups of elderly: first, the current transportation-dependent group who would use it for relatively short-distance social and shopping trips and longer-distance medical trips, and second, those who could be considered choice riders—elderly residents who have access to a personal auto but are concerned about driving and would welcome a flexible alternative. The second group might well include some residents with higher incomes. The physical deterioration that comes with age affects all regardless of income. There was no correlation between income level and concern about driving in the nine-county Iowa-Missouri study. The national accident figures for the very elderly certainly reflect people with all income levels. Nevertheless, elderly individuals who are not accustomed to relating to social service agencies will not ride in a social service van. They typically insist on driving even when they have difficulty seeing or are not sufficiently alert to drive. The more personalized service of a rural jitney (a shared-ride rural taxi) would, however, potentially appeal to them.

Fortunately, the majority of survey respondents indicated a willingness to contribute toward a flexible transportation system. Those who are able to pay can, in fact, indirectly provide a cross-subsidy to others and play a part in maintaining the system. No innovation of this type can be effective, however, in attracting elderly riders without a sensitive proactive marketing program. Plans for such a marketing system must be developed at the same time as the system is being developed.

In the final analysis, a rural transportation system will only be an effective alternative to driving a car when it begins to serve purposes that the elderly themselves consider high priority—visiting, personal recreation, and shopping. Those are trip purposes for which many seniors are reluctant to request a ride from a friend or relative and trips that are not accommodated by most current rural transit systems. Yet these trips are important to maintaining the quality of life of rural elderly residents. They represent the continued mobility that the rural elderly equate with personal independence.

PART III

Physical and Mental Health

8

In Sickness and in Health

Age, Social Support, and the Psychological Consequences of Physical Health Among Rural and Urban Residents

SUZANNE T. ORTEGA
MARTHA J. METROKA
DAVID R. JOHNSON

Research on mental health routinely finds that physical health status is a powerful predictor of depression among community residents; individuals who perceive their physical health as poorer, who have physical disabilities, or who have more disease symptoms all report higher levels of depressed mood (Aneshensel, Frerichs, & Huba 1984; Berkman et al.,1986; Carpiniello, Carta, & Rudas, 1989; Dean, Kolody, & Wood, 1990; Frerichs, Aneshensel, Yokopenic, & Clark, 1982; Haug, Breslau, & Folmar, 1989; Kennedy, Kelman, & Thomas, 1990; Turner & Noh, 1988). Research consistently shows that older persons have more chronic health conditions than younger persons (Turner & Noh, 1988); somewhat less consistently, data also show that rural residents have higher levels of chronic illness and impairment than do urban dwellers (Lassey & Lassey, 1985; Reitzes, Mutran, & Pope, 1991; Sotomayor, 1981; but

AUTHORS' NOTE: This research was supported in part by Grant R01-MH44317-01 from the National Institute of Mental Health.

see also Krout, 1986; Stoller, 1984). Given these findings and all else being equal, one would expect that older rural residents would have the highest levels of depression. Of course, all else is seldom equal and mental health research does not, in fact, consistently demonstrate the expected age and rural/urban effects. Instead, studies generally find that older persons report higher levels of well-being (Gove, Ortega, & Style, 1989) and are less likely to experience depressive disorders (Blazer, Hughes, & George, 1987; George, 1989) than younger persons; and if rural residents are not in unequivocally better mental health than urban residents, they are not clearly in poorer mental health either (Bull & Aucoin, 1975; Ortega & Johnson, 1990).

Few attempts—theoretical or empirical—have been made to explain the seeming paradox that rural residents and the elderly, groups with relatively poor physical health, do not have concomitantly high levels of depression. With respect to the rural/urban effect, the literature on social support provides a possible clue. As this literature makes abundantly clear, social support systems can provide an effective buffer to stressful life events such as marital loss, economic hardship, and perhaps ill health (Pearlin, Lieberman, Menaghan, & Mullen, 1981; Sherbourne & Hays, 1990). If, as many have suggested, rural communities provide a more supportive environment than cities (Reitzes et al., 1991), the rural social support advantage may simply buffer or counteract the rural disadvantage in physical health status (Schooler, 1975).

The age paradox is somewhat harder to explain. It is possible that older persons are better able to mobilize social support during periods of illness than are younger persons. Although older persons are scarcely isolates, this interpretation seems unlikely. First, the social support networks of older persons tend to be slightly smaller than those of younger persons (Babchuk, 1979). Second, there is a positive association between age and long-term illness; it seems likely that the longer the duration of illness, the greater the probability that social support resources will be depleted. Indeed, there is some support for this hypothesis in the literature on financial hardship and the elderly; researchers report that as the duration of financial difficulties increase, social ties and emotional support actually weaken (Krause & Jay, 1991). Consequently, differences in level of social support are unlikely to explain the relationship between age, physical health status, and mental health. It remains possible, however, that social support and age interact in such a way that the mental health consequences of physical impairment are attenuated in old age (Dean et al., 1990; Turner, 1983). Alternatively, age may interact with physical health; physical health may simply have a different meaning and thus different mental health consequences across the life course. Although few studies have systematically explored this hypothesis, there is some evidence that the association between psychological distress and physical symptoms varies at different stages of life (Aneshensel et al., 1984; Hansell & White, 1991; Turner & Noh, 1988).

In this chapter, we adopt a life course perspective and test both additive and interactive models of the relationships among place of residence, age, physical health, social support, and depression. Specifically, we begin by using multiple classification analysis to describe and compare the social support, physical, and mental health status of rural and urban residents and older and younger respondents. We focus on symptoms of depression (1) because of its prevalence and (2) because some studies report it to be the most common psychiatric disease associated with physical illness (Kathol & Petty, 1981).

Next, we use multiple regression to specify the indirect effects of age and community type on mental health; indirect effects are hypothesized to operate primarily through physical health status and social support. In order to test the hypothesis that the effects of physical health vary across age strata and across the rural/urban continuum, models are estimated that include two-way interactions between place of residence, age, social support, and physical health.

Finally, multiple regression is used to assess which has the greater effects on depression—change in health status or level of health. The hypothesis that *change* in physical health status has different mental health consequences for the young and old is also tested.

The study contributes to the gerontological mental health literature by specifying the extent to which the community context impacts the physical or psychological well-being of older persons. The study also contributes to the literature on rural elderly by systematically describing and explaining rural/urban differences in three basic quality-of-life indicators—health status, depression, and social support. Last, data from the panel component of the study bear on one other unresolved question in the current literature: Is it change in health status or health status per se that has the strongest effects on mental health?

Study Design

This study is based on a representative sample of Nebraskans, 18 years of age and older. Cross-sectional analyses are based on the approximately 2,500 respondents, who were interviewed in 1989 (T_2); change analyses are based on the 1,411 respondents who had also been interviewed in 1986 (T_1). Johnson and Ortega (1992) provide a detailed description of the study design and report finding no evidence of significant response bias to either the cross-section or panel components of the survey.

Dependent Variables

The major dependent variable in this study is depression in 1989. Depression was measured by the 18-item Warheit depression subscale (Schwab, Bell, Warheit, & Schwab, 1979). Reliability and validity tests conducted by Schwab et al. (1979) found that the scale was able to differentiate clinical and nonclinical populations, was consistent with the judgments of psychiatrists, and had an alpha reliability coefficient in excess of .80.

Physical health serves as both a dependent and an explanatory variable. Health, at both T_1 and T_2 is measured by a single item that asks respondents to rate their health as excellent = 4; good = 3; fair = 2; and poor = 1. Although subjective evaluations of one's own health may be confounded with depression, research shows that perceived health items correlate well with functional status indicators and other objective measures of health status (Fillenbaum, 1979; Mor-Barak, Miller, & Syme, 1991). It is also the case that results from studies using objective indicators of health closely parallel those of studies using perceived health measures.

Independent Variables

The two major independent variables are age and rural/urban place of residence or community size. Age is a respondent's actual chronological age in 1989; in descriptive analyses, age is collapsed into five categories: 18-34, 35-49, 50-64, 65-81, and 82 and over, representing periods of early, young, middle, older, and late adulthood, respectively.

In order to take into account the heterogeneity of rural life, we use a categoric measure of community size that reflects five points on the rural/urban continuum: farms, rural (open country and towns with populations less than 2,500), towns with populations of 2,500 to 10,000, cities with populations from 10,000 to 50,000, and metropolitan areas larger than 50,000. In all multiple regression analyses, community type is entered as a series of dummy variables, with metropolitan being the omitted category.

Explanatory Variables

In addition to physical health status, the major explanatory variable is social support. Blazer (1982) and Deimling and Harel (1984) have demonstrated the importance of distinguishing between objective and subjective indicators of social support. Thus, two measures of social support are included in this study. One measure reflects the perceived adequacy of social support; the other is a more objective measure of the actual support received. Both measures are derived from the 40-item Interpersonal Support Evaluation List developed by Cohen, Mermelstein, Kamarek, and Hoberman (1985). The Available Social Support Index is a count of the number of different types of support the respondent perceives to be available to him or her through their existing support network. Scores on this index range from 0 to 13, but the variable is highly skewed. Consequently, scores of 0 through 7 are set equal to 7. The Actual Social Support Index is a tally of the number of different types of support the respondent actually received within the last year. Scores on this index range from 0 to 8.

Control Variables

Because they are associated with both depression and community size, in all analyses we control for the effects of education, gender, and marital status; education is the actual number of years of schooling completed by the respondent, and gender and marital status are both dummy variables, with male and married coded as 0 and female and not married coded as 1.

Findings

Multiple classification analysis (MCA) was used to explore the relationship between age, community type, and each of the dependent and

explanatory variables. Results are presented in Table 8.1. Unadjusted
mean values for each variable are presented in Column 1 (UNADJ).
Column 2 (ADJC) displays the mean value for each community type
and each age category, controlling for gender, marital status, and education. Mean values, adjusted for the control variables and the other
independent variable, are arrayed in Column 3 (ADJC+I).

Looking first at the top panel and at the zero-order effects of age,
there is no evidence that older people have higher (or lower) levels of
depression than middle-aged or younger adults. Although the results are
not statistically significant, the trend, with the exception of individuals
82 and older, is for depression to decrease with age. In contrast to results
for depression, however, age is significantly and inversely related to
each of the other three variables; these relationships are substantively,
as well as statistically, significant. People in the oldest age category are
much more likely to rate their health as fair to good ($X = 2.67$), whereas
individuals in young adulthood are more likely to rate their health as
good to excellent ($X = 3.39$). Compared to the oldest respondents,
individuals in the youngest age group report having more types of
support available to them (11.03 and 12.25, respectively). Similarly,
young adults report having received, on the average, at least one more
type of support over the course of the last year than older persons (4.81
compared to 3.42). Although age-related decreases in social support are
meaningful, it is important to keep in mind that persons of all ages report
having nearly the maximum number of supports available; even among
the oldest category, where potential supports are lowest, the average
respondent reports having 11 of 13 potential types of support available.

Perhaps more significant than age-related reductions in available
support is the decline with age in received support. Although the results
reported in Table 8.1 do not control for *need* for support, it is reasonable
to conclude on the basis of age-related changes in health that need for
support increases with age. At the same time, the actual receipt of
support appears to decrease. We will address this point more directly in
the regression analyses reported later. Suffice it to say at this point that
chronological age does appear to effect perceived physical health and
social support and, as findings in Column 2 show, these effects are not
a result of age/cohort differences in education or in the gender or marital
status composition of the population.

Column 2 displays health ratings and social support scores by age
category, adjusting for the effects of sex, education, and marital status.
Compared to the zero-order effect, introduction of controls somewhat

Table 8.1 Mean Depression, Health, and Social Support by Age and Community Type, Controlling for Marital Status, Education, Sex, and Other Independent Variable (MCA)

	Depression			Perceived Health			Available Support			Received Support		
	UNADJ	ADJC	ADJC+I	UNADJ	ADJC	ADJC+I	UNADJ	ADJC	ADJC+I	UNADJ	ADJC	ADJC+I
Age												
18-34	13.96	14.08	14.30	3.39	3.38	3.37	12.25	12.18	12.19	4.81	4.82	4.82
35-49	13.32	14.23	14.19	3.30	3.24	3.24	12.09	11.95	11.96	4.28	4.28	4.32
50-64	13.03	13.13	13.07	3.04	3.05	3.05	12.09	11.09	11.90	3.43	3.43	3.51
65-81	12.89	12.15	12.02	2.83	2.90	2.91	11.66	11.82	11.82	3.20	3.20	3.13
82+	13.48	11.92	11.74	2.67	2.78	2.80	11.03	11.32	11.32	3.42	3.42	3.09
Eta/Beta	.06	.12**	.13**	.30**	.25**	.24**	.19**	.13**	.13**	.33**	.34**	.34**
Community Type												
Farm	13.13	13.17	13.23	3.25	3.25	3.26	12.16	12.15	12.12	3.89	3.97	4.02
Rural	13.26	13.08	13.16	3.08	3.12	3.10	11.95	12.01	12.04	3.80	3.83	3.93
Town	13.47	13.46	13.53	3.18	3.18	3.18	11.88	11.89	11.89	3.91	3.92	3.98
City	13.40	13.51	13.50	3.11	3.09	3.07	12.03	11.99	11.97	4.07	4.02	3.98
Metro	13.53	13.71	13.06	3.13	3.13	3.11	11.98	11.93	11.88	4.17	4.08	4.01
Eta/Beta	.02	.04	.03	.08*	.07*	.08*	.06	.05	.06	.07	.05	.02

NOTE: UNADJ = Unadjusted. ADJC = Adjusted for Control Variables. ADJC+I = Adjusted for Control Variables and Independent Variable.
*p < .01; **p < .001

reduces the effect of age on perceived health and available support; for health, the eta of .30 is reduced to a beta of .25, and for available support the coefficients change from .19 to .13. Age effects are virtually unchanged for received support (eta/beta of .33 and .34). For both health and social support, then, age effects are significant and the net effects of age, with or without controlling for basic demographic variables, are highly similar (compare unadjusted and adjusted means in Columns 1 and 2). For depression, however, introduction of controls actually doubles the size of age effects. After adjusting for sex, marital status, and education, the effects of age are clearly significant, inverse, and monotonic, with average scores ranging from 14.08 among 18- to 34-year-olds to 11.92 among individuals 82 years of age and older. Thus, even without taking changes in health or social support into account, the general trend is for individuals in this sample to become less, not more, depressed with age.

Note that neither the findings for depression nor the findings for health status and social support are significantly impacted by the residential characteristics of our respondents; results are basically unaffected by the introduction of an additional control for community type (see Column 3). This is not surprising given the finding that community type is, by itself, unrelated to three of the four major dependent and explanatory variables in this study.

In the bottom panel of Table 8.1, mean scores on depression, health, available support, and received support are arrayed by community type. There are no rural/urban differences in depression or social support. However, community type is related to perceived health. Before and after controls, individuals living on farms report the best health. Interestingly, respondents living in towns of 2,500 to 10,000 populations report the next highest level of health. After adjusting for demographic variables, rural/open country area residents and metropolitan residents have very similar levels of health; after controls are introduced, city dwellers perceive the worst overall level of health. The patterns we find are generally consistent with Krout's 1984 study (as cited in Krout, 1986), in which he found that nonmetropolitan elders perceived their health as better than those living in larger communities. However, two points are in order. First, although community differences in health are significant, they are not particularly strong; most people, regardless of community type, perceive their health to be in the good to excellent range. The second point is that the relationship between community type and health is neither linear nor monotonic; thus, community effects cannot be interpreted as a direct function of community size. This is a particularly important finding, given the tendency to treat place of residence as a simple dichotomous variable—metropolitan/nonmetropolitan or urban/rural—or to treat rural/urban differences as though the only important distinctions among communities stem from population size and density. We shall return to this point in closing.

In sum, although age has consistent additive effects on each of the health and social support variables, there is little variation across community type on these variables. With the exception of perceived health, farm residents, residents of small towns, cities, and metropolitan areas are very similar to one another. There is no evidence, either, of community interaction effects. In none of the MCA's summarized in Table 8.1 were the age*community type interaction terms significant. Controlling for differences in gender, marital status, and education, there is no support for the proposition that the mental health, health, and social support consequences of aging are different for rural and urban residents; although farmers perceive their health to be better than city dwellers, older farmers are no more and no less likely to do so than younger farm residents.[1]

In order to assess the extent to which age and community type impact mental health, indirectly, through physical health and social support, a series of multiple regression analyses were conducted. Results are reported in Table 8.2.

Consistent with MCA results, the simple bivariate relationship between age and depression (Column 1) is not significant, but the relationship after controlling for demographic variables and community type (Column 2) is.

Column 3 shows the results of the regression in which perceived health is added to the equation. After adjusting for health, age effects become even more pronounced; the size of the regression coefficient for age almost doubles, with a beta of $-.094$ before the health control is introduced and $-.183$ after controls. On the one hand, these results suggest that if it were not for age-related declines in health, the tendency for depression to decrease with age would be even more pronounced. On the other hand, the data clearly show that health is the single strongest predictor of depression. Health effects (beta $= -.358$) are nearly twice as strong as those of the next strongest predictor—age—and the increment to R^2 due perceived health is .113. To the extent that age is accompanied by declines in health, we would expect somewhat higher levels of depression among older populations. This is particu-

Table 8.2 Standardized Regression Coefficients Testing the Effects of Age, Health, Community Type, and Social Support on Depression

	Model 1	Model 2	Model 3	Model 4
Age	−.039	−.094***	−.183***	−.153***
Gender		.035	.040*	.049**
Marital status		.128***	.105***	.054**
Education		−.133***	−.078***	−.050**
Community type				
Farms		−.016	.009	.022
Rural		−.010	−.006	.006
Town		.004	.016	.011
City		−.002	−.008	−.003
Health			−.358***	−.268***
Available support				−.335***
Received support				.156***
R^2	.002	.037	.150	.257

* $= p \leq .05$; ** $= p \leq .01$; *** $= p \leq .001$

larly important to note since data suggest that health effects are only partially mitigated by social support (see Column 4 of Table 8.2). Although introducing controls for social support reduces the size of the regression coefficient (from −.358 to .268), health status remains a strong predictor of depression. Social support, especially perceived support, however, is an even stronger predictor of depression than health.

Both available support and received support are significantly related to depression. Together, the two social support indicators add an additional .107 to the variance explained by the overall regression equation. Note, however, that their effects are in the opposite direction. Although perceived availability of support is strongly and inversely related to depression ($B = -.335$), received support bears a more modest, but still significant, positive relationship to depression ($B = .156$). The somewhat counterintuitive result for received support makes sense once we take into account the fact that depressed persons are more likely to *need* support; they are, therefore, also more likely to receive it. In sum, social support has two important kinds of effects on depression. As regression results reported in Table 8.2 indicate, social support has strong direct effects on depression. However, as previously noted, social support also has indirect effects on depression through "buffering" individuals from the mental health consequences of decrements in physical health; introducing controls for social support substantially reduces the effects of health.

It is also interesting to note in Table 8.2 that introducing controls for social support only slightly decreases the effects of age; although age is related to social support, the effects of age on depression are largely independent of it. This is true not only in analyses based on a simple additive model but also of models that include age*social support, age*health, or age*community type interaction terms; in no instance did these interaction terms reach statistical significance when they were added, individually, to regression models (data not shown).

In order to test the possibility that age and health affect depression primarily because their effects differentially impact social support, two final regression models were estimated. In addition to each of the independent and control variables, age*health interaction terms were added to equations predicting each of the social support measures. Although findings from these analyses clearly show that health status impacts social support, there is no evidence that the impact of health on social support is any different for older persons than it is for younger, and this is true for both the available support and received support measures. It is worth noting, however, that health status, independent of age, is positively related to available social support; people who perceived their health to be better report higher levels of available support ($B = .214$). Despite reporting a smaller pool of potential supports, people who report their health as poorer actually do receive *more* different types of support ($B = -.118$).

Change Analysis

To differentiate between the effects of level of health and *change* in health between 1986 and 1989, two new health variables were created. The first, designed to measure average level of health status over the last 3 years is the sum of the respondent's health status in the two waves ($HS_1 + HS_2$). The second measure is an indicator of change between the two waves and was created by subtracting health status in 1989 from health status in 1986 ($HS_1 - HS_2$). The higher the score on this second variable, the greater the change in health; positive scores signal declines in health and negative scores signal an improvement in health.

Table 8.3 Standardized Regression Coefficients From Regression, Testing the Effect of Health Change on Depression

	Depression
Age	−.154***
Gender	.052*
Marital Status	.057**
Education	−.020
Community type	
Farm	.019
Rural	.003
Town	.017
City	.003
Health	−.309***
Health change	.067***
Available support	−.354***
Received support	.156***
R^2	.304

*$p < .05$; **$p < .01$; ***$p < .001$

Typically, change is measured in regression analysis by including measures of health status at T_1 and T_2. The method used here yields precisely the same R^2 as the more conventional approach but has the advantage that the coefficients for the added and subtracted terms can be directly interpreted as the effects of (1) level of health status and (2) change in health status (Judd & McClelland, 1989). Results from this analysis are presented in Table 8.3.

Both the level of health and change in health significantly affect depression. However, the effects of health status per se are stronger than those of the change variable; betas are −.309 and .067, respectively. As demonstrated in previous analyses, individuals with better perceived health have lower depression. The sign and magnitude of the health change coefficient indicates that declines in health status lead to higher levels of depressive symptoms, whereas improvements in health lead to lower levels. In none of the analyses were age*health change interaction terms significant. Although social support has very strong direct effects on depression, there is no evidence for the hypothesis that the effects of health change on social support or depression vary across the life course (data not shown).

Summary

Results from our study are consistent with most of the previous literature on the relationship between age, health, and depression, but our results for community type are not. Age is significantly and inversely related to depression, once controls are introduced for gender, education, and marital status. If it were not for the tendency for health status to decline with age, age effects would be even more pronounced. Of course the incidence of ill health and widowhood *do* increase with age and each has significant independent effects on psychological well-being; the married are somewhat less depressed than the not married, and certainly those who perceive their health as better experience fewer symptoms of depression. Health status is, indeed, one of the two strongest predictors of mental health. Many of the "natural hazards" of aging—health problems and widowhood, for example—do increase the likelihood of depression. Nevertheless, overall, even without controlling for any of these factors, older people are no more depressed than younger—the zero-order relationship between age and depression is simply not significant.

Our analysis of social support and interaction effects has done little to advance our understanding of this paradox. Although the effects of health status are profound on both depression and social support, they are apparently no different for people at different stages of life. Thus, failure to find the expected overall positive association between age and depression does not, at least in our data, stem from age-related differences in the "meaning" or the social support consequences of health. Similarly, our data provide no support for the hypothesis that change in health, or age variation in the impact of change in health, accounts for the age/mental health paradox.

Clearly, the simple additive models we have tested provide a good explanation of depression; together with age, social support, and the demographic control variables, health status and health change account for over 30% of the variation in depressive symptoms. Nevertheless, important theoretical and empirical questions remain, and these questions derive as much from the variables that were not significant as from those that were.

Sociologists have long argued that community contexts impact the nature and quality of our lives. There are good theoretical reasons to expect that the social and psychological consequences of growing older will differ in rural and urban communities, yet there is no evidence in our data that rural elders are any more or less depressed than their town or metropolitan counterparts. Despite all that has been written about the problems of out-migration, isolation, and lack of services, there is no indication that community type significantly impacts either the availability or receipt of informal social support for either young, middle-aged, or older adults. The unresolved question is, of course, WHY NOT?

Conclusions

As many scholars have suggested, it is possible that over time there has been a convergence in rural and urban life-styles. Given modern modes of transportation and mass communication, a uniquely rural way of life simply may no longer exist. From the standpoint of those who have argued for the salubrious effects of rural life, the implication of such a convergence might be that the protective advantage rural residents once received from larger, more densely knit social support networks has simply disappeared. As a result, one would expect, and indeed we found, no mental health differences across the rural/urban continuum.

From the standpoint of the farm crisis literature of the mid-1980s and from the standpoint of others who have discussed the implications of rural agricultural decline, it appears that the social and psychological consequences of the very real economic dislocations of this period have been exaggerated. Rural out-migration, particularly of the young, increased levels of rural poverty and financial distress, and decreases in the availability of formal services including health care are undeniable. However, our results do not indicate any net, or even gross, mental health consequences of these processes, not for rural populations, in general, and not for the rural elderly, in particular. Again, theory gives us little guide in interpreting these results. It is possible, of course, that there are a number of compensatory processes taking place, which buffer residents of smaller towns and communities from the psychological consequences of rural change. These could involve psychological processes of dissonance reduction or fatalism or they could involve social processes, such as an increased reliance on the church. Clearly, such factors could lead to an apparent convergence in rural/urban social support and mental health; clearly we have not measured these variables, and clearly they warrant further research.

Finally, it is quite possible that the way we have measured community type is not sensitive enough, or simply obscures, meaningful differences. We are certainly not the first to caution against treating rural communities as though they were all alike and, in fact, we believe the typology we use in this study is a first step towards recognizing differences between farmers, residents of small towns, and other rural residents. However, we do not believe that a more sensitive measurement of community size, alone, will help us to understand the ways community type matters. Our results, for instance, show that farmers and farm families report their health to be better than other individuals. They certainly do not tell us how or why. Perhaps since farming is an occupational, as well as a residential, category, individuals whose health is declining move off the farm and into towns and cities. If so, our health findings might simply be an artifact of a selection process. Alternatively, it may be more threatening for farmers to admit a health decline, given the close tie between health and their ability to maintain their livelihood. If this is the case, then our results might reflect a kind of response bias. Perhaps individuals assessments of their own health are influenced by the availability of health care, in which case community variation in access to physicians and other health professionals/facilities is the critical issue. Whatever the case might be, and our data provide us with little help in this regard, it is clear that future research must give more systematic attention to the operationalization of community type and to the conceptually relevant distinctions underlying the measures. Our research needs mandate such attention, but in closing we would note that social policy does, as well.

Research in the health policy and health services arena clearly shows that rural residents and rural elders are medically underserved. Research shows that transportation and a host of other problems create access problems for the rural elderly. Research also shows that accidents and injuries are more common among farmers than among city dwellers. If these variables do not translate into a health disadvantage for residents of smaller communities, and using measures of perceived health it appears they do not, then it would be prudent for policymakers to identify those factors or processes that allow individuals to overcome these problems. The policy goal, of course, would be to find ways to encourage these strengths in larger communities or metropolitan areas.

If, however, failure to find community differences in perceived health reflects a form of denial, a kind of psychological coping mechanism that "what will be, will be" or that "there is no sense worrying about things that can't be changed," then "faulty health perceptions" may constitute yet one more barrier to adequate health care among rural populations. Lacking a clear theoretical model of the way in which community type impacts social support, health, and mental health, we cannot hope to develop measurement models that are sensitive enough to yield good policy advice.

Note

1. Because fewer degrees of freedom are used to estimate interaction effects in multiple regression than in MCA, when age*community type interaction effects are assessed in a multiple regression framework, two significant interaction effects emerge. The age*farm and age*rural terms are significant in an equation that regresses perceived availability of social support on age, community type, education, marital status, and gender. Results indicate a more substantial social support decrease with age in metropolitan than in farm or rural communities. At age 65, for instance, the average level of support available to metropolitan residents would be .568 lower than that available to farm residents; by age 80, the difference would be .693. The trend is the same for rural residents vis-à-vis metropolitan residents as it is for farmers, but the effect is somewhat weaker. Although findings *may* indicate that the social support networks of rural residents are somewhat more resilient to the effects of age than those of metropolitan residents, we are reluctant to place too much emphasis on these results. First, the increment to R^2 due to the interactions is small—.0035. Second, out of the dozens of interaction terms we tested, these are the only two that reach significance; by chance alone, we would expect several significant terms.

9

Health Promotion
and Disadvantaged Elderly

Rural-Urban Differences

MARGARET J. PENNING
NEENA L. CHAPPELL

There is increasing attention to targeting health promotion programs and policies to older adults (Estes, Fox, & Mahoney, 1986; Schweitzer, 1989). This is not surprising given that the major causes of death and disability (including cancer, heart disease, arthritis and rheumatism, and diabetes, for example) are increasingly those for which traditional medicine has proven relatively ineffective and the causes of which are known to be largely social, environmental, and behavioral in nature (Estes, Fox, & Mahoney, 1986; Kar, 1989; Lubben et al., 1988). It is also not surprising given concerns over the increasing costs associated with providing traditional health care services (Berkanovic, Hurwicz, & Lubben, 1989; Weiler, Lubben, & Chi, 1987).

AUTHORS' NOTE: Data collection for this study was sponsored by the Manitoba Council on Aging and funded through the Seniors' Independence Program of Health and Welfare Canada. However, the results and interpretations presented here are the sole responsibility of the authors and do not necessarily reflect the views of the Manitoba Council on Aging or Health and Welfare Canada.

Research in the area of health promotion remains underdeveloped with greater emphasis on the development and demonstration of the service components of such programs (Rakowski, 1992). This is particularly true with regard to the abilities of such programs to meet the needs of those in different segments of the older adult population, including those living in rural and urban areas.

This chapter examines rural-urban differences in the effectiveness of a health promotion program directed primarily towards economically disadvantaged adults aged 55 to 74. The impact of rural-urban residence on the nature and extent of changes in health-related knowledge, attitudes, and behavior is addressed using data from a longitudinal study of older adults living in Manitoba and Saskatchewan, Canada.

Health Promotion and Empowerment

The concept of health promotion, like the concept of health, lacks a widely agreed on definition (Kar, 1989). In practice, however, two approaches to health promotion are often differentiated. An individual approach focuses on changing individuals' health behaviors and lifestyles. Strategies adopted to bring about change include improving health-related knowledge and motivation through information, education, or counseling; increasing health potential through nutrition, exercise, immunization, smoking-cessation, or other training programs; and offering screening and referral services for the early detection and treatment of disease.

A community health approach, in contrast, seeks improvement in "the health resources of the economic, social, cultural, natural, and technical environments" (Noack, 1987, p. 19). Proponents of this approach argue that a focus on individual life-styles and behaviors obscures structural problems underlying unhealthy life-styles and behaviors and also ignores the potential importance of decision makers and others for helping create environments conducive to health (Minkler & Pasick, 1986). As noted by Minkler (1987, p. 310), for example, "it makes little sense . . . to advocate life-style behaviors that delay death, prevent the onset of disability, or promote wellness when the barriers to adopting healthful practices are numerous."

Minkler and Pasick (1986) and others point to the need for a more comprehensive approach, one that is directed toward influencing both individuals' health-related knowledge, attitudes, and behavior and the ability of the environment to support individuals' health (Flora, Jackson, & Maccoby, 1989; Noack, 1987). One such approach conceptualizes health promotion in terms of empowerment.

According to the World Health Organization, health promotion is "the process of enabling people to increase control over, and to improve their own health" (World Health Organization, 1984, p. 101), including their abilities to realize aspirations, satisfy needs, and cope with the environment. Similarly, the Canadian government has proposed a framework for health promotion in which inequities between individuals would be reduced, prevention efforts widened, and individuals' abilities to cope enhanced (Epp, 1986). This framework considers health promotion as a mediating strategy between individuals and their environments, synthesizing personal choice and social responsibility in health. The particular mechanisms through which this can be achieved include self-care (decisions and actions individuals take in the interests of their own health), mutual aid (actions people take to help each other cope), and healthy environments (the creation of conditions and surroundings conducive to health). Consequently, health promotion focuses on enabling rather than prescribing solutions and on rights and abilities rather than on deficits and needs. To be effective, individuals and communities must increase their control over their health. Thus, as noted by Minkler (1985), a meaningful approach to promoting health involves empowering elderly individuals to reduce and eliminate barriers so that individual choices are possible.

The Importance of Area of Residence

The concept of empowerment suggests the study of people in context (Rappaport, 1987); it implies an interactive process between the person and his or her environment. Settings can serve to enhance opportunities for empowerment, acting as mediating structures, but they can also inhibit empowerment. Diversity in the expression and extent of empowerment is therefore expected in different settings. The level of resources available and options for choice are likely to vary considerably (Clark, 1987). As a result, "empowerment will look different in its manifest content for different people, organizations, and settings" (Rappaport, 1981, p. 122).

One element of context that may be important for determining the effectiveness of programs to promote health is area of residence. Despite contradictory findings (Chappell, Strain, & Blandford, 1985; Shapiro & Roos, 1984), research frequently reveals significant rural-urban differences when looking at various indicators of objective well-being, particularly health, income, and the availability of health services. Rural elders often emerge as disadvantaged when compared with their urban-dwelling age peers (Blieszner, McAuley, Newhouse, & Mancini, 1987). They are reported to be less healthy, more impaired in their daily activities, and less likely to receive help when they need it (Ahearn & Fryar, 1985; Coates, 1981; Halpert, 1988; Matthews & Vanden Heuvel, 1986; Wright & Jablonski, 1987). They have more health problems but fewer options for medical treatment (Lubben et al., 1988). Perhaps as a result, it is also believed rural elders feel more powerless (Ontario Advisory Council on Senior Citizens, 1980, p. iv).

The importance of rural-urban residence to the effectiveness of alternative strategies for health promotion remains unknown. Rural elders have had less access to health promotion services than have those living in more urban areas (Bender & Hart, 1987; Lubben et al., 1988), and although needs for a more comprehensive approach are recognized, only rarely is this applied in rural areas. Comparisons of the relative effectiveness of such programs for older adults living in rural and urban areas are virtually nonexistent. However, because of the tendency to develop programs and services for rural areas based on knowledge obtained from models developed and tested in urban areas, differences between rural and urban dwelling elderly (including sociodemographic characteristics, the structure of their kinship and friendship networks, etc.) may well result in programs that do not fit the needs, life-styles, or living arrangements of rural elders (Blieszner et al., 1987).

This study examines the results of a relatively extensive evaluation of a community-based health promotion program directed at empowering economically disadvantaged older adults in two provinces, Manitoba and Saskatchewan, in Canada. The specific research questions addressed include: (1) What, if any, impact does rural-urban residence have on the effectiveness of the program—that is, to what extent does it influence changes in health-related knowledge and attitudes, social support, linkages to community organizations, and self-development? and (2) To the extent that the program was effective in these areas, what impact does this have on health behavior?

The Discover Choices Program

"Discover Choices" was launched in September 1988 by the Health Promotion Directorate (Prairie Region) of Health and Welfare Canada and ran for a 2-year period throughout Manitoba and Saskatchewan. The overall goal was to encourage economically disadvantaged older adults to make informed choices about their health through increasing their knowledge of factors affecting health as well as through social support, community development, and self-development. The primary short-term objectives of the program were to increase older adults' knowledge (of ways to maintain health, cope with common problems, and resources available); to increase their perceptions of themselves as able and entitled to work with others for mutual benefit and to work for changes leading to increased opportunities and reduced barriers to personal and shared goals; and to increase recognition of interdependence and knowledge of the skills and resources available to promote the benefits of interdependence.

The program also sought to increase involvement by disadvantaged older adults in community-based programs and services as well as in informal interactions with family members and friends. Longer-term objectives were to increase participation and leadership in organizations and activities designed to achieve social and environmental change; to increase feelings of personal worth, control over lives and choices, and satisfaction with health and well-being; and to improve the health, social and psychological well-being, and ability of older adults to deal with changes in old age.

The primary target group included those aged 55 through 74 living in Manitoba and Saskatchewan whose personal annual incomes were $10,000 or less (or family incomes $18,000 or less), whose formal education was grade 12 or less, and who were not working full-time. Secondary target groups included family and friends of the primary group, other older adults, and others involved with older adults.

The program had four major components: television, print, support and promotional materials, and community development. A series of television programs dealing with topics relevant to health and quality of life (including myths and stereotypes of aging, health, dependency and interdependency, family relationships, consumer protection, personal relationships, elder abuse, housing issues, and death and loss) were developed. These were aired weekly in the fall of 1988 and once again beginning a few months later.

Print material consisted of articles, written by seniors, on a variety of health topics distributed in a kit, along with a guide to resources, listing the programs and services available within the two provinces. A variety of promotional materials were also distributed. Finally, a community development component was implemented to build on existing programs and activities as well as to stimulate new activities.

Data and Methodology

Sample

Data for this study were drawn from personal interviews conducted with a stratified (by age, education, income, and area of residence) random sample of 720 individuals aged 55 through 74. Interviews lasted about $1\frac{1}{2}$ hours. Respondents were initially selected from random listings of all those in this age group living within large urban or other areas of the two provinces, obtained from the government bodies responsible for processing provincial health insurance claims. Telephone screening procedures were then used to identify those belonging to the primary target group as identified above.

Overall, 1,235 people were identified as belonging to the primary target group. Of these, 720 (58%) participated in the first interview, which took place (in the summer of 1988) prior to implementing the Discover Choices program. The refusal rate was 33%. The analyses reported here focus on all those who participated in the initial interview who were successfully re-interviewed approximately 18 months later, following the completion of all aspects of the program. This sample includes 532 respondents (74% of those originally interviewed).

At baseline, just over half (54%) of the sample was aged 65 to 74. Sixty percent were female and about one fifth (22%) were widowed while over two thirds (69%) were married. Most respondents (83%) indicated having been born in one of the two provinces, with very few (12%) born outside of Canada. Protestant religious affiliations were the most frequently reported (67%) followed by Catholic (26%). Almost three quarters (74%) of the respondents reported having either no ethnic identification (41%) or an ethnic identification as Canadian (33%).

Table 9.1 Sample Distribution—Rural/Urban Areas of Residence

Population Size	N	Percentage
Fewer than 500 residents	93	17.5
500-4999 residents	123	23.1
5000-99,999 residents	63	11.8
100,000-499,999 residents	126	23.7
More than 500,000 residents	127	23.9
Total	532	100.0

Measurement

Rather than dichotomize area of residence as rural or urban, the size (number of residents) of the city, town, or area in which respondents lived was used. No distinction between rural farm and nonfarm residents was possible. Table 9.1 shows the distribution of the sample by size of area. The majority live either in or near small towns and villages with fewer than 5,000 inhabitants (40%) or in relatively large urban areas of 100,000 or more residents (47%).

Dependent variables of interest in these analyses include health-related knowledge and attitudes, social support, organizational involvements, and attitudes towards self. Health knowledge was assessed using a 23-item true-false test constructed specifically for the study from information disseminated by the program. Items referred to knowledge in such areas as nutrition, exercise, smoking, drug use, sleep, weight, and social integration. Examples include: "One can do little to reduce or control the problem of high blood pressure" and "As we get older, drugs like alcohol take longer to move through the bloodstream." Scores range from 6 to 22 at baseline and from 4 to 23 at Time 2 with average scores of 17.1 (baseline) and 17.4 (Time 2; see Penning, Blandford, & Chappell, 1991).

Health attitudes encompassed beliefs in the importance of preventive health behaviors and health-specific locus of control. To elicit opinions regarding the importance of various preventive health behaviors, respondents were asked how important (on a 3-point scale ranging from not at all important to very important) 20 different behaviors (for example, regular exercise, vitamins, having close friends, avoiding stress, eating a balanced diet, and so forth) were in order to stay healthy. The responses were summed and divided by the number of items answered. Inter-item reliability for this measure reached .71 (Time 2). Overall scores ranged from 1 (no importance attributed to any of the preventive health behaviors) to 3 (all preventive health behaviors considered very important).

Respondents were also asked to indicate whether they agreed or disagreed with a series of 22 statements designed to assess medical skepticism and health-specific locus-of-control beliefs (Lau & Ware, 1981; Segall, 1983, drawing on Freidson, 1961; Wallston, Wallston, Kaplan, & Maides, 1976). Factor analyses (principal axis, varimax rotation) revealed three different factors corresponding with dimensions labelled internal or self-control, medical skepticism, and external or chance control. Three separate measures were therefore created, based on the factor scores. In each case, a higher score indicates a greater belief in the particular dimension under consideration.

To assess social support and organizational involvements, several indicators were used. Involvement in leisure activities was assessed using the number of activities (including indoor, outdoor, and other recreational, social, and political activities) respondents reported participating in at least occasionally. Size of the informal social network referred to the total number of family members, friends, and neighbors (including household members) available to the respondent. Respondents were also asked how many people they were able to count on for help in time of need, providing a somewhat more direct measure of potential for support.

In addition, respondents were also asked about their knowledge of various organizations, programs, and services available to older adults within their province. Over 78 resources were listed including 48 in Manitoba and 41 in Saskatchewan (some services overlapped). Overall familiarity with seniors' organizations was assessed based on the proportion of organizations that respondents reported being at least somewhat familiar with.

To examine the effectiveness of the program for enhancing self-development, a modified version of Rosenberg's (1965) self-esteem scale was used. Respondents were presented with a series of 10 statements reflecting self-worth and were asked how often they agreed with each. Responses ranged from never (1) to always (5). An index was constructed by summing these items and dividing by the number of questions answered. Inter-item reliability for this measure was .75 (Time 2).

Health behavior was assessed based on the frequency respondents reported engaging in various preventive health behaviors (as listed earlier). Responses ranged from a low of 1 indicating they never engaged in any of the preventive health behaviors listed to a high of 3, indicating they always engaged in all of them (alpha = .76, Time 2). Table 9.2 reports the sociodemographic characteristics of respondents by area of residence. Given their potential importance for health programming, the analyses include controls for education, marital status, province of residence, and health status, as well as gender. Education is measured in years of schooling. Marital status contrasts those who are married with those who are not (married = 1, not married = 0). Gender was coded as 1 for women and 0 for men and province as 1 for Manitoba and 0 for Saskatchewan.

Measures of health include levels of chronic illness and functional disability. Respondents were presented with a list of 15 chronic health problems drawn from the U.S. Health Insurance Study (U.S. National Office of Vital Statistics, 1957) and were asked whether or not they had experienced any of them in the last year or still had aftereffects from having had them earlier. Problems reported as being experienced were summed with possible responses ranging from 0 to 15. However, few respondents reported no chronic conditions (9% at both baseline and Time 2) and the average number of conditions reported was 3.2 (baseline) and 3.4 (Time 2).

Functional disability was measured on the basis of respondents' reports concerning the extent of their ability to perform various basic and instrumental activities of daily living (Cronbach's alpha = .68 at Time 2). The majority of respondents reported no disability (81% at baseline and 77% at Time 2). Therefore, to maximize the contrast involved, responses were dichotomized with respondents reporting at least one area of disability receiving a score of 1 and others receiving a score of 0.

Data Analysis

The focus of these analyses is on rural-urban differences in the effectiveness of the Discover Choices program in meeting its objectives with regard to specific aspects of health-related knowledge, attitudes, social support, organizational awareness, and self-development. The analyses begin with an examination of rural-urban differences among

Table 9.2 Selected Sociodemographic Characteristics by Rural/Urban Residence ($n = 532$) (in percentages)

	Area of Residence				
	1 Small	2	3	4	5 Large
Gender					
Male	37.6	44.7	41.3	34.9	40.9
Female	62.4	55.3	58.7	65.1	59.1
($X^2 = 2.81$; df = 4; p = n.s.)					
Marital status					
Married	81.7	70.7	65.1	66.7	61.4
Other	18.3	29.3	34.9	33.3	39.6
($X^2 = 11.3$; df = 4; $p < .05$)					
Age					
55-64	32.3	34.1	25.4	39.7	37.8
65-74	67.7	65.9	74.6	60.3	62.2
($X^2 = 4.7$; df = 4; p = n.s.)					
Education					
0-6 years	15.1	12.2	15.9	9.5	11.8
7-9 years	50.5	54.5	49.2	41.3	36.2
10-13 years	34.4	33.3	34.9	49.2	52.0
($X^2 = 16.6$; df = 8; $p < .05$)					
Income					
<$750/month	21.4	27.1	24.6	12.3	22.0
$750-$999/month	22.6	19.6	15.8	19.3	16.9
$1000-$1249/month	34.5	27.1	29.8	23.7	28.0
$1250-$1749/month	13.1	18.7	22.8	29.8	22.9
>$1750/month	8.3	7.5	7.0	14.9	10.2
($X^2 = 21.2$; df = 16; p = n.s.)					
Province					
Manitoba	55.9	47.2	50.8	0.0	100.0
Saskatchewan	44.1	52.8	49.2	100.0	0.0

NOTE: No significant differences emerged with regard to ethnic identification, language, religion, or health status (chronic conditions or functional disability).

the various health indicators at baseline, at Time 2, and, finally, from baseline to Time 2. Change is assessed through the use of residuals. To determine whether rural-urban differences are due to confounding with other related differences as well as to determine whether familiarity with the Discover Choices program can explain the differences observed, multivariate (regression) analyses are conducted where the bivariate analyses reveal significant differences in the amount of change observed over time in relation to rural-urban residence.

Findings

The results of the bivariate analyses of relationships involving the health indicators and area of residence are reported in Table 9.3. They reveal no differences in health knowledge by rural-urban residence at either point in time. Overall, however, health knowledge increased from baseline to Time 2, particularly among respondents in more rural areas including small- to average-sized towns and villages.

In terms of health beliefs, those in smaller, rural areas attributed significantly greater importance to preventive health behaviors at both baseline and Time 2 when compared with those living in larger urban areas. Also, they were more likely to have increased their belief in the importance of such behaviors over the course of the study. With regard to health locus of control, the analyses reveal that on two of the three dimensions (a belief in chance outcomes and a belief in the efficacy of self-care) there were no differences associated with rural-urban location at either point in time and no difference in change over time. However, those living in smaller rural or larger urban centers were somewhat more skeptical of medical care at both baseline and Time 2 than were those in centers of more moderate size.

Greater involvement in leisure activities and greater access to informal networks (including family, friends) as well as to caregivers was evident among rural than urban elders. The differences in involvement in leisure and access to caregivers also increased over the duration of the study. In contrast, familiarity with seniors' organizations was greater among larger urban residents. This too increased over the one and a half year study period.

No differences were found with regard to feelings of self-esteem over the course of the study or between groups. Turning to health behaviors, however, those living in more rural and smaller urban areas were more likely to report engaging in preventive health behaviors at both baseline and Time 2. As well, the extent of preventive health behavior engaged

Table 9.3 One-Way Analyses of Variance: Health Indicators by Area of Residence at Baseline, Time 2, and Change Over Time

	Small Rural 1	2	3	4	Large Urban 5	F
A. *Health knowledge*						
Baseline	17.0	16.7	17.2	17.2	17.3	1.1
Time 2	17.8	17.7	17.9	17.3	16.9	2.2
Change	.8	1.0	.9	.3	−.1	5.2***
B. *Health beliefs*						
1. Importance of preventive health behaviors						
Baseline	2.5	2.5	2.6	2.5	2.5	3.0*
Time 2	2.6	2.6	2.6	2.5	2.5	7.5***
Change	.0	.0	−.0	−.0	−.0	6.2***
2. Health locus of control: Chance control						
Baseline	.3	.4	.5	.3	.2	1.9
Time 2	.0	.1	.1	−.1	−.0	1.0
Change	−.5	−.5	−.5	−.6	−.4	1.2
3. Health locus of control: Medical skepticism						
Baseline	−.1	.2	−.1	.1	−.1	2.5*
Time 2	−.0	.1	.1	.0	−.2	2.5*
Change	.0	.1	.1	−.0	−.1	1.5
4. Health locus of control: Self-efficacy						
Baseline	.4	.3	.5	.4	.5	.9
Time 2	.1	−.0	−.0	−.1	.0	.7
Change	−.5	−.6	−.7	−.7	−.6	1.0
C. *Social/organizational involvements*						
1. Leisure/activities						
Baseline	4.5	4.5	4.0	3.9	3.8	6.3***

in by those living in the smaller rural and urban centers increased significantly from baseline to Time 2 in contrast with those living in average to larger urban centers.

Overall, the bivariate analyses reveal that area of residence is unrelated to health knowledge or self-esteem of disadvantaged older adults in the two provinces. Residents of larger urban centers are more knowledgeable about seniors' organizations, not surprising given that most of those organizations are located in such centers. Residents of smaller rural areas, however, are more likely to believe in preventive health behaviors, to practice preventive health behaviors, to pursue more

Table 9.3 (Continued)

	Small Rural				Large Urban	
	1	2	3	4	5	F
Time 2	4.9	4.8	4.4	3.8	3.8	13.2***
Change	.3	.2	.2	-.4	-.3	7.4***
2. Network size						
Baseline	146.8	176.2	142.1	113.8	76.0	3.7**
Time 2	290.7	244.9	236.9	99.6	62.6	9.1***
Change	112.9	61.2	60.1	-71.5	-100.8	7.9***
3. Number of caregivers						
Baseline	3.4	3.2	2.9	3.0	2.9	3.7**
Time 2	3.5	3.5	3.2	3.0	3.3	4.3**
Change	.1	.1	-.0	-.2	.0	2.8*
4. Knowledge of seniors' organizations						
Baseline	33.9	30.4	30.7	31.5	38.5	2.2
Time 2	31.5	26.4	25.3	33.0	40.1	6.1***
Change	-.9	-4.3	-5.4	1.8	5.3	4.3**
D. Self-development						
1. Self-esteem						
Baseline	4.3	4.3	4.4	4.3	4.2	0.8
Time 2	4.3	4.3	4.4	4.3	4.2	0.4
Change	.0	-.0	.1	-.0	-.1	0.5
E. Health behaviors						
Baseline	2.5	2.5	2.6	2.5	2.4	5.1***
Time 2	2.6	2.6	2.5	2.5	2.4	9.5***
Change	.1	.1	-.0	-.0	-.1	6.3***

*p < .05; **p < .01; ***p < .001

leisure activities, and to have larger informal networks. In all of these areas, residents of smaller rural areas were also likely to have increased their beliefs and activities from baseline to Time 2. It is noteworthy that the greater belief in and practice of preventive health behaviors is not reflected in greater health knowledge or self-esteem.

Table 9.4 reports findings obtained from multivariate (regression) analyses conducted using each of the health-related indicators in which change was found, as a dependent variable. The findings reveal increases in health knowledge over time are negatively associated with being older and with residence in larger urban areas but positively

Table 9.4 Predictors of Change in Health-Related Indicators: Standardized Regression Coefficients

Predictors	Health Knowledge	Importance of Preventive Health Behaviors	Leisure Activities	Familiarity with Seniors' Organizations
Age	-.10*	-.05	.07	.03
Education	.19***	.01	.09*	.15***
Married	-.09*	-.01	-.01	-.03
Manitoba	-.08	-.12**	.07	-.03
Rural/Urban	-.20***	-.17***	-.23***	.11*
Chronic conditions	.01	-.08	-.06	-.00
Change in chronic conditions	-.09*	.02	-.10*	.00
Functional disability	.00	-.02	-.08	.12**
Change in disability	-.02	-.07	-.04	-.05
Familiarity with Discover Choices	.10*	.00	.12**	.12**

*$p < .05$; **$p < .01$; ***$p < .001$

associated with having higher levels of education and familiarity with the Discover Choices program. Rural-urban residence is the strongest predictor.

For the most part, similar factors emerge as significant predictors of change in the importance attributed to preventive health behaviors and in involvement in leisure activities. Those with higher levels of education, living in smaller, more rural areas, and reportedly familiar with the Discover Choices program tend to report change in a positive direction. Rural-urban residence is the strongest predictor of change in both the importance of preventive health behaviors and in participation in leisure activities. In terms of familiarity with seniors' organizations, however, increases over time are found to be positively associated with residence in larger urban areas and with greater functional disability as well as with higher education and familiarity with the Discover Choices program. Education is the strongest predictor.

Given findings indicating that changes in health-related knowledge and attitudes did take place over the duration of the program and that both area of residence and familiarity with the Discover Choices program are significant predictors of this change, it is of interest to explore the impact, if any, that these factors as well as the changes in knowledge and attitudes have on actual health behaviors.

Table 9.5 Predictors of Change in Preventive Health Behaviors: Unstandard-
ized and Standardized Regression Coefficients

Predictors	b	beta
Age	.00	.09*
Education	−.01	−.05
Married	.05	.09*
Manitoba	.03	.06
Rural/urban	−.01	−.09*
Chronic conditions	.00	.04
Change in chronic conditions	−.00	−.04
Functional disability	−.13	−.07
Change in functional disability	−.27	−.12**
Change in health knowledge	−.00	−.03
Change in important preventive health behaviors	.64	.43***
Change in leisure activities	.02	.11**
Change in familiarity with seniors' organizations	.00	.06
Familiarity with Discover Choices	−.01	−.02

*$p < .05$; **$p < .01$; ***$p < .001$

Table 9.5 reports the results of analyses conducted to assess the
impact of rural-urban residence, familiarity with the Discover Choices
program, and changes in health knowledge, attitudes, and beliefs, on
changes in preventive health behavior. The findings reveal increases in
the frequency of preventive health behaviors over time are positively
associated with various sociodemographic characteristics (age, being
married) as well as with living in smaller urban or rural areas and with
changes over time in health attitudes and involvements. Those whose
functional disability did not decline over the duration of the program,
who increased in terms of the importance they attributed to preventive
health behaviors, who increased their involvement in leisure activities,
and who became more familiar with health-related organizations, also
increased their preventive health behavior. No changes were found in
relation to familiarity with Discover Choices directly. By far, the strongest predictor of increased preventive health behavior is an increased
belief that such activities are important, providing strong empirical
support for the argument that a change in attitude leads to a change in
behavior.

Size of place of residence is a significant predictor in all of the
analyses and is the strongest predictor for change in beliefs about
preventive health behaviors and participation in leisure activities. In

turn, a change in beliefs about the importance of preventive health behaviors is a strong predictor of change in actual behavior.

Discussion

These analyses offer only limited support to the view that rural elders are comparatively disadvantaged. Rural elders did have significantly lower levels of education and income than those living in the larger urban areas, even though these factors were largely controlled for by the particular sampling strategy employed. Rural elders, therefore, did emerge as more economically disadvantaged than urban elders even within a sample selected to represent those who are disadvantaged. However, similar differences were not evident with regard to any of the health-related indicators examined. Additional analyses (not reported here) revealed rural and urban dwelling elderly individuals did not differ with regard to their objective (levels of chronic illness and functional disability) or perceived health status. As well, rural elders were no less knowledgeable about health matters and no more likely to feel negatively about themselves or their abilities to exert control over health matters than those living in larger urban areas. There is little evidence here to support conclusions regarding a greater lack of empowerment (powerlessness) among rural elders.

Where differences between rural and urban elderly did exist prior to the program, rural elders tended to hold the advantage: rural elders attributed greater importance to preventive health behaviors than those living in more urban areas; engaged in more extensive preventive health behavior; had significantly larger social networks; had greater access to caregivers for assistance in time of need; and engaged in more leisure activities. In fact, the only area in which urban elders held the advantage was in familiarity with community-based health-related organizations, resources, and services for seniors.

According to the findings presented here, elders living in more rural, smaller urban areas benefited more from the Discover Choices program than those living in the larger urban areas. No differences were found on any of the direct empowerment measures (dimensions of health locus of control and self-esteem), but there were differences with regard to changes in health knowledge, beliefs in the importance of preventive health behaviors, community involvement, and actual preventive health behavior. Those in less urban areas were more likely to report positive changes over the course of the study in all domains except familiarity with community-based organizations and services. Therefore, where the program appears to have been particularly effective was with regard to health education and attitudes among those living in less highly urban areas. The study may have needed a longer follow-up period to show effects in empowerment.

Familiarity with the program tended to emerge as a significant predictor of change but did not explain away the rural-urban difference. In fact, those in urban areas report greater familiarity with the program. This suggests that the program may have had an impact, yet individuals were not aware of their exposure to it. Another possibility is that something else took place in the less urban areas of the two provinces at about the same time as the Discover Choices program that produced the same effect. It may be, for example, that our study served to educate those being interviewed.

When the impact of exposure to Discover Choices, rural-urban residence, and changes in health knowledge, attitudes, and beliefs on health behavior was assessed, the findings revealed the major predictors of change in behavior were changes in health functioning, attitudes, and organizational involvement. Therefore, to the extent that Discover Choices had an influence over attitudes and involvements, it succeeded indirectly, in influencing behavior as well.

10

The Rural Aged, Social Value, and Health Care

JAMES A. THORSON
F. C. POWELL

Modernization theory (Cowgill, 1974) is at the heart of any discussion of rural versus urban comparisons of aged persons, their status, and their place in American society. As described by Passuth and Bengtson (1988), modernization theory, "is a functionalist perspective in that it suggests that the status of the elderly derives from their relationship to evolving systems of social roles which vary across societies depending on the degree of industrialization. . . . Modernization theory argues that the status of the aged is inversely related to the level of societal industrialization" (p. 337). Earlier, presumably rural, societies held older individuals in high esteem and respect because of their knowledge of an agricultural way of life and, perhaps, because of their control of land and resources (Hanawalt, 1986). Cowgill (1974) detailed four areas of modernization—health technology, economic technology, urbanization, and education—all of which result in decreased status of the aged in modern industrial societies.

Glaser and Strauss (1968), among others, describe the phenomenon of prioritization of health care (in this instance, to the terminally ill) in what can only be called *triage* in crisis settings:

In such a case, the patient's social value may play a strong part in the decision. Age, education, social class, race, marital status, parenthood, and occupation, as well as physical condition and temporal shape of the trajectory become involved in who shall be saved now and who shall be saved later or not at all. Patients are, in effect, competing for life on the basis of their social value. (p. 106)

If these theorists are correct, what is happening with respect to health care delivery to the aged in rural America may involve what Streib (1985) describes as *status discrepancy*: the differential loss of status. The aged might in fact be seen as the least important members of a segment of society that is itself losing importance in an industrial economy. If resources, in this case health care, can be seen as being apportioned (Glaser & Strauss, 1968) on the basis of social value (at least in some situations), then the rural aged might be *expected* to receive inferior, infrequent, or at least inconvenient access to health resources. The rural aged may indeed hold such expectations themselves.

Numerous researchers from a variety of different disciplinary perspectives have described situational variables in terms of health care delivery among the rural aged (Brubaker, 1985; Cutler & Coward, 1988; Krishan, Drummond, Naessens, Nobrega, & Smoldt, 1985; Krout, 1986; Miller, Stokes, & Clifford, 1987). The rural aged, variously, have fewer practitioners from which to choose, less access to primary health care providers and hospitals, and differential health care outcomes, as a few examples. Lassey and Lassey (1985), however, point out that efforts need to be made to sort out such variables as social networks among the rural and urban aged as they relate to health outcomes and practices. Health beliefs may also have an important influence on health care and utilization of health services (Strain, 1991). Research is needed that helps explain the paradox of less adequate health care services but high levels of satisfaction among the rural aged.

Related Literature

There are a number of ways to compare relative health, including issues of urban versus rural access and adequacy (Lassey & Lassey, 1985). Other measures might include outcomes, ratings of relative satisfaction and well-being, utilization of services, morbidity, and mortality. When a number of these factors are taken together, the resulting overall matrix of health status and health well-being makes it evident that simple urban-rural comparisons are not adequate. What, for example, is a better measure of health status: number of miles to the hospital or length of life? Given that doctors and hospitals in rural areas are fewer and farther between, are the older persons living in rural areas any worse (or better) off because of it? Do life-style approaches or health habits or beliefs have more to do with intrinsic health than does access to medical care?

A variety of approaches has been taken to differentiate older persons living in rural areas from those who are urban-dwellers vis-à-vis different aspects of health and well-being. One direction has been to investigate possible differences in subjective well-being and psychological health. Meddin and Vaux (1988) sought to determine relationships between psychosocial factors and self-reported well-being among rural old people. They interviewed 140 senior center participants in four small towns in the Midwest (mean age = 70, 69% female, 81% white), and produced usable data from 100 of the interviews. Information included dependent variables relating to subjective well-being: positive affect, negative affect, and a composite well-being measure that included the Center for Epidemiologic Studies Depression Scale. Independent variables included an inventory of 53 life events, two indices of social support, measures of coping resources, and demographic items including a self-assessment of physical health. Health problems had the strongest correlation ($r = -.40$, $p < .001$) with global satisfaction. Regression analyses indicated that well-being is predicted by psychosocial variables, particularly a sense of mastery and perceived health. They note that the profile of these rural respondents differs little from subjective well-being profiles of the general and of other elderly populations.

On the basis of this study, then, there is some evidence on which to conclude that elements of well-being may be similar for many older persons, urban or rural, and that one of the most important of these elements is perception of physical health. Health and income have in fact been shown in study after study of the elderly over the past four decades to be the most consistent predictors of well-being. One might say that gerontologists have a propensity in this regard to belabor the obvious: prosperous, healthy older people as a general rule tend to be happier than those who are poor and sick. There should be no particular reason for this to be more (or less) true of urban- or rural-dwelling older persons.

Given the relative importance of health to overall perception of well-being, a number of researchers have sought to determine whether older people living in rural areas for some reason lead a healthier life-style. Some contributing variables in this regard might, however, be seen as both exceedingly difficult to measure and be in conflict with the way they might contribute to a health paradigm. How do, for example, presumed availability of ample amounts of fresh air and sunshine, freedom from stress and hassles of city life, and settings more free of environmental pollutants balance off against lack of access to health services, providers, and institutions? That is, who is better off and why?

Health life-style behaviors and attitudes might be more easily measured than environments, and a recent study sought to determine urban-rural differences in health life-style among the aged. Speake, Cowart, and Stephens (1991) investigated six elements that may have an influence on overall health (stress, exercise, nutrition, health responsibility, self-actualization, and interpersonal support) among 106 rural- and 237 urban-dwelling people (mean age = 71.4), concluding that place of residence, controlling for education and income, was not independently predictive of any of the six life-style practices examined. This finding, they concluded, is consistent with other research that indicates that urban-rural health differences may be more closely related to respondents' education and income level than rural or urban residence.

Social Networks and Support

A number of authors have examined the influence of social ties and the availability of support networks on the health and well-being of older persons. A major study on depression and older adults living in urban and rural areas, for example, sought to differentiate the effect of social ties. Johnson and his colleagues (1988) interviewed 315 non-metropolitan and 678 metropolitan randomly selected older persons from 45 states and the District of Columbia, using the Center for Epidemiologic Studies Depression Scale as a dependent variable. Independent variables included measures of intimate social ties, primary attachments, secondary attachments, stressful events, perceived health, and demographic items. No overall differences were found in the average depression scores of older urban or rural respondents, nor was any social network variable found to have a direct effect on depression. Such a statement, however, is not to denigrate the importance of social networks among the aged, merely to note the lack of urban-rural differences in measures of depression and social ties. Isolation remains an important variable in the well-being of the aged, often in curious ways. Lawton, Moss, and Kleban (1984) found, based on their analysis of three large samples, that older people living alone tended to be *healthier* but much lower in subjective well-being. However, social ties have been shown to be directly and significantly related to overall rates of survival: "Proportional hazard analyses indicate that social ties are significant predictors of lower 17-year mortality risks for those aged 70 or more" (Seeman, Kaplan, Knudsen, Cohen, & Guralnik, 1987, p. 714).

One might, then, seek to determine differences in social ties, which may in fact be seen as critically important to the well-being of the aged. As an illustration, Tennstedt, Sullivan, McKinley, and D'Agnostino (1990) studied 635 frail older persons and found that (1) 79% received most of their needed assistance from informal caregivers, 2) living alone is the consistent predictor of the use of formal services, and, 3) those who live with a spouse are likely to use no formal services regardless of how frail they are.

Because of these findings, it might be concluded that isolated elders, urban *or* rural, are particularly vulnerable. This conclusion has been suggested by previous research: Coe and his colleagues (1984) analyzed 401 interviews from a sample of noninstitutionalized older persons and concluded that those lacking a family or neighborhood social network had a much higher rate of visits to physicians. It is difficult to determine with any precision, however, the relative availability of social networks and associated health status among samples of urban and rural elders from available studies.

Health Status, Disability, and the Use of Services

An analysis of differences in relative health of urban and rural elders might well take use of services—both health services and supportive social services—into account, as well as factors such as self-assessed health and relative levels of disability. Again, however, prior research reveals as many paradoxes as it does direct relationships. Wan and Arling (1983) found a number of predictors of the use of physician and social services among a sample of 772 older persons who had at least one limitation of their activities of daily living; transportation barriers had no predictive validity in terms of their use of services, but perceived health had the greatest predictive value. Perception of health may, in fact, be among the most important variables in relative terms. Idler, Kasl, and Lemke (1990) provide clear, significant longitudinal findings demonstrating the relationship between self-assessed health and mortality among two large samples of the aged in New Haven, Connecticut, ($N = 2812$) and in two Iowa counties ($N = 3673$). They further conclude that health professionals need to respect what people, especially the elderly people they treat, are saying about their health (Idler & Kasl, 1991).

Wolinsky (1990) suggests that most of the variation in the use of health services remains unexplained, and points to the observation of Shanas and Maddox (1985) that one way to define health among the elderly is level of functioning. Thus, the emergence in recent years of research on functional ability using measures of ADLs and IADLs (activities of daily living and instrumental activities of daily living). A series of studies recently published by the National Center for Health Statistics (NCHS) confirms the relationship between level of disability and perceived health status among the elderly. Ries and Brown (1991) analyze NCHS data and demonstrate that among white persons 65+, only 9.2% of those without an ADL limitation indicate that they feel they are in poor or fair health, whereas 20.1% of older whites who have an ADL limitation rate their health as fair or poor. Similarly, among African-American respondents 65+, 14.3% with no ADL limitation rate their health as fair or poor, whereas 32.9% with limited ADLs indicate a self-rating of health that is either fair or poor.

Ries and Brown, however, point out another paradox: Although those (of all ages) who reside outside Metropolitan Statistical Areas (MSAs) tended to give a more negative self-rating of health, regardless of level of disability, those persons living in nonmetropolitan areas also tend to spend fewer days in the hospital, have fewer days of restricted activity, and fewer total physician contacts (1991). Is it the case that rural people are healthier but less likely to admit it? These data and others we will cite later suggest that there may be some evidence to support this contention.

NCHS data give a profile of what the relative level of disability is among the U.S. population aged 65 and above. Of the ADL limitations, 6.2% of the aged had difficulty bathing, 4.4% with dressing, 2.4% with

Table 10.1 Level of Functional ADL and IADL Dependencies, U.S. Population
Aged 65+ (in percentages)

	All Dependencies	5-7 ADL	3-4 ADL	1-2 ADL	IADL
White	28.4	4.9	2.5	14.0	6.9
African American	36.4	5.2	3.4	18.2	9.6
Hispanic	30.3	6.0	4.1	14.5	5.6
Married	21.5	2.7	1.8	11.7	5.2
Not married	37.5	7.5	3.5	17.2	9.3
Above poverty	25.4	3.4	2.3	13.0	6.7
Below poverty	49.5	13.7	4.8	21.5	9.6

SOURCE: From Hing & Bloom, 1990, p. 23.

use of the toilet, 3.2% with physical transfer, and just 1% had difficulty
eating. With reference to IADL limitations among the noninstitutionalized aged, 3.9% had trouble preparing meals, 7.5% with shopping, 3.3%
with money management, 1.9% with use of the telephone, and 4.9%
doing light housework (Ries & Brown, 1991). Additional NCHS data
(Hing & Bloom, 1990) give an indication that level of ADL and IADL
dependencies are related to social condition and race. As reported in
Table 10.1, African-American and Hispanic elders, those who are not
married, and those living below the poverty line have the greatest
relative rates of functional disability.

In summary, it is evident that there are issues that go beyond simple
urban versus rural comparisons that are relevant to public policy issues
related to the health of the aged and delivery of health and social
services to the older population. Poverty, race, income, social network,
and marital status are all important variables, as are relative levels of
disability and subjective perceptions of health.

There Is No Place Like Nebraska

The authors of this chapter were asked to begin a series of studies of
the relative health of older persons living in the Omaha area beginning
in 1988. In the first report to the funding agency, the Eastern Nebraska
Office on Aging (ENOA), a profile of 278 randomly selected elderly
African-American residents of Omaha's North Side indicated that they

were less likely to have a primary care physician than were white elders in the community, but that they did not differ significantly from whites in terms of episodes of illness, use of hospital emergency rooms, or delays in seeking needed health care services (Powell & Thorson, 1989). Their overall responses were comparable to an earlier study of a sample of older African-American citizens of Cleveland, Ohio (Petchers & Milligan, 1988); in general, the respondents were quite satisfied with health care services available to them.

Subsequently, we were asked to do a follow-up in Omaha and Douglas County, both of which might be considered urban, to determine relative levels of ADL and IADL impairment, self-perception of health, access to health care facilities and providers, and health practices and beliefs. Our Douglas County sample consisted of 196 randomly selected individuals, average age 73.8 years, 72% female, 7% minority, and 55% married. Our university's Center for Public Affairs Research provided funding to draw a random sample of the elderly living in the very rural Sandhills counties in the western part of the state ($N = 200$). They were significantly older (76.6 years) and less likely to be married living with a spouse (47.5%); the proportion of females (73%) was comparable; there were no racial minorities represented in this group (Powell & Thorson, 1991; Thorson & Powell, 1992). Many of the comparisons that conclude this chapter deal with the similarities and differences that were found among these urban and rural samples.

It should be noted that Nebraska is a unique state in many ways, not the least of which is that by far the greatest portion of its population resides within 60 miles of its Eastern border. It has two cities (Omaha, with a MSA of over 500,000, and Lincoln, with over 200,000); the next largest town has a population less than 30,000, and there are 9 counties with fewer than 1,000 residents each. The 5 counties served by ENOA have a combined total population of 591,452 (1990 census), and the 11 counties in the Sandhills area have a combined population of only 11,206. Thus, there is a truly urban area in the state and a genuinely rural one to compare it to. The Sandhills counties are exactly that: sand hills unfit for farming, made up for the most part of cattle ranches each of which is several thousand acres. Most of the Sandhills counties have no resident physician, hospital, or health department. Despite these differences, there is general agreement that ethic and attitudes are largely homogeneous throughout the state, and Nebraska is by and large an exceedingly healthy state. It has a relatively high longevity rate compared to other states and, as an indicator of public health, the lowest

Table 10.2 Percentages: Self-Assessed Health, Rural and Urban Respondents Aged 65+

Sample & Health Status	Rural	Urban	
Rundall & Evashwick, 1982 (Seattle)		$N = 869$	
Good/excellent		61.7%	
Fair		24.6	
Poor		12.1	
Johnson et al., 1988 (45 states)	$N = 315$	$N = 678$	
Good/excellent	67.0%	73.5%	
Fair	25.0	20.5	
Poor	8.0	6.0	
Idler & Kasl, 1991 (New Haven)		$N = 2812$	
		M	F
Good/excellent		60.1%	57.9%
Fair		31.5	33.7
Poor		8.4	8.4
Garrett, 1991 (Omaha)		$N = 200$	
Good/excellent		84.4%	
Fair		15.1	
Poor		0.5	
Powell & Thorson, 1991 (Omaha and Sandhills Counties, Nebraska)	$N = 200$	$N = 196$	
Good/excellent	59.5%	68.9%	
Fair	29.0	20.9	
Poor	11.5	10.2	

tuberculosis rate among the states. This is true in the urban as well as the rural areas; Omaha is among the five cities with the lowest TB rate nationally (Metropolitan Life Insurance Company, 1991). Thus, intrastate comparisons can be made among persons with many similarities despite differences in residence.

Our first comparison (see Table 10.2) was of self-assessed health status among our urban and rural Nebraska samples with other studies available that asked the question in the same manner, requesting that respondents rate their health today as either excellent, good, fair, or poor. Consistent with previous studies, rural respondents from Nebraska tended to give a slightly more negative assessment of personal health. Comparing the present data with prior studies, however, there is a disparity between samples equal to or greater than the difference within samples; it appears that the answer to that question will be determined largely by "who is asked."

Garret (1991), for example, asked 200 retired school teachers living in Omaha for a self-assessment of health; 84% said that it was good or excellent and less than 1% rated their health as poor. Our random sample, taken in the same city during the same month, rated good or excellent health among only 69% of respondents and fully 10% as being in poor health. The two groups were comparable in age and marital status and proportionate by race and gender, but Garret's sample contained persons who had a significantly higher average number of years of education.

Similarly, Johnson et al.'s national sample (1988) found 73.5% of urban respondents rating their health as good or excellent, whereas Idler and Kasl (1991) in their New Haven sample found only 60% of their male respondents and 58% of the women who rated their health as good or excellent. So, although there may be a trend among some studies to find a more negative self-rating of health among rural respondents, the differences between other social characteristics of the research subjects may account for a greater proportion of the variance.

Comparing self-rated health of the 196 respondents in Douglas County with the 200 in the Sandhills drew no differences that were statistically significant, nor were there significant differences in subjective rating of health compared to others their own age.

The urban dwellers were slightly, but significantly ($t = 2.4, p < .05$), more likely to have a primary health provider than were those living in the Sandhills. And the urban group had been with their primary provider for a longer time (12.1 years versus 9.2 years) than those in the rural area ($t = 2.52, p < .01$). The urban sample also expressed slightly higher satisfaction with their primary provider ($t = 2.02, p < .05$); however, only 5.6% of the entire group indicated that they were dissatisfied with the care they received from their primary health care provider. As might be anticipated, the largest difference was in mean travel time to primary provider (urban = 15.9 minutes; rural = 42.3 minutes).

The mean number of months since last physical exam (28.3 months and 28.1 months, respectively) did not differ between urban and rural subjects, nor did their rating of overall health care satisfaction. Although fully half of the respondents had seen a physician during the previous 3 months, the mean number of months since the last visit for the sample as a whole was 9.8. This mean was skewed by several persons at one extreme—there were at least 3 hearty individuals who had not seen a doctor in the past 25 years. Again, there were no urban/rural differences in this comparison. Of the 38 total subjects in both samples who reported delaying needed health care for any reason, only 3 said it was because of a transportation problem; 12 said they were too busy.

The samples did not differ in their use of hospitals, incidence of illness, or use of emergency rooms. There were, however, significant differences in terms of length of stay once hospitalized: the 42 urban-dwellers who had been hospitalized during the previous year had a mean stay of 11.3 days; the 41 in the Sandhills were in the hospital for an average of only 6.6 days. Despite a significant difference in distance to hospital (6 miles versus 43.7), there were no differences between the two groups in terms of expressed satisfaction with hospital care available. Self-assessed health did not correlate significantly with travel time to primary provider ($r = -.07$), travel time to hospital, or urban/rural residence. ADL and IADL scores did not differ between urban and rural respondents, either.

The Sandhills group, however, was less likely to report having someone available to help with performance of ADLs ($t = 2.92$, $p < .004$). This might be interpreted in either of two ways: It may be that the very rural residents have fewer persons to help, or it could be that, because of distance from neighbors, they feel they should rely less on others for help. Regardless, there were no intergroup differences in availability of someone to help for those who reported needing help.

A forced-entry multiple regression procedure suggested that the primary predictors of inability to perform activities of daily living are age (disability increases with chronological age), self-reported health status, and being a member of a minority group. Living alone and being male also contribute slightly to the variance. About 8.7% in the urban sample and 6.5% in the rural group felt that they needed help with performing one or more of the activities of daily living; however, only 9 and 10 respondents, respectively, felt that they needed help but had no available assistance.

Summary

Random samples of 196 older residents of Douglas County, Nebraska, and 200 older persons residing in 11 rural counties of the Sandhills area of western Nebraska were interviewed for this study. Although the rural residents were on the average about 4 years older than their urban counterparts, they reported a lower incidence of illness and shorter hospital stays if they were hospitalized. Other than travel time and distance to primary providers and hospitals, there were few differences between the urban and rural samples. Less than 1% of either group reported delays in obtaining needed health care because of cost or transportation. On the average, most had not had an annual physical examination, yet most have a family doctor, are highly satisfied with that doctor, and had seen that doctor within the previous year. Two thirds rate their health as good or excellent. The rural residents were no less satisfied with their health care than were the urban. There were virtually no differences in terms of self-ratings of health, comparison of health today to 5 years ago, health compared to others of own age, use of emergency rooms, hospitalization episodes during the previous year, or rate of Medicare and supplemental health insurance coverage.

In conclusion, it is difficult to find support for any theoretical position such as differential prioritization of health care resources or modernization theory in the Nebraska data. In fact, much of these data are consistent with other studies in the literature: Urban versus rural differences in satisfaction with health care services and usage seemingly have greater anecdotal than empirical support. Income and education differences seem to have much more influence on health care received than does residence. A conclusion that might be made from the present study is that conventional stereotypes of the health status of the rural elderly may lack support. As Nyman, Sen, Chan, and Commins have found in their recent study of rural and urban home health patients in Wisconsin (1991), it is difficult to demonstrate evidence for problems of access. Although many rural older persons no doubt have great difficulty in obtaining adequate health care, the same could be said for many urban-dwelling older persons. The difference for many older persons seemingly is a drive of an hour rather than one of 15 minutes. For the most part, however, both groups report receiving the services that they need and high levels of satisfaction with those services.

11

Rural Geriatric Mental Health Care

A Continuing Service Dilemma

ELOISE RATHBONE-McCUAN

The purpose of this chapter is to identify the major issues contributing to the lack of adequate mental health services for the rural elderly and to suggest steps to address the critical shortage of these resources. It is estimated that 15% to 25% of those over 65 years of age have significant mental health problems, yet 85% go without the mental health care they need (Dorwart, 1990). According to Durenberger (1989), research from Minnesota shows that about 20% of the rural elderly population present significant mental health problems whereas only 1% seek mental health services. The place of residency may influence the estimates of mental health service utilization among the elderly, however, all research points to need for and lack of service provision to meet mental health needs of older Americans.

Many of the concerns about how to provide more cost-effective mental health care to the aged cut across all residential locations and represent an equally critical problem for metropolitan and nonmetropolitan areas as well as having some unique features in the context of rural life. Whenever possible, program planners and researchers should attempt to develop programs adapted for the particular area and population. At the same time, local innovations need to be supported by national structures and mechanisms for service delivery.

Perspectives and Assumptions

The declaration that "the elderly will not use mental health services" can be challenged by virtue of the fact any vulnerable target population cannot be expected to use what is not available. Documentation of the elderly population's stigmatized attitude toward psychiatric illness and non-utilization of services may be little more than a justification for failing to provide them with adequate service resource access. Until professional service providers confront this situation the expansion of appropriate services and outreach efforts will remain a low priority.

Some of the major issues most central to planning and delivering mental health services to the rural aged include the following:

1. The mental health needs of rural elderly cannot be met through only the informal social support networks even though these may be essential components in the majority of successful case interventions. Usually too many bio-psycho-social factors combine to contribute to mental health risks making it impossible for informal resources alone to meet care needs (Gurian, 1982).

2. No one agency such as the Area Agency on Aging (AAA) or the community mental health clinic should claim rural mental health as an independent service domain because coordinated health, social, and psychiatric services are often required to address the mental health needs of older clients (Shane, 1987).

3. Psychiatric care or its equivalent carries a deep-seated confusion among the rural elderly and "myths of madness" are well established in the community culture of rural America and are often passed down from one generation to the next.

4. Financial and personnel shortages to plan, implement, and sustain special geriatric mental health programs are interconnected to the larger mental health picture in rural America. In turn, the larger issues of rural health care impact on psychiatric care.

5. All of the documented service shortages and recent macro economic and demographic trends impacting on rural America have some association with the mental health needs of the aged population and the solutions that might be created to meet needs. Demographic aging, the increased dependency-ratio in small towns, and the declining economic base result in a higher proportion of rural residents drawing on fewer community resources.

6. The complexity of rural mental health service provision results from policy, reimbursement, organizational, and clinical variables that must be

factored into the resolution of mental health care dilemmas for older citizens. At this time, there is no evidence of a consensus-building effort to develop resolutions to service shortages.

7. Mental health concerns should be included in the social policy and service provision priorities established for rural elderly.

The implications to be drawn from these ongoing issues are foreboding in so far as framing an effective action plan adaptable among rural communities. Area Agencies on Aging have demonstrated effectiveness in mobilizing the informal community resources that support elderly in times of crises and help prevent unwarranted institutionalization. However, few have opted to address mental health care needs if it draws the agency into the realm of politically charged and stigmatized public psychiatric care. The increasing involvement of AAAs in the development and delivery of health and long-term care has less stigma even though this service initiative is being questioned in some communities because other agencies wish to dominate health care delivery. To be associated as part of the mental health system is thought by some AAA administrators to reduce the effectiveness of outreach to older persons for home health, adult day care, and health status assessment.

The distancing of AAAs from the mental health problems of the elderly has made it more difficult for cooperation to develop and sustain in the face of multiple mandated service functions assigned to public mental health programs. Local community human service agencies have been destabilized from the economic and social pressures of rural life over the past decade so many agencies place their own survival first. Maintaining an economic base for agency operations may justify either cutting expensive underutilized services or not expanding into service areas where no profit margin is predicted. These conditions do not foster the resource exchanges needed to provide comprehensive mental health services to rural elders and may actually impede the creation of solutions projected as too costly for underfunded agencies.

Psychiatric Disorders and Mental Health Concerns

Viewing needs of the elderly within the psychiatric disorder framework places the issues of treatment and care in the domain of psychiatry, which maintains its professional place in the medical care dominion. For example, an acute hospital-based assessment clinic supporting an

interdisciplinary team within the hospital staff may be a more acceptable medical care model than hiring rural outreach workers. This association implicates mental health care with the spiraling costs of the
medical care industry. A psychosocial scheme leads to a broader interpretation of human needs, problems, and solutions that extend services
beyond the biomedical base of health care but draws mental health into
the unstable financial and politically unpopular public social service
arena. There is widespread resistance to defining community mental
health programs with adult protective services associated with county
welfare.

Because rural communities are increasingly without professional and
highly specialized psychiatric care, it is necessary to plan delivery
strategies to have the psychiatric knowledge available in the treatment
of specific aspects of patient care without dominating the actual delivery of care. The community mental health movement has accomplished
this through involvement of psychologists and social workers rather
than psychiatrists. These staff deliver all facets of treatment except that
which is linked to medication therapy or some other medical-based
treatment. These nonmedical professions are trained to work within
both frameworks even though their greater professional legitimation
comes from a psychosocial perspective because they are treating/coun-
seling the client in the environmental context.

Organic mental disorders are the most prevalent psychiatric disorders
of late life and the most costly both in terms of patient care costs and
quality of life issues (Raskind, 1989). The organic mental syndromes
that are of primary importance in the elderly population are these:

1. *Dementia:* impairment of memory and breakdown of intellectual thinking
2. *Amnestic syndrome:* impairment of memory secondary to a specific organic condition in some part of the brain
3. *Delirium:* clinical profiles related to organic etiology creating distorted
   attention
4. *Organic mood syndrome:* the depression type that is attributed to an
   underlying organic factor (Cohen, 1990; Raskind, 1989; Solomon, 1990)

There is limited information from which to conclude that rural residence is a factor that directly influences the distribution of psychiatric
disorders among the elderly. Without epidemiological studies that provide information about the distribution of mental disorders and risks,
both states and local communities are in a difficult position to plan for

the mental health care of older adults. Blazer (1989) notes that such data could contribute to case identification, understanding historical trends of mental illness, identifying the etiology of psychiatric disorders, and planning for the use of psychiatric care and mental health services. The case identification function can not rely solely on epidemiological data, however, and should not be confused with the clinical information that practitioners gather when working in communities to identify clients at risk. It is through that worker-in-community knowledge-building process and qualitative studies of specific rural communities (Bartlett, 1990) that we have learned most about the intimate influences of social factors extended into the context of mental health problems in late life.

Studies by Brown (1990) and Rowles (1990) confirm some of the important aspects of the elderly person-in-environment that seems so essential for managing life crises and adapting to major intrapersonal, interpersonal, and environmental change associated with the gains and loses of the aging process. For example, connection to nonkin groups such as civic, fraternal, women's leagues, and religious groups give many elderly people continued social contacts that partly compensate for the most recent historical cycle of residential destabilization of rural extended families. Personal identification with land, culture, and history give some rural elders a symbolic attachment to their environment and helps to buffer them from the isolating forces of community change.

One of the most recent contributions for studying the general mental health status of the elderly has been proposed by Aldwin and Stokols (1988). Scheidt and Norris-Baker (1990) and others have found their approach, developed through a broad transactional paradigm, to be most helpful in understanding acute and environmental stress associated with rural crises (e.g., farm crisis, renewed out-migration of younger community or regional cohorts and family members, closures of rural hospitals and loss of familiar health personnel). Their hypotheses (Scheidt & Norris-Baker, 1990) about the impact of stress include both positive and negative outcomes that occur at the micro psychophysical and macro physical environmental levels and impact on well-being (Aldwin & Stokols, 1988).

Using the broad transactional paradigm to understand the environmental stress of rural women and their aging processes affords an excellent foundation for designing services to address the complex impact of female poverty in rural area where 1 in 4 older women live in poverty (Coward, 1987b). Gender and age interact to create special mental health issues for older women such as social isolation, depression, and self-neglect (Rathbone-McCuan & Bricker-Jenkins, 1992).

A comprehensive review of the rapidly growing knowledge base of older women prepared by Kivett (1990) gives useful direction to the mental health professionals. She challenges professionals to recognize the heterogeneity of older rural women while also seeking to understand their commonalities. Programs that validate the personal worth of older women need to be offered as part of formal service provision and fostered where they exist beyond the boundaries of social service systems such as within rural churches. Kivett encourages the provision of services that support independence and personal control in adapting to changing self-images, increasing adaptation to dependencies in later life, enhancing personal relationships, and participating in self-advocacy to expanded needed social supports.

Demythologizing life in rural America has been one of the most formidable tasks facing rural specialists who have applied various research methodologies to describe the strengths and limitations of old age and rural residence. "The lack of access to mental health services in rural areas, especially in the face of increasing need, is an issue that has received less attention but that is of great concern" (Human & Wasem, 1991, p. 223). Groups at greater risk of mental disorder (the full range of mental health needs) are the elderly, the chronically ill, the poor, and those who are dependent (Wagenfeld, 1990). The demographic correlations among factors of age, poverty, illness, and functional dependency are known to extend across regional sectors of this country.

Another area of important social research relevant to mental health and the elderly falls under the multidimensional conceptualization of social support. This area of study has helped provide practitioners with a better understanding of the actual social connections with friends and family and peers that act as sources of social resource. Those social supports influence the elderly client's perception of social connection. Involving the older person in a process of specifying their perceived sources of support give direction for involving a larger, more diverse helping network (Piazza, 1989). Case management and improved professional service coordination models have also directed professionals to follow-up on the social supports enacted on behalf of the older person, which helps monitor the actual availability of supportive assistance (Streeter & Franklin, 1992).

Current Issues in Rural Mental Health Care

Almost 30 years ago, Congress passed the Community Mental Health Centers Act (PL 88-164, Title II). This legislation supported the development of community mental health centers (CMHC) that grew in number to more than 500 between 1965 and 1973, and 40% of these served catchment areas in one or more rural counties (Human & Wasem, 1991). By the late 1970s there was national concern about how well the CMHC model was meeting all the needs that were considered of immediate priority and those looming on the horizon as growing unmet needs were documented in rural America.

Some of the most persistent problems in the provision of mental health services to the aged included the following: (1) mental health professionals often lacked any specialized training or interest in aging; (2) recruitment of specialists in aging and/or for rural agency settings was difficult; (3) funding to support special innovative programs for the elderly were often grant-based and could not be continued after grant funds ended; (4) formal mental health care was a source of stigma to the elderly; (5) other high-risk populations such as children were as underserved as were the elderly and their needs were placed in competition for services; (6) labor-intensive community outreach and multiagency coordination was necessary to make contact with older people; (7) interagency working agreements formed to strengthen the cooperation of rural agencies were often a proforma administrative gesture; (8) elderly people identified with their physician as the first line of intervention for a mental health problem and/or sought counsel from ministers; and (9) advocacy groups and state mental health policies were turning toward the younger, chronically mentally ill population to prevent costly long-term institutionalization. These factors continue to influence the design, provision, and utilization of mental health services among rural elderly in this decade.

Illustration of Early Rural Mental Health Service Approaches

Amendments to the Community Mental Health Centers Act provided funding designated to help agencies target on underserved at-risk groups. In the mid and late 1970s a small number of rural community mental health centers expanded their service delivery capacity to the aged. Although there was no one single effective scenario, some common program characteristics were in evidence: (1) Recruitment for a geriatric mental health specialist to work in a rural community was very difficult, so specialist positions were filled by psychologists or social workers who had to learn on the job; (2) initial strategies to bring elderly clients into the community mental health center as in-office therapy clients failed to a large extent, so outreach was required in places in the community where elderly were to be found; (3) developing programs in the community took place in settings where there were larger numbers of elderly, such as rural senior centers, and these usually involved some form of age-peer group to encourage socialization and late life problem solving; (4) specialists were invited or positioned themselves to provide no-cost/low-cost community education to different service providers, such as in-home health workers or information and referral staff that served a number of elderly, in order to give them information about the psychological needs of the elderly and establish a referral channel; (5) some liaison work was attempted with physicians and churches, for example, since these were key gatekeepers for the elderly; and (6) efforts were made to interest other CMHC staff in the potential of older persons to be successful psychotherapy clients.

These initiatives were often successful and the "practical wisdom" of these approaches is now documented in the professional literature. The programmatic achievements of an earlier era usually involved incorporating extensive community organization skills into the role of the mental health worker and these professionals built on the strengths of the informal helping network and centrality of cooperative agreements in the agency service network. So what happened that prevented proliferation of these early aging and mental health efforts and discouraged more rural community mental health centers from developing programs targeted for the aged?

Hiatus in the Rural Mental Health Field

Murray and Keller (1991) have outlined a number of trends that began in the 1980s and continued to exert major influences on rural mental health service provision. The optimism for new federal leadership in mental health (Keller & Murray, 1982) fell away quickly when the Congress shifted the leadership from the federal to state and local governmental control. Had the role of NIMH continued to expand it is probable that a major research and demonstration initiative would have been launched (Bergland, 1988). Unfortunately, in 1981, the Alcohol, Drug Abuse, and Mental Health Block grant statute enacted by Section

901 of the OBRA of 1981 (PL 97-35) not only mandated transfer of the community mental health program to states but also discouraged NIMH from maintaining a rural mental health focus (Human & Wasem, 1991). Categorical community services such as consultation and education that supported the type of geriatric mental health specialist described above were dropped. Decisions not to continue these services were usually related to cost-effectiveness decisions when administrators faced no source for reimbursement. In their place came the block grant funding that allowed states to reestablish priorities for the distribution of federal mental health dollars. According to Murray and Keller (1991), "At the very least , this has typically meant redirecting staff efforts toward more fee-for-service reimbursement. . . . Although we are not aware of any comprehensive national data, we believe that, overall, rural mental health practice has been narrowed, focused more on ability to pay, and has moved further away from the broad goals of the original community health centers movement in the 1960s" (p. 226). Community mental health centers have been drawn into the "managed mental health care" agenda that took hold during the 1980s so that psychiatric care costs might have some controlled increases. This agenda will grow throughout the 1990s to the extent that some sources predict that within only a short time 3 out of every 4 psychiatric patients will have their care overseen by some type of organized system of managed care (Dorwart, 1990).

   In the midst of current pressure for mental health service cost-containment and a pervasive limbo among community mental health centers there are federal initiatives underway that again capture attention to the special health and human service needs in rural areas. The Office of Rural Health (ORHP), established within the Health Resources and Services Administration of the Department of Health and Human Services in August 1987, is charged with the responsibility to coordinate within and among federal agencies and with other organizations and state governmental units the addressing of health care (including mental health care) in rural communities (Human & Wasem, 1991). An important outcome of ORHP has been the grant support to create seven rural health research centers each with a specialized area of concern related to rural needs. Another recent funding initiative for rural health and aging centers was awarded by the National Institute on Aging. According to Hutner and Windle (1991), NIMH is seeking increased funding for rural research and demonstration projects. New federal money would be coordinated with the rural mental health agenda of other national organizations advocating for rural mental health concerns. Working together, these academic research, policy, and educational organizations have the potential to provide more cost-effective care for the rural aged.

Considerations for Future Planning and Response Sets

This section summarizes what is understood about the circumstances of rural elderly and service provision efforts that could address their needs. The reader, however, is cautioned against assuming that the data bases from which to draw information are adequate for comprehensive planning and program implementation. The mental health care system and the aging network are essential agencies in order to develop solutions for the underserved elderly. Some service provision steps will require that state planning requirements draw aging and mental health systems together with reimbursement and grant incentives attached for demonstration program implementation. Other solutions involve training to develop a comprehensive client assessment shared between aging and mental health service providers (Shane, 1987).

Lack of Specialized Mental Health Services

Legislative changes and severe budget reductions during the 1980s led CHMCs to reduce special at-risk population initiatives. Community education and prevention programs and specialized clinical services for the elderly were either cut back or ended. In the few communities where these services had been available, they were not continued as part of the long-range planning of most agencies. It is known that rural children and elderly have needs that are different from the adult populations that CMHCs serve as their client majority. Currently, the two major client service streams are (1) the psychotherapeutic clients who receive individual, family, and group therapies and are able to pay for the service or have third-party insurance, and (2) the case management clients who are individuals with chronic mental illness that are paid for by state funds intended to keep them in the community. Fiscal problems haunt many community mental health centers, leaving them in a position of being unable or unwilling to venture into new service provision areas. Where there is only adequate sources of public funding through short-term grants or contracts, there is resistance to increasing the dependent patient caseload especially those who are without the means to pay. State mental health funds are appropriated according to priorities for community supervision and maintenance for younger patients. Even in those states where there is advocacy for the mental health needs of older citizens, it is difficult to get their needs given priority over the younger long-term population.

Other sources of psychotherapy provision that could extend services to the rural elderly face a nonviable patient market. Private practitioners are looking for a paying client group upon which to build a stable client fee base. This financial need will preclude most rural elderly from being seen by private practitioners. The continuing closure of rural hospitals further erodes the availability of acute short-term psychiatric bed space. A shortage of evaluation and short-term crisis treatment beds also characterizes the care shortages in public psychiatric institutions. To an increasing extent, these settings are a dying breed in the world of public psychiatric service. Restrictive admissions policies help institutions defend against becoming overwhelmed by aged clients that might backlog bed space. The misdiagnosis of Alzheimer's disease has been recognized recently as a problem that may have very serious consequences for rural elderly persons having no access to diagnostic expertise (Rathbone-McCuan & Fabian, 1992). There may be a proliferation of "specialized" nursing home beds established in costly for-profit facilities seeking to make a profit from family caregiving crises, but few public local alternatives to care for the cognitively impaired aged.

Attitudes of Mental Health Professionals

Among the CMHC therapist practitioners there continues to be a lack of interest in serving elderly clients. This attitude is perpetuated by a lack of training in aging as well as recognition of the severe limitations of these clients as a source of fee-for-service payment. Many of these rural clinicians have progressed in their career to an in-office-based practice adapted to the willing, mobile, insured client. Techniques of practice that address community mental health issues are often limited to those that will help recruit paying clients, which does not include the majority of the rural elders.

The casemanager side of CMHC mental health practice is not especially welcoming of the elderly chronic mentally ill patient. The older the patient the less likely to be perceived as benefiting from existing group socialization or specialized vocational supports. Elderly patients are harder to place in contract board-and-care situations that often exclude patients needing routine self-care and mobility assistance. Furthermore, casemanagers are not eager to have clients who require attention from medical care facilities where poor clients of all ages are increasingly less welcome as patients as well as being harder to access for patient care.

Lack of Mental Health Priorities within AAA Networks

The decade of the 1980s saw the mandated service functions of the Older Americans Act increase and diversify without substantial funding increases to support expanded core service provision. Like community mental health centers, AAAs are unable to offer new service programs for which there is no funding. Poor interorganizational relationships may characterize connections between a AAAs and CMHCs because each sees the elderly mentally ill client as a responsibility of the other agency, which makes cooperation more difficult (Rathbone-McCuan, 1981). When these agencies engage in the planning process it may be cut short because of no information on the prevalence and incidence of geriatric mental health needs.

Five Years into the Future

Despite the current discussion of rural human service delivery crises, there continues to be too little advocacy for geriatric mental health care. Perhaps better research data will become available to substantiate unmet needs and research can stimulate practitioners to design innovative service models. This would require, however, more funding for mental health research on aging issues, collecting data and analyzing secondary data on rural aging populations, and giving attention to mental health risk variables as well as a service project funding.

Budget projections for the 1990s will reconfirm that community mental centers are rarely in a position to provide specialized comprehensive care to the elderly. The lack of financing and the inability of some rural CMHCs to build a client base through a strong fee-for-therapeutic services may lead to the continued reduction of experienced clinical staff. Other CMHCs will remain open because of further program conversion to support case management for chronic mentally ill.

Only through increased advocacy will it be possible to promote the notion that mental health services for children and aged persons are not a privileged entitlement from CMHC facilities. In this area there is need for better intergenerational advocacy for the elderly and children.

The new initiatives of "the Eldercare Campaign" announced in 1991 by the Administration on Aging reflects a "do more with less" agenda. This service provision philosophy has the long-range impact of discouraging innovative models of service delivery. Policy directives need to establish a realistic limit regarding the extent to which new models of coordination and innovation among beleaguered and underfunded rural agencies are proposed. In reality, too often they go nowhere but on paper and in the files. Although models of community organization to better integrate the formal and informal resource networks of rural agencies are very helpful, they do not offer much hope of reviving depleted informal and voluntary community resources to offset what formal agencies lack the funds to provide.

Aging inplace among the elderly without alternatives or willingness to leave the rural area will have the consequence of leaving the rural AAAs with a steady increase in the cases of highly vulnerable elderly. A proportion of these individuals will be very isolated (Rathbone-McCuan & Hashimi, 1982) and caught in a cycle of self-neglect (Rathbone-McCuan & Bricker-Jenkins, 1992). Self-neglect cases may be more frequently ignored or unrecognized in rural areas because of geographic isolation and values of autonomy and right-to-be that lead to failure to report cases of high risk. There may be no integrated service network interventions that adequately connect public social services, legal and financial advocates, and mental health specialists.

The elderly with Alzheimer's disease and their aging caregiving kin will become more recognized as "high risk" clients who are set adrift among the medical, psychiatric, and public social service agencies. New federal initiatives are now being planned to encourage states to develop comprehensive support programs for caregivers. It remains to be seen whether or not these programs will include a strong mental health focus. Cost-containment for in-home services will become a means of further rationing community maintenance care whereby social care attendants are hired to keep the cognitively impaired elderly at home. Money for these individuals is already limited and their wages are shockingly low. It is likely that these underpaid "home-makers" will become less available if rural home health care agencies have to pay registered nurses "rural duty supplements" to attract them to rural agencies. Hiring much needed professionals who demand high salaries often cuts down the pool of equally valuable nonprofessional care staff.

The discontinuation of public housing development from the federal government has left both rural and urban communities with shortages in housing for all special needs groups. These "naturally occurring retirement communities," now referred to as NORCs, are already very much in evidence throughout rural America. More professional services, including more mental health services, will be needed to sustain these "community elderly" in apartment settings. It is a reality for many rural communities that no nursing home alternatives are readily available where and when they are needed as a next step in long-term care. Many rural communities do not have the economic market potential to attract for-profit investors that can create buy-in long-term care continuums. There may be some AAAs that try to find financing for these alternatives, but economic and demographic factors will work against their success. The rural elderly will continue to be interested in purchasing long-term care insurance, which remains a relatively untested long-term care financing mechanism, but uninformed rural elderly remain a target market. Furthermore, there has been limited attention to the coverage these policies will provide for geropsychiatric needs that often combine with higher levels of institutional care.

Mental health needs that leave the elderly person without cognitive capacities will further necessitate conservators/guardians. Without nearby family and friends to provide this function, greater public costs will be evident to provide for such conservators/guardians. This fact may force a new linkage between county-level adult social services and AAAs because of the growing numbers of frail, isolated elders who need personal life management assistance. Mental health agencies will be drawn into more "competency determination" functions for elderly clients. These evaluations often require that professional experts be paid to complete assessments for court competency decisions. There will be a pattern of "client passing" for the cognitively impaired elderly who are not welcome or well suited for the services available from either the aging network or the community mental health center. Far too many of these elderly will fall into the background.

In summary, the provision of mental health care for the rural elderly is a continuing human service dilemma. The range of human needs that are encompassed by the psychosocial perspective of mental health needs broaden the perspective of what should be included in the continuum of mental health services to the aged. The medical/psychiatric illness perspective narrows and refines the focus of geriatric mental health care. However, such care is too often costly and requires a more comprehensive definition of third-party service coverage. Both perspectives have their role in the provision of needed services to the vulnerable rural elderly through further expansion of both public and private care resources that are well integrated into a multisystem care provision model.

12

Elder Abuse

A Rural Perspective

NOVELLA PERRIN

One in every two households will experience some form of domestic violence this year (Strauss, Gelles, & Steinmetz, 1980). The tragedy of domestic violence was first brought to national attention during the 1960s with the publication of *The Battered Child Syndrome,* by Kempe et al. (Kempe, Silverman, Steele, Droegemuller, & Silver, 1962). Spouse abuse and elder abuse were then "discovered" in the following two decades.

Although elder abuse researchers and reformers have benefited from the scientific and public attention given to other forms of domestic violence, they have been confounded with some of the same problems, not the least of which is the definition of abuse (Pedrick-Cornell & Gelles, 1982). Much has been written regarding this definitional dilemma (Douglass & Hickey, 1983; Galbraith, 1986; Johnson, 1986; Pedrick-Cornell & Gelles, 1982). In fact, Pedrick-Cornell and Gelles (1982) suggest the lack of a clear definition of abuse is "perhaps the most significant impediment in the development of an adequate knowledge base on intrafamily violence" (p. 458). Without a clear definition, one cannot compare the results of extant research, document its incidence, or determine the causes of the behavior (Pedrick-Cornell & Gelles, 1982).

The Definition of Elder Abuse

Definitions of elder abuse tend to be much broader than those used in relation to child abuse. Abuse as related to children almost always is restricted to physical maltreatment (Yin, 1985). Definitions of elder abuse, however, also include psychological abuse (Block & Sinnot, 1979; Lau & Kosberg, 1979; O'Malley et al., 1979), financial abuse (Block & Sinnot, 1979; Lau and Kosberg, 1979; Select Committee on Aging, 1981), and violation of rights (Lau & Kosberg, 1979). Other definitions have made a distinction between abuse and neglect and some definitions have subdivided neglect into passive and active categories (Douglass & Hickey, 1983; Douglass, Hickey, & Noel, 1980; Hickey & Douglass, 1981; Select Committee on Aging, 1981; Sengstock, Hwalek, & Moshier, 1986). This lack of a uniform operational definition makes comparison between studies most difficult. For example, the physical abuse category of Lau and Kosberg (1979) coincides with the category of neglect in the study of Douglass, Hickey, and Noel (1980).

In an attempt to simplify the definition problem, the Select Committee on Aging (1981) adopted five categories of elder abuse. These are (1) physical abuse whether caused by deliberate or negligent action, (2) psychological abuse, (3) financial abuse, (4) violation of rights, and (5) self-neglect. Because the victim and the perpetrator are one and the same in the self-neglect category, this category is frequently omitted from current research.

Although gerontologists are beginning to reach consensus on broad categories of abuse, the range of abuse within each category still confuses the issue. For example, withholding food, biting, hitting, sexually abusing, and murdering an older adult all fall within the category of physical abuse. Psychological abuse may include name calling, insulting, threatening violence or nursing home placement, demeaning the older person's sense of dignity and worth, or isolating the individual. Financial abuse includes theft or misuse of money or materials. Violation of rights includes attempts to adjudicate the individual as incompetent when that is not true or to in any way reduce or remove the inalienable rights guaranteed to every American citizen (Select Committee on Aging, 1981).

Given the number of categories, the determination of intention, and the degree of severity within each category, it is easy to understand why the definitional dilemma remains a significant problem for elder abuse researchers and reformers.

Incidence of Abuse

Just as the lack of a universal operational definition impedes comparability of existing research, lack of a uniform definition inhibits accurate and comparative reporting of abuse cases. Estimates of elder abuse range from 4% to 10% of the older adult population or from 500,000 to 2.5 million cases annually (Pedrick-Cornell & Gelles, 1982). Adopting the lowest estimate (which excludes self-neglect cases), the Select Committee on Aging (1981) concluded approximately 1 million, or 1 in every 25 older adults, are being abused annually, only slightly lower than the estimated number of child abuse cases. However, data reveal 1 of 3 child abuse cases is reported but only 1 of 5 elder abuse cases is reported. Although 40% of all abuse cases are adult cases, these cases receive only 4.7% of the state's protective services budgets. States spend $22 per child on protective services compared to $2.90 per case on elder abuse (Subcommittee on Health and Long-Term Care, 1985).

It must be stressed that these incidence figures are *estimates* of elder abuse. All states do not have mandatory reporting laws for elder abuse and there is discrepancy from state to state regarding the definition of abuse. These estimates have come from known reports to agencies or extrapolations of data from small nonrepresentative samples to national figures and are based on number of cases rather than number of incidents. Elder abuse tends to be recurrent rather than an isolated event and the abuse most generally encompasses multiple categories (Select Committee on Aging, 1981). Thus, an older adult whose rights are violated and who is physically and psychologically abused every day may count only as one case.

Abuser/Abused Profiles

Although the elder abuse research is fraught with definitional discrepancies and methodological problems it has produced a fairly consistent profile of the abuser and victim. The abuser is generally a relative of the victim, most frequently a son, daughter, or spouse. The abuser is experiencing great stress due to the demanding needs of the impaired older adult. Alcohol and drug abuse is also a frequent characteristic of the perpetrator (Block & Sinnot, 1979; Hickey & Douglass, 1981; Lau & Kosberg, 1979; O'Malley et al., 1979; Select Committee on Aging, 1981).

The elder abuse victim is most often a female of advanced age (75+), who is physically and mentally impaired and who is dependent on the abuser with whom she lives (Block & Sinnot, 1979; Galbraith, 1986; Lau & Kosberg, 1979; O'Malley et al., 1979; Rathbone-McCuan, 1980; Select Committee on Aging, 1981).

Theories of Abuse

Again, borrowing from and building on the early child and spouse abuse research, elder abuse researchers have offered a number of theoretical explanations of elder abuse. These theories tend to fall into one of four major categories outlined by Henton, Cate, and Emory (1984). Their four categories are (1) personal characteristics of the abuser and victim, (2) interpersonal factors of the relationship between the abuser and victim, (3) situational factors that increase the likelihood of abuse, and (4) sociocultural factors that are related to the acceptable use of violence.

Personal Characteristics of the Abuser and Victim. Included in this category would be the personality disorder theory. The basic assumption of this theory is that the abuser has a personality problem that causes him or her to be abusive (Douglass, Hickey, & Noel, 1980; Hickey & Douglass, 1981). Characteristics of the pathological deviant include lack of self-control, psychotic or sadistic compulsion, passive-aggressiveness or displaced aggression, and undifferentiated types of mental illness (Galbraith, 1989). This category would also include the perpetrator that is an alcohol and/or drug abuser (Select Committee on Aging, 1981).

Interpersonal Factors of the Relationship Between the Abuser and Victim. One of the common themes related to elder abuse is the cycle of violence theory. This theory basically states that parents and children abuse each other throughout their lifetimes. Conflict is resolved through violence, is learned, and is passed from generation to generation. Thus, the abused child becomes the abusive parent (Hickey & Douglass, 1981; Steinmetz, 1977). In writing on wife and child abuse, Gelles (quoted in Galbraith, 1989, p. 17) argues the more violence an abuser

> experiences in growing up, the more likely an individual is to use violence as an adult. . . . Children who see and experience violence when growing up tend

to use these experiences as guides for dealing with problems in their adult families.

Steinmetz (1978) supports this statement as she found only 1 in 400 children reared in nonviolent homes abused their parents, whereas 1 in 2 children reared in abusive homes abused their parents. Other researchers have explained the abuse of the parent by the child as simple revenge for real or perceived wrongdoing (Galbraith, 1986; Rathbone-McCuan & Hashimi, 1982) or the failure of the adult child to resolve filial crisis (Block & Sinnot, 1979; Lau & Kosberg, 1979).

Situational Factors That Increase the Likelihood of Abuse. Much of the current gerontological literature focuses on caregiver burden and caregiver stress. Although caregiver stress obviously does not always result in elder abuse, stress is often the precipitating factor in elder abuse (Block & Sinnot, 1979). The older adult is dependent on the caregiver. This often places a great economic, psychological, and social burden on the caregiver. As Steinmetz reported to the Select Committee on Aging:

> The bottom line is that if you increase the stress on family members without adding supports to help them cope with it, you increase the likelihood of violence because a person and a family can handle only so much. (Select Committee on Aging, 1981, p. 64)

This dependence of the older adult on the caregiver is a recurring idea throughout the early research (Block & Sinnot, 1979; Douglass, Hickey & Noel, 1980; Lau & Kosberg, 1979).

Sociocultural Factors That Are Related to the Acceptable Use of Violence. The American society glorifies violence. Violence is viewed as societally acceptable and may be perceived to be less harmful when directed toward a group already devalued by society (Block & Sinnot, 1979). The devaluation of older adults is part of the "ageism" concept described by Butler (1969).

Assessment of Elder Abuse

Unlike abused children who are in daily contact with persons who may be able to help them, the abused older adult is often quite isolated

(Wolf & Pillemer, 1984). When a professional does come into contact with the victim, he or she may not recognize the abuse. Because the abuse may take many forms, educating professionals to properly assess abuse is of vital importance. Research has indicated that protective service workers may adopt their own "profile" of an abuse victim and thereby overlook certain indicators of abuse (Bookin & Dunkle, 1985; Douglass, Hickey, & Noel, 1980; Galbraith, 1989; Hickey & Douglass, 1981). To assist workers, a number of screening instruments have been developed to assess for elder abuse. Perhaps the most thorough of these is the Sengstock-Hwalek Comprehensive Index of Elder Abuse (Sengstock & Hwalek, 1985).

Even if the professional accurately identifies that abuse has occurred, it is likely the older adult will not assist the worker by talking about the abuse situation. The victim may fear more severe abuse or nursing home placement. In the eyes of many, a known abusive home is preferable to an unknown nursing home.

Other older adults may deny the abuse is occurring. It is difficult for some parents to admit their child is harming them. Some may feel a need to protect the abuser. Yet others may feel they deserve the treatment and therefore, never report the abuse.

Older adults may not be aware of the protective services that are available to them. Or, if aware of the service, the victim may mistrust the protective agencies. Others fear the situation will not change even if it is reported, and, for many of the isolated elders, they feel have no options (Bookin & Dunkle, 1985; Quinn & Tomita, 1986). For whichever of these reasons, this lack of cooperation may hinder appropriate intervention.

Intervention Strategies

Once the older victim is identified, an intervention strategy may be developed. Hooyman and Lustbader (1986) believe it is imperative for professionals to

> recognize that they can easily make the situation worse if they cannot offer better alternatives. . . . To be beneficial, interventions must be preceded by a careful attempt to understand why the abuse is occurring, why it is tolerated, and what alternatives can be provided. (pp. 102-103)

Developing an appropriate intervention strategy is often difficult because older adults are autonomous and have the right of self-determination (Phillips, 1989). Unless the older adult has been found incompetent, he or she has the right to determine which intervention strategy, if any, is best. Also, there may be few alternatives or services available for older adults. A lack of in-home services, support groups, respite care, or other options may mean the victim is removed from the home and placed in a long-term care facility.

State Regulations

In an attempt to assure that older victims do receive attention and necessary services, 43 states and the District of Columbia have adopted statutes on adult abuse reporting or comprehensive adult protective services. As may be expected, there is significant variation on the definition of abuse, who is protected under the statute, how the abuse is investigated, and the penalty for the abuser (Traxler, 1986). As stated earlier, this makes interstate comparison extremely difficult and often misleading. Missouri, for example, consistently reports more cases of abuse than Iowa (Missouri Division of Aging, 1992). One could erroneously conclude there is more abuse occurring in Missouri when, in actuality, the discrepancy is due to definition and reporting laws.

As one would imagine, the lack of a national elder abuse data base hampers interstate comparisons and rural-urban comparisons. Without national data, rural-urban comparisons are almost always limited to intrastate analysis.

The Rural Perspective

Interestingly, a review of the literature does not reveal significant differences in the number of abuse cases in rural versus urban areas of the same state. Most state reports simply indicate abuse occurs in both rural and urban areas but exact numbers or percentages are not given. The Missouri Division of Aging (1992) has more systematically investigated the rural-urban differences. Missouri has a toll-free statewide hotline to which abuse reports are made. When a call is received, the county of the alleged victim is recorded. Between January 1, 1990 and December 31, 1991, the Division received 79,272 abuse calls. Based on

1990 census data, it was determined that 10 of Missouri's counties could be classified as urban and the others could be classified as rural. Within the 10 urban counties there were 42,507 abuse calls, 85.6% of which were for persons over 60. There were 36,766 abuse calls in the rural counties, 82% of which were for persons 60 and over. This translates to 4.95 per 1,000 population in urban areas and 4.89 per 1,000 in rural areas. Only a slight difference between rural and urban incidence rates can be detected.

A profile of the alleged victim in both rural and urban areas was similar to that found in national studies. In the urban areas, 69% of the alleged victims were women and 31% were men and 70% were white. In the rural areas, 64% were women and 36% were men and 95% were white. Fifty-two percent of the alleged urban victims lived with their spouse, other relative, or nonrelative. Forty-two percent lived alone. Fifty-one percent of the rural alleged victims lived with another person and 44% lived alone. Again, the profile of the victim, although consistent with national data, does not indicate any significant rural-urban distinctions.

However, when the complaint was investigated some differences began to emerge. In Missouri, the seriousness of the complaint is recorded as either life-threatening or non-life-threatening. Fourteen percent of the urban cases were determined to be life-threatening compared to 18% of the rural cases. The cases are also judged as to whether there is reason or not to believe the abuse did occur. Forty-nine percent of the urban life-threatening and 38% of the urban non-life-threatening cases were judged reason to believe. Sixty-five percent of the rural life-threatening and 50% of the rural non-life-threatening cases were judged reason to believe. These figures indicate that the reported cases in rural areas are slightly more serious and that there is a higher rate of accuracy in the report. However, based on the earlier discussion of the professional's own view of the abuse case, one might question whether it is a rural-urban difference or an investigator difference.

One other small difference in the findings between rural and urban areas was found regarding the alleged perpetrator. In both areas, the older adult was most frequently the perpetrator (i.e., self-abuse). The spouse, however, was slightly more likely to be the perpetrator in urban than in rural areas.

The significant differences between urban and rural abuse do not seem to be in incidence rates or abuser/victim profiles. The differences appear to be in service options and intervention strategies once the abuse is verified.

The very factors that define an area as rural—space, geography, and dispersed population—work to collectively obstruct provision of services to rural people. Much has been written regarding the lack of health and social services in rural areas. Regardless of the type of service being examined, rural areas simply have fewer services (Krout, 1986; Nelson, 1980; Taietz & Milton, 1979). Deficits in number of trained personnel (New York State Senate, 1980), a lack of organizational structural complexity (Steinhauer, 1980), and low funding levels and tax bases (Ecosometrics, 1981) all contribute to the low number of services available.

Even those services that are available may be difficult to reach because of topography, distance, and lack of adequate transportation. Or, if the service is available and the older adult has easy access to the service site, there is considerable evidence that rural older adults generally do not like to use formal services. Independence and self-reliance are basic and important values of rural individuals (Coward, 1979). It appears that rural older adults have a greater reliance on family and other informal support networks. To use the services would imply that the person could not take care of himself or herself or that there was no family member on which to rely. Remembering that the older adult has the final say in determining the appropriate abuse strategy, it may be that the service is simply rejected based on learned rural values.

Of course, not all older adults refuse the service options. Many indicate they would have used the service earlier had they known about it. However, the rural persons' isolation may prevent them from knowing about the service (Coward & Rathbone-McCuan, 1985).

The problems of service availability, accessibility, awareness, and attitude are not just problems for the victim. These are also problems for the perpetrator. The rural older adult is more likely to look to the family for help (Krout, 1986) and the more dependent the person the more help is needed. If there is a lack of adequate services such as adult day care or in-home service, then there may be a greater burden on the caregiver. Even if the services are available, the distance to the service may be too great to make its use practical. Though a caregiver may benefit from a support group or respite care, the underlying distrust of formal services or the attitude of independence may make the service undesirable.

Conclusion

Today in rural America there is an older woman who is living with her abusive alcoholic son. He beats her every day and steals her meager monthly Social Security check. She is unaware that help is only a phone call away but it makes no difference, for she has no phone and no close neighbor to hear her screams. The closest hospital, abuse shelter, and nursing home are all 150 miles away, and even if she could get to one her pride makes her reluctant to go. After all, he is her son and she loves him.

The rural perspective on elder abuse is not necessarily quantitatively different than that of urban counterparts, but as the data above suggest, rural elder abuse may well be qualitatively more severe and hopeless. Wherever it occurs, elder abuse is a national tragedy.

PART IV

Social Supports

13

Formal Long-Term Care

Case Examples

BETTY HAVENS
BEVERLY KYLE

A rationally organized long-term care continuum for seniors starts with health promotion for the well elderly and moves through to institutional care for the acutely ill. The full continuum of health and social services includes not only informal care, support services, home care (including adult day care and respite care), nursing home care, extended and rehabilitative institutional care, day hospitals, acute care, and care from physicians and other health professionals but also the broad spectrum of social services including pensions, affordable housing, senior centers, senior educational programs, and all the age-integrated social programs (Havens, 1987).

Within this context, seniors move back and forth on the continuum of services from programs for the well to those for the ill and require the flexibility to take advantage of services as their individual needs require and change. The challenge to the long-term care system, and society in general, is to provide services that will allow seniors to "age in place," with place being anywhere from a single-family dwelling to a tertiary care hospital. Oregon has developed a comprehensive definition of aging in place:

"Aging in Place" means the process by which a person chooses to remain in his/her living environment ("home") despite the physical and/or mental decline that may occur with the aging process. For aging in place to occur, needed services are added, increased or adjusted to compensate for the physical and/or mental decline of the individual. (Oregon, in press)

It is important to note that this definition acknowledges that deficits *may* occur but that they are not automatic and also that service levels should not be assumed to remain static.

Linking the Components of the Service Continuum

The most essential element in long-term care is assessing the individual's type and level of care. Only then, as a last step in the assessment process, should the most appropriate location for that care be considered. The assessed need and level of care decision is totally different from the location or site of care decision. If the location decision, that is, whether or not the individual is eligible for nursing home care, is made first, then that decision will come to drive the whole system. When this type of decision occurs, long-term health care costs will necessarily escalate as it becomes necessary to build, staff, and operate additional nursing homes in lieu of using the more cost-effective solution of providing care in the elderly person's home (Havens, 1990a). Even more cost-effective solutions may be provided collectively to elderly persons by the community-at-large, in the community.

It is essential to have a continuum of services available to ensure that a range of required services is provided in the most appropriate location. Table 13.1 illustrates the range of services available to seniors in Manitoba. Manitoba has developed a broad array of services for the well elderly. These services typically provide the initial entry point(s) into the continuum. Information and referral services play a critical role in the appropriate access to and use of other services.

The programs that address the area falling between the well elderly and the frail elderly, who are living in the community and using the formal system, were the last to be developed in the Manitoba system. In the last 6 years, with the development of meals programs and community and tenant resource programs through the Support Services to Seniors initiative, communities have become able to develop their

Table 13.1 Continuum of Services

Well Elderly	Frail/Functionally Disabled Elderly		Ill Elderly
	Living in Community	*Living in Institution*	Acute Care
Information Referral	Continuing Care/Home Care	Personal Care Home	Hospital
Manitoba Senior Citizens' Handbook	Home Support	Levels 2, 3, & 4	
A&O, MSOS, Seniors Directorate	Aides/Orderlies	Extended Care/	
All Senior Centers	Nurses: LPN & VON	Chronic Care	
Medication Info Line	Community Therapy Services		
Education	Day Care		
Creative Retirement	Respite Care		
U. of W. Senior Programs	Medical Equipment & Supplies		
All Senior Centers	Personal Care Home Paneling/		
Counseling: Age & Opportunity	Waiting List		
Senior Centers: 13 Centers in Manitoba	Day Hospital		
Advocacy:	Geriatric Assessment Units		
Manitoba Society of Seniors	Public Trustee		
Travel: A&O, MSOS, Lions Place	Office of Residential Care		
Seniors Job Bureau	Meals on Wheels		
Fitness Programs	Homebound Learning		
YM/YWCA	Alzheimer Resource Center		
Mall Walking			
Victim Services: A&O			
Senior Clubs			
Legal Services			
Meals Programs			
Transportation Services			
Handi Transit—Urban			
Program for Mobility			
Disadvantaged—Rural			
Home Maintenance Services			
Community Home Services			
S.S.C.O.P.E.			
Community Resource Programs			
Seniors Home Maintenance			
Community Resource Programs			
Tenant Resource Programs			
Community Health Facilities			
Mount Carmel Clinic			
Nor'West Co-Op			
Klinic			
Personal Emergency Response Systems			
Elder Abuse Resource Center			

Basic Entitlements

Financial
  Old Age Security
  Guaranteed Income Supplement
  Spouse's Allowance
  Canada Pension Plan
  55+ Manitoba Supplement
  Manitoba Property Tax Credit
  Pensioners School Tax Assistance

Housing
  Elderly Persons Housing
  Shelter Allowance for Elderly Renters
  Critical Home Repair

Health
  Ambulatory Care:
  Physicians
  Pharmacare
  Eyeglass Program

own unique, local responses to the needs of seniors in this borderline area (Kyle, 1991).

Case Example 1—Community Supports

Simple, collective solutions are often overlooked or ignored by "the system". For example, Mrs. Jones may not be able to do her own shopping, and her neighbor, Mr. Smith, may not be able or wish to do any cooking; but if Mr. Smith does the shopping, and Mrs. Jones does the cooking, they *both* avoid malnutrition. Expanding this dual solution to a larger number may lead to a congregate meals program in a local community.

As another example, what happens when Mrs. Blanchard cannot take care of her garbage? If she does not have garbage pick-up, can no longer walk to the dump, and does not have *frequent* visits from younger family members, or teenage neighbors, garbage begins to accumulate. First, in the shed, then in the garage, then in the porch, then in the back hall, and finally in the house proper, usually starting in the kitchen. If the rats did not arouse complaints from the neighbors during outside "storage", the public health inspector or nurse will be called when it is inside because even an infrequent visitor will complain about the smell. The "official" systems will usually say, "Mrs. Blanchard, you cannot live here anymore, you will have to sell your home or farm and move into a nursing home".

It is more effective to find all the Mrs. Blanchards in the community and set up a volunteer community solution to garbage pickup. Virtually any community has someone with a pickup truck and an older teenager who loves to drive, who will take the garbage of several frail neighbors to the dump just to drive that truck (Havens, 1992a). This is also one productive contribution to the community that can be performed by the "town drunk" with his run-down truck.

Likely the most familiar and generic example of programs appropriate to the well elderly are those available through senior centers, whether in urban settings or smaller rural communities. Some senior centers include a noon meal program and various community outreach services; but they are essentially focused on the well elderly and on maintaining their wellness. Home care and the various institutional options are focused on the frail and ill elderly as components within the formal care system.

The informal networks of the at-risk older population have been expected to fill the gaps along the continuum. The first example, above, is essentially that informal network in action, namely, a pair of neighbors helping each other (Rosow, 1967). Experience indicates that such "person to person" examples are far more prevalent in rural communities or local urban neighborhoods.

Derived from these simple idiosyncratic solutions and based on usual community development principles (Marris & Rein, 1973), collective solutions to inhibit inappropriate use of the formal system have evolved in response to collective needs. The plight of Mrs. Blanchard highlights the way in which many small rural communities have addressed and solved a typical collective need. Congregate meals programs represent another popular collective solution. Again, these examples are more prevalent in rural communities, senior citizens housing units, and localized urban neighborhoods (Regnier, 1976). A multisectoral response establishes viability and use of minimal staffing ensures continuity to preclude volunteer "burnout" and enhance volunteer satisfaction (Payne & Bull, 1977).

Support Services to Seniors Program

The Support Services to Seniors Program is an example of all sectors cooperating to ensure a senior's ability to remain independent. The community owns and operates the project through the managing body. It provides the operating capital, very often through donations-in-kind such as rent-free office space and through fund-raising.

Individuals in the community may be involved as service providers either on a volunteer basis or a modest fee-for-service basis. Municipal governments very often contribute expertise through membership on the community board and many municipalities assist in the operating costs. The provincial government provides assistance through a grant that ensures continuity of the project by providing the salary and benefit costs of a resource coordinator, usually the sole staff person and that, often, on a part-time basis. The federal government, through the New Horizons Program, assists with equipment costs. It is still the community that identifies the services to be provided, but all of the other players accept their responsibility to ensure the delivery of those services (Interagency Committee, 1985). Table 13.2 provides examples of the kinds of services communities have developed in their Support Services to Seniors projects.

A Community Resource Council (CRC) provides an overview of needs in the community and the identification of resources, both those available and those that may be missing. A council is developed to have a broad-based membership that includes existing community groups,

Table 13.2 Support Services

Transportation
Escort
General housecleaning
Heavy cleaning
Yardwork
Handiperson chores
Shopping
Friendly visiting/Phone a friend
Translation
Information
Referral
Foot clinic
Personal emergency response system
Garbage pickup
Income tax
Filling out forms
Errands
Meals
Companion
Wheelchairs
Vacation home check
Congregate meals

SOURCE: Adapted from Kyle, 1987a.

consumers, local business, and service providers. The council assesses local community needs; plans on a communitywide basis; ensures coordination and effective use of existing local resources; assists in the development of additional resources; facilitates proposals for new services; and reviews the effectiveness of existing services (Interagency Committee, 1985).

Although the services may be similar, the way in which each community has designed its service delivery reflects the uniqueness of the community and the flexibility of the support services program in responding to that uniqueness. The following examples demonstrate how differently four communities chose to meet the need for home maintenance services.

Case Example 2—Four Community Resource Councils

CRC 1 applied for a summer jobs grant from the provincial government to hire four students. Fliers advertising the availability of yard services and heavy cleaning help were distributed. Referrals were solicited from agencies dealing with the elderly. One central dispatch location (the CRC) took calls and deployed workers. No fees were charged to seniors but donations were solicited. Workers were paid through the job grant and supervision was supplied by the CRC. To maintain a service beyond the summer, students interested in part-time work were placed on an availability list and dispatched as before. Donations banked through the summer were used to supplement current donations in order to pay students beyond the summer jobs program grant.

CRC 2 interviewed students interested in yard work. A list of dependable workers was developed. The CRC provides names of several students to the senior who selects one for the job. A modest per-hour fee is paid by the senior directly to the student. The CRC also identified people in community willing to do housecleaning and painting. Names are provided to the senior who hires the worker and pays the fee directly to that worker.

A local service club provides labor as a fund-raising mechanism. The members will do carpentry, painting, odd jobs, and the like for a modest fee. The CRC 3 acts as a broker in linking the senior with the service group. A contract is arranged, directly between the senior and the service club, determining the work to be done, the payment mechanism, the purchase of supplies, and the duration of the project.

An arrangement has been made through CRC 4 that links a community facility for mentally handicapped young adults with seniors requiring assistance. The facility residents provide the home maintenance service under supervision as part of a job-training program. An interesting reciprocal benefit has evolved with the seniors providing the experience and the mentally handicapped providing the labor (Kyle, 1987b).

Home Care Program

Having developed community resources to meet the independence needs of seniors, higher levels of disability have become those that require a more traditional formal system response to ensure that the health and safety needs of the resultant frailer seniors can be met in the community. These more frail individuals are addressed by the Continuing Care Program.

Unlike Medicare and Medicaid, the Manitoba Continuing Care Program is a provincewide, *universal,* no-cost-to-consumer program that was initiated by the provincial government in 1974 and gradually expanded throughout the province by 1975. The program staff in Manitoba are known as case coordinators rather than casemanagers (Havens 1985). This distinction is important, because the Manitoba approach is that one coordinates services not manages clients. In general, clients can manage themselves or with the assistance of their informal caregivers, if given support through coordinated services. The program staff assess persons requiring care, whether for placement in nursing homes or for home care. The program delivers home care services to those who remain at home. It should be noted that home care is available to persons of all ages, although seniors constitute over three quarters of the clients.

Program guidelines call for each person to be fully assessed using a comprehensive multidimensional assessment instrument including the identification of those activities that the person can perform himself or herself; those that family members, friends, or neighbors can realistically perform; and those that require placement of services (Shapiro, 1987). A care plan is developed to provide needed services that exist within the program. When needed services are not available within the program, every effort is made to secure services from other community sources such as meals programs and CRCs as part of the care plan. Services provided by the program are to be the minimum required to meet need and to foster independence. Delivery is to be organized so that services are provided by the person with the minimum skill required to perform the task. That is, a nurse will not be used to provide a service that can be performed by a home support worker (Chappell, 1988).

The following two examples highlight the strengths of clients and their informal support networks. They also portray the enabling role of the formal system. The ability of an assessment to identify the strengths, initially, and then to proceed to identifying weaknesses that inhibit independence, allows the assessment team to develop a care plan and assign a case coordinator who will provide only those services that fill gaps in supporting a client's independence and in maintaining his or her informal support network.

Case Example 3—Mr. Sawchuk

Mr. Sawchuk is 88 years old and lives alone on a small farm at the edge of a small village. He has lived on this farm all of his life, he never married, and his siblings have predeceased him. His only relatives, nieces and nephews, live many miles away and seldom visit. Mr. Sawchuk had been coping relatively well on his farm until he suffered pneumonia 8 months ago. Since that time, he has been unable to haul water from the well and chop the necessary firewood for cooking. He also had not built up his stock of wood that he uses for heating in the winter.

A niece referred him for placement in a nursing home. The assessment for care indicated that he did need care but none of the staff in the neighboring nursing home spoke Ukrainian and Mr. Sawchuk spoke very little English. In any case, he did not want to leave his farm. The assessment team had grave concerns about providing home care to him without water or reliable heat in the house. Mr. Sawchuk was not opposed to having water and plumbing in the house, he just had not needed them.

The case coordinator, a Ukrainian-speaking social worker, began to negotiate with the local municipality for assistance with bringing water into the house under a special senior citizen's assistance program. In the meantime, the case coordinator found a neighboring teenager who agreed to haul water from the well on a daily basis. The case coordinator also helped Mr. Sawchuk arrange with the electrical utility company to install electric heating and a hot water tank in the house. The public health nurse added him to her caseload to monitor his continued recovery and general health status.

Finally, late in the fall, water was brought into the house and Mr. Sawchuk contracted with a local plumber to install a kitchen sink ordered from the Sears catalogue and to attach the hot water tank. A toilet with an external septic holding tank was installed.

His neighbor continues to visit Mr. Sawchuk a couple of times a week, helping a bit around the place even though the water no longer needs to be hauled. After all this work was completed, the case coordinator closed the case as Mr. Sawchuk is able to continue living at home on his own without any home care services and is no longer a candidate for an unwanted placement in a nursing home. (Havens, 1990a)

Maintaining the balance between supporting independence without incurring dependence is critical and seldom easy to accomplish. If the case coordinator had not been committed to maintaining and supporting independence, Mr. Sawchuk would likely have been placed in a nursing home at the request of his niece. The creativeness of the case coordinator in assisting Mr. Sawchuk to modernize his house not only allowed him to remain at home but in fact even made it unnecessary for home care services to be provided in his home. This solution enabled him to maintain his home, his health, and his independence (Havens, 1986).

In another community, a solution was more difficult because fewer resources existed. Also, although the family is larger in this second case, none of the family members, except the spouse, live in the same community, let alone in the same household.

Case Example 4—Mr. and Mrs. White

Mr. and Mrs. White live in a small town and Mrs. White has been a home care client for several years because of her emphysema. More recently, she has been experiencing periods of disorientation. The nurse assigned to Mrs. White monitors her emphysema, assists with her bathing, and does her foot care. A homemaker assists with household maintenance 3 days a week. The Whites' grandson and wife, who live on a farm in the area, pick them up for Sunday dinner.

Mrs. White's disorientation has caused Mr. White to stay at home, because he is fearful that Mrs. White will wander off and get lost. A neighbor contacted Mrs. White's nurse because he had not seen Mr. White in town for several weeks and his phone calls had been unanswered. On her next visit the nurse asked Mr. White if he had been in town recently. He replied, "I've been afraid to leave Sara alone since she wandered off 2 months ago while I was raking leaves at the back of the house." The nurse reported this to the case coordinator who visited the Whites to reassess the situation.

It became obvious that Mr. White was not sleeping or eating well and was very anxious about his wife. Mr. White complained that no one had called and, other than an old friend who often stopped on his way to town, he had not talked to anyone in about 6 weeks. The case coordinator checked the telephone and discovered that the bell had been turned down accidentally.

The case coordinator, in discussion with Mr. White, decided that an adult day care program for Mrs. White would make it possible for Mr. White to continue caring for his wife. The problem was that the nearest adult day care program was in a neighboring town 15 miles away.

The case coordinator began negotiating with a nursing home in the Whites' home town to provide an adult day care program for Mrs. White and three other home care clients in or near the town. This negotiation took many months because the nursing home had virtually no activity programming for the residents and was very insecure about starting any new programs.

In the meantime, a temporary solution was initiated by increasing the homemaking time assigned to Mrs. White. Over a year later, the local nursing home finally started an adult day care program and Mrs. White began attending regularly 3 days a week and the homemaker's time was decreased. Mr. White began to take a renewed interest in the community and became a volunteer driver for the local adult day care program. He drives two other participants to the nursing home along with his wife. (Havens, 1986)

The Strengths of Community Care in Rural Areas

These two case examples highlight the ingenuity of staff and the responsive resourcefulness of rural communities in the face of geographic isolation and distances that complicate transportation to secure services. They also provide some sense of the social isolation in rural communities, in large part occasioned by the "demographic thinning" of the adult population (Havens, 1992b) and the migration of the labor force cohort to secure employment in urban areas. Although the range of service options is often larger in urban centers, the human resourcefulness in rural communities often enables more flexible solutions to be tried and to succeed. Community development principles, which are the backbone of the Support Services to Seniors Program, are also used by home care staff in developing resources to address individual client needs in a locally appropriate manner. The case coordinators in rural areas are able to facilitate idiosyncratic solutions based on the strengths of local social networks, traditional neighboring, and informal interpersonal service provision.

These examples and those described earlier place home care and support services as conceptual extensions to the informal care provided to the elderly historically and in the present. Women have been and are still the primary providers as well as consumers of this care (Maclean, 1985). The care provided by the formal system augments and supports the informal care, thus enabling the informal network to carry on even in extremely difficult situations.

The most effective home care programs will have evolved from social, as opposed to medical, models of care (Chappell, 1985, 1988; Estes, 1986; Shapiro, 1986) and will have developed strong linkages across all the components of the continuum, as shown in Table 13.1, enabling solutions, such as those described in the case examples, to be created *with* the client and his or her informal support network and to be changed or modified as and when required. The maintenance of these linkages creates a type of functional reciprocity throughout the system. This process is more successful and easier when a common multidimensional assessment for service or care is used by all the components (Shapiro, 1987). The maintenance of service and care solutions is more effective when all services are coordinated on behalf of the client and his or her informal support system by one person in the formal system— that is, the case coordinator. Further, this role is equally important whether home care is viewed as care in its own right or as an alternative to other care components (Havens, 1990a).

The Bridges Between Community and Institutional Long-Term Care

Seldom does a long-term care client need a single service to remain in his or her own home in the community. Day-care programs are just one of the essential elements in the long-term care continuum.

The range of programs that may be classified as day care is very broad and varies considerably from one jurisdiction to another. As a general rule, day-care programs can be distinguished from home care in that they are congregate programs that occur in various community facilities outside the individual's homes. Adult day-care programs are usually located in nursing homes but are also found in senior citizens' housing units, health centers, senior centers, and local churches. In these programs, the participants have the opportunity to socialize, share a nutritious meal, and have their health care monitored and their medication supervised.

Respite care programs are usually located in a nursing home but may occur in a local hospital, in the home of a volunteer, or in the client's own home and provide complete care for the client for a few days, as scheduled within the care plan, or up to a few weeks to provide often much-needed holiday relief. Finally, day hospital programs provide multidisciplinary clinical assessments, medical supervision, and therapeutic treatments (occupational therapy, physiotherapy, speech therapy, and psychotherapy) in addition to the elements of adult day care. Any of these programs may be used alone or in combination depending on the assessed need and based on the care plan that incorporates the care required to maintain the informal support system, typically family caregivers, as well as providing direct care to the client.

The universality of home care and insured nursing home care is a further guarantee of support by families, not a deterrent. In Manitoba, 80% of the care provided to people over age 65 is still maintained by the family or by other members of the informal support system. This rate was 80% before Manitoba had a long-term care system and it is still 80% (Shapiro, 1986). Virtually all of the literature in the United States and Europe also indicates that approximately 80% of elder care is provided informally, as is shown in Table 13.3 (Havens, 1990b).

This is an issue that is constantly raised as something that it is feared will change when alterations are made to insure nursing homes or other forms of long-term care. This fear is particularly common if one proposes to create insured community-based programs to provide home care. It is feared that families will just desert their elders, by "dumping" them in a home care program or in a nursing home. This has not been Manitoba's experience at all. As a matter of fact, there are many clients whom one would not think could be maintained in the community. At such time as care needs can no longer be met safely or economically in the community, personal care home (nursing home) placement becomes the next step in the continuum.

Table 13.3 Research on Informal Care

Author(s)	Percentage of Care Received from Informal Support Networks
Liu et al. (1985)	
Liu et al. (1986)	75% solely informal
Bressler et al. (1984)	80%
Shanas (1979)	80%
Community Council of Greater NY (1978)	77%
Rubin (1986)	75%
Comptroller General of the United States (1977)	70%-80%
Stone et al. (n. d.)	Nearly 75%
Brody (1985)	80%-90%
Wilson & Battino (1987)	80%
Soldo (1983)	75%
Senate Special Committee on Aging (1987-1988)	84%
Gurland et al. (1978)	80%
National Center for Health Statistics (1979)	80%
Morris et al. (1984)	Nearly 90%
Tobin & Kulys (1980)	Nearly 90%
Doty et al. (1985)	60%-85%
Morginstin (1987)	86%
Chappell (1985)	
Chappell & Havens (1985)	94%
Chappell (1988)	
Chappell (1991)	78%
Chappell & Horne (1988)	66% of hours of care
Executive Directors Report (1987)	Nearly 75%
Kelman (1987)	Nearly 75%
Doty (1987)	Nearly 75%

SOURCE: This table was prepared by Betty Havens, Manitoba Provincial Gerontologist, and colleagues (Neena Chappell and Audrey A. Blandford from the Center on Aging, University of Manitoba, and Analee E. Beisecker, National Center of Extension Gerontology, University of Missouri-Kansas City) (Kane, 1990).

Institutional Long-Term Care

The Personal Care Program, managed by Manitoba Health provides *insured* benefits to residents of nursing homes. The program was implemented in July 1973. The benefits under the program, unlike Medicare and Medicaid, are those provided for the care and well-being of all persons who meet care requirements, specific residency requirements, and are approved for placement by an assessment panel of the Continuing Care Program. The average age of entry is 84.3 years of age. The residents pay a daily residential charge, which represents approximately 25% of the facility budget, government funds making up the remaining 75%.

The program provides for care of individuals assessed at one of four levels; the level of care refers to a person's degree of dependency on nursing staff time for activities of daily living and basic nursing care. The multidimensional assessment that determines the level of care of a nursing home resident uses the same instrument as is used for determining the level of care for home care. When these levels are applied to the institutional setting, they become defined by the amount of time required to meet the applicant's needs.

In this context, a Level 1 resident requires 30 minutes of care per day. The care at this level is primarily of a supervisory nature, unlike Levels 2 through 4 wherein care is primarily a combination of personal care and skilled nursing. A Level 2 resident is deemed to require 2 hours of care per day, and the care required by Levels 3 and 4 residents is averaged to 3.5 hours of care per day. By relating the levels of care to time units, comparisons are possible across jurisdictions and facility types. It is worth noting that all of these levels of care are also able to be delivered in the community through home care, providing there is an available primary caregiver or other backup system in the community, usually in the client's household. The majority of facilities provide all levels of care, thus eliminating the need to transfer a resident to another facility should their care level change. The facilities provide 24 hours a day of professional nursing care; however, the majority of the personal care is provided by nonprofessional staff, that is, nursing assistants.

Some personal care homes in rural areas are juxtaposed to small rural hospitals or health centers; other personal care homes are juxtaposed to seniors' housing units. However, the majority of these homes are freestanding and are either proprietary (including a few that are owned by multinational health care chains) or nonproprietary (i.e., religious, ethnic, or service or fraternal ownership). Personal care homes also vary in size from 14 residents in the smallest facilities to 320 in the largest home. Regardless of these variations, they all operate under the same provincially administered standards and within the same insured-funding guidelines based on the assessed levels of care of the residents.

There are two large urban facilities that provide chronic hospital care in conjunction with nursing home care. Further, most urban and several of the larger rural hospitals have a unit designated for chronic care.

These patients pay the same daily residential charge as do residents of personal care homes; however, in the case of chronic care the residential charge represents less than 10% of the budgeted cost. The residential charge is equivalent to approximately 80% of the minimum public pension.

Housing to Support Long-Term Care

Although there is a broad range of options in Manitoba, there are still many barriers to aging in place. In the last 5 years there has been a "boom" in housing and services for seniors, but there is still a long way to go (Manitoba Health, 1992). The ability to age in place requires better planning of future elements of the housing and formal care systems.

The vacancies now being experienced in the older seniors' housing units provide an incentive to plan with flexibility. Those units reflected the needs of the senior population in the 1950s and 1960s when affordability was identified as the major concern (Manitoba Housing, 1991).

The vast majority of seniors' housing units available today were built to the Canada Mortgage and Housing design specifications of the late 1950s. The standard design was a 400-square-foot suite that included a bed-sitting room, a small kitchen with space for a table, and a bathroom with some safety features. Typically, there was a common laundry facility and a storage area in the basement. Some of these complexes also included a small lobby area and in more recent buildings (i.e., those built in the 1970s or later) a lounge with a small kitchen has been included.

The typical occupants of these units in the 1950s and 1960s were largely never-married or long-time widowed individuals who relied almost exclusively on public (i.e., not employment derived) pensions. More recent applicants for seniors' housing still have limited incomes but are more accustomed to privacy and space and have found the bachelor suite unacceptable.

In the urban centers, more options for commercial age-segregated as well as age-integrated apartments have been built since the mid-1970s. These broader options have led to a higher vacancy rate in the larger urban areas (9%) as compared to the more rural centers (5%) where the traditional seniors' housing unit is still likely to be "the only act in town" (Manitoba Housing, 1991).

Seniors' housing units were built traditionally for the poor but well elderly and do not lend themselves to aging in place. If those units had been able to take advantage of today's technology, they could be adapted to meet the individual's changing needs (Kane & Kane, 1986). Therefore, current planning is beginning to consider modifying seniors' units. Height-adjustable kitchen cabinets and appliances can now provide adaptation at the press of a button. The same kitchen can be made easily accessible to an individual in a wheelchair, an individual who requires a stool for support, and an individual with no disability. Add the new emergency response devices that, at the push of a button, ensure that help is on its way, and suddenly a currently unmodified vacant apartment can accommodate a frailer senior. By combining the currently available technology with the services already existing in the system, aging in place becomes a reality wherever that "place" may be.

Conclusion

Maintaining seniors in the local community supports the tax base, creates jobs for those providing goods and services, and provides care or services in the appropriate setting. It is not possible or desirable to have a nursing home in every community, but it is possible and desirable to encourage "aging in place" by assisting communities to develop an array of long-term care and service options.

Coordination of those options is the key to making the continuum responsive to individual need. With the "system" providing the coordinating role, there is one locus of responsibility for examining all available options to develop the right mix of services to keep each individual functioning at the most independent level possible. Even with the support of the formal long-term care system and all of the new technologies available, it will still be the strength of the informal, interpersonal networks in rural communities that will provide a long-term care continuum uniquely adapted to meeting the needs of individuals, albeit differently in each community (Chappell, 1985; Chappell & Havens, 1985).

14

The Rural Factor in Developing State and Local Systems of Home and Community Care

GARY M. NELSON
MARY ANNE P. SALMON

Developing comprehensive state and local systems of home and community care services for older adults in general presents a challenge. Developing such systems in rural communities presents a unique challenge, at the heart of which is isolating a rural factor or factors that can be calculated into their design and development. The job of isolating these factors is made difficult owing to the variability in both the objective and self-perceived circumstances of rural older adults and the communities in which they live. The task of this chapter is to address issues associated with developing a continuum of services in rural communities.

To provide a context for this discussion, the chapter begins by defining the concept of a rural continuum of long-term care. It then reviews research on the availability of various rural elements of this continuum and explores the influence of community capacity factors on their availability. It is against this backdrop of findings that the chapter concludes, presenting a series of recommended strategies for developing comprehensive home and community care systems for older adults in rural communities.

A Rural Continuum of Home and Community Care

The concept of a *continuum of care* generally recognizes that older adults need different social and health services at different ages and different stages of the chronic health and social conditions for which they are at risk (Huttman, 1987). The continuum should include diagnostic, preventive, therapeutic, rehabilitative, supportive, and maintenance services (U.S. Health Care Resources Administration, 1977) and allow for a choice of service preferences in a variety of living arrangements (Byerts, 1982). These preferences range from services at home (e.g., in-home aide services, home health or home-delivered meals), to community-based services (e.g., adult day care, senior centers, assisted independent living), to congregate housing, and institutional care.

An examination of in-home, community-based, and institutional long-term care options for older adults in rural settings shows no clear linear relationship between a community's level of rurality and the presence or absence of a comprehensive continuum of long-term care. The breadth and depth of the continuum in rural counties is highly variable. Central, however, to this finding is the observation that the variability among communities is only partially explained by rurality and other ecological need variables. It is necessary to look to other county characteristics to understand this variance.

Variability of Community Care Services in Rural Communities

The research of the 1980s suggested that older adults in rural communities had less access to services than their urban counterparts (Coward & Cutler, 1989; Coward & Rathbone-McCuan, 1985; Cutler & Coward, 1988; Nelson, 1980). More recently Gibbons, Camp, and Kaiser (1991) found a larger mean number of services in urban Kansas counties than in rural ones but also that some rural counties in fact had a broader range of long-term care services than could be found in some urban counties. Salmon, Nelson, and Gralen-Rous (1991) found similar variability in long-term care resources in North Carolina's rural counties. These recent findings fit with Taietz and Milton's (1979) decade-old observation that rural-urban differences in service availability were declining in upstate New York.

In-Home Services

Research that specifically examines the provision of in-home services from an urban-rural perspective is limited. Most researchers (Gibbons et al., 1991; Nelson, 1980; Taietz & Milton, 1979) examine the urban-rural factor from the perspective of number of services available to communities rather than from the perspective of specific classes of services such as in-home, community-based, or institutional care. However, Salmon et al. (1991) provide a state-specific comprehensive analysis of various in-home service funding patterns, and Benjamin (1986), Hammond (1985), Swan and Benjamin (1990), and Nyman, Sen, Chan, and Commins (1991) have conducted state and national examinations of home health service provision under Medicare.

In examining total in-home skilled and unskilled services for older adults, funded through such sources as Medicare, Medicaid, the Social Services Block Grant (SSBG), and the Older Americans Act (OAA), Salmon et al. (1991) found that rural counties were receiving more federal and state in-home service dollars than urban counties. The per capita in-home service spending in the most rural counties was $175, compared to $148 for the second most rural counties, followed by $128 and $130 per capita for the more and most urban counties. However, rural-urban differences in spending differ according to funding source. In the same study, the authors found that the 11 most urban counties received the highest Medicare per capita funding but among the lowest from Medicaid, SSBG, or OAA sources. By contrast, the completely rural counties received the second lowest funding from Medicare home health services but received high per capita funding from Medicaid, SSBG, and OAA sources. In addition, the standard deviations indicate much more variation in spending among rural counties than among urban ones.

To get a better idea of the predictive effects of the urban-rural factor, Salmon et al. (1991) estimated linear regression equations for skilled in-home services spending, both Medicare and Medicaid, paraprofessional in-home services, and a composite of both scores. A multivariate analysis of the provision of skilled home health services demonstrates that although rurality is positive in its impact, it was not a statistically significant predictor of higher spending. Only poverty was found to be significant. A multivariate analysis of the provision of paraprofessional in-home services such as chore and homemaker shows that rurality is a significant and positive predictor but not as strong as minority composition of the county. A multivariate analysis of composite per capita spending for both skilled and unskilled in-home services does not show rurality to be a significant predictor, despite higher average spending in rural counties—both poverty and minority status of older adults are the only significant predictors.

In national research on state-level provision of Medicare home health benefits, Benjamin (1986), Hammond (1985), and Swan and Benjamin (1990) found that the distribution patterns are highly variable and complex. Urban and rural status of the state plays only a minor role in explaining these differences. In a national examination of county-level home health benefits, Hammond (1985) developed a multivariate model that accounted for 25% of the variance. Service availability, measured by the number of registered nurses and licensed practical nurses employed by certified home health agencies, was the most powerful predictor in the model. Urbanization accounted for only 0.4% of the variance, compared to 5.8% for region and 3.3% for population need characteristics.

Benjamin (1986) and later Swan and Benjamin (1990) also found that home health expenditures vary significantly from state to state with much of the variance due to provider variables. Factors of home health agency supply, case mix severity, and availability of such service substitutes as nursing home beds emerged as important in understanding variations in number of users and expenditures per user across the states. Particularly noteworthy was the impact of the size and the character of the home health market on service availability and expenditures. In a follow-up study of Medicare home health utilization, Swan and Benjamin (1990) again point to the influence of provider variables, most notably a nursing home substitution variable. The authors assert that demand for home health benefits is, in part, generated by relative scarcity of nursing home beds, a relationship made stronger by the implementation of prospective pay reimbursement to hospitals.

Nyman et al. (1991) examined urban and rural differences in home health patients and services in Wisconsin and found that urban patients received more home health visits and perhaps a greater variety of services than rural patients. Rural residents were more likely to be admitted as skilled nursing care patients, demonstrated by a higher share of the overall visits falling into this category. However, Nyman and colleagues performed regressions using three different definitions of urban and found that variable significant for only one of the definitions.

In that one instance, where 37% of the variance in home health visits was accounted for by the model, the urban variable accounted for 0.8%. Although the study did control for alternate sources of services such as available nursing home beds in the community, it did not control for the relative supply of home health service providers. The significance of more visits by single home health users as opposed to higher numbers of individuals using the services is also difficult to assess. The authors conclude that it is difficult to compare services received in urban and rural areas because differences in received services may stem not only from differences in the types of services needed by clients in the two communities but also from differences in provider service patterns in each place and from differences in consumer service preferences and life-styles.

Community-Based Services

Community-based long-term care services for older adults include supportive social and health services provided in community settings outside the home, such as adult day care, mental health services, congregate meals, and senior center services. They also include congregate housing arrangements such as assisted independent living arrangements and congregate public housing. An additional important community-based services for older adults is transportation. Even more so than for in-home service, there is little comparative research on the availability of specific community-based services across the urban-rural community residence continuum.

Nelson (1980) early identified some of the biggest differences in urban-rural service provision by a national sample of Area Agencies on Aging (AAAs) as falling in the area of community-based services. Rural AAAs were much less likely to be engaged in providing adult day care services, foster care, and protective services and only somewhat less likely to provide housing services, legal services, meals, and recreational services. The frequency with which they provided transportation and employment and education services was very similar among rural and urban AAAs. Similarly, Gibbons et al. (1991) made an interesting finding in examining urban-rural service provision in Kansas. Such community-based services as recreation programs, adult education, escort services, support groups, friendly visitors, and retirement counseling were ranked by local experts as the least difficult to establish, even though they were largely absent in rural communities. More expensive services such as acute hospital care, home health care, skilled and intermediate nursing homes, and transportation were more likely to be uniformly present in urban and rural communities.

In a recent state-level analysis of the comparative urban-rural provision of community-based services to older adults, Salmon et al. (1991) found that the relationships vary depending on the service. Per capita spending on mental health services and meals (both congregate and in-home) increase from the urban to most rural counties, whereas adult day care decreases dramatically as counties become more rural. In North Carolina's 100 counties, all urban counties have adult day care programs, whereas 46% of the semiurban, 22% of the semirural, and only 10% of the totally rural counties have them. Per capita spending on transportation was found to increase from urban to rural counties, although the highest mean spending was found in semirural counties. However, when these community-based services were examined separately using a multivariate model, rurality was found to be a significant predictor only for the provision of meals. When the different community-based services are aggregated into a composite community-based per capita spending figure, rurality is not a significant predictor of higher spending—only poverty is.

Housing is an essential, although generally ignored, component of community-based services and the long-term care continuum (Harrington, Newcomer, & Estes, 1985; Newcomer, Lawton, & Byerts, 1986). Older homeowners, urban or rural, clearly prefer to "age in place." Having affordable, safe, and adaptable housing is a central factor determining whether they can do so. The quality of housing is a risk factor for many rural older adults. Eighty percent of severely inadequate housing is in rural areas, and 65% of all inadequate housing in rural areas occurs in their most remote parts (Redfoot & Gaberlavage, 1991).

Housing resources consist of both rehabilitation measures (e.g., maintenance, repair, and home modification) and alternative noninstitutional housing arrangements outside the older adult's home. Home repairs can be funded through various funding streams, such as the Community Development Block Grant (CDBG), the Social Services Block Grant (SSBG), and Title III of the Older Americans Act. However, CDBG funding has declined significantly, and there is a great deal of competition for SSBG and Older Americans Act funds. Only Section 504 of the Farmers Home Administration has focused specifically on older homeowners. Outside of Gibbons et al. (1991), who found that home repair services were one of the most underrepresented support services in rural communities, there has been little research on rural-urban differences in home rehabilitation services.

A development in federal assistance for alternate non-institutional housing is the Congregate Housing Services Program (U.S. Congress, 1987). This program recognizes the need for housing redesign and the integration of housing and services to serve public housing residents who have aged in place. The Department of Housing and Urban Development (HUD) estimates that roughly 45% of all federally assisted housing units (funded through HUD's Section 202/208 or Section 8, the Farmers Home Administration, or other housing funds) were occupied by older adults in 1986. This amounts to over 1.5 million units. Comparative information about counties' ability to integrate service packages into housing programs for older adults is unavailable.

Institutional Care

Institutional care services for older adults is the third broad classification in the continuum of community care for older adults. Institutional care services include intermediate and skilled nursing home care, rehabilitative and chronic care hospitals, state mental hospitals, and acute care hospitals. Both nursing home care and acute hospital care are institutional service categories that are seen as universally essential components of urban and rural community care continuums for older adults.

Weiner (1987) has noted that although there is a perception of a shortages of nursing home care in rural communities, some of the highest ratios of nursing home beds to population occur in predominantly rural states. Harrington, Swan, and Grant (1988) examined the nursing home bed capacity of states for the period 1978 to 1986 and lend substantial support to the finding that what marks nursing home bed supply across states is its variability and that assigning this variability to one particular cause, rurality included, was difficult. For example, although the national average bed supply ratio in 1986 was 52 per 1,000 adults age 65 and older, Minnesota had a bed supply of 89.6 and North Carolina, 32.2. Both are predominantly rural states. A major factor that accounts for high nursing home bed supply, particularly in Northeastern states, rural or not, is a cold climate (Harrington et al., 1988). Although Minnesota's climate is certainly different from North Carolina's, the reported difference does not take into account a more important structural factor—that in North Carolina there are nearly as many adults and older adults in domiciliary care homes as in nursing homes, primarily owing to the state's ceiling on nursing home bed construction and the consequent substitution of domiciliary care for intermediate level nursing home care. North Carolina's overall supply of nursing home beds in 1989 was 34 per 1,000 people 65 and older and of beds in domiciliary care homes, 27.8, totaling 61.8 institutional beds per 1,000 people. Although this is still less than Minnesota's 89.6 nursing home beds, the difference is much smaller than it might appear to someone unaware of North Carolina's overall bed supply.

Salmon et al. (1991) examined both the nursing home and domiciliary care home bed supply in North Carolina's 100 counties and identified some interesting patterns. The relationship between bed supply and rurality in North Carolina is curvilinear but slightly negative overall. If counties are divided into quartiles according to their per capita bed supply, rural counties are overrepresented in both the top and bottom quartiles, although more heavily in the bottom. The most urban counties, by contrast, are disproportionately found in the middle 50%. Both poverty and proximity to urban areas are significant positive predictors for nursing home and domiciliary home bed supply in a multivariate model for North Carolina.

Hospitals are a major component of the health care infrastructure in rural communities and play a significant role in the local economy. However, rural hospitals, beset with a number of pressures, face an uncertain future. Bernstein, Kolimaga, and Neuschler (1988) observed that in the 15-year period prior to publication of their article, over 700 rural hospitals closed. Between 1983 and 1987, small rural hospitals, those with 25 to 49 beds, were the most likely to close (American Hospital Association, 1989), and more still are projected to close in the next few years. A major factor for rural hospital closures is uncompensated care, which amounts to 5.5% of the total cost of care, compared to 3.5% for nonrural hospitals (Ermann, 1990). Rural hospitals rely more heavily on publicly supported patients—through Medicare and Medicaid among those who do have coverage, but many of the rural poor lack coverage. An estimated 25% of the poor in rural areas receive Medicaid coverage, compared to 43% in urban areas (Rowland & Lyons, 1989). Reimbursement rates for Medicaid and Medicare are lower than private reimbursement rates. In addition, rural hospital occupancy rates have dropped significantly: one third, with fewer than 50 beds, had occupancy rates of only 40% in 1986 (AHA Report, 1987). Beds that are filled are increasingly filled with clients on Medicare: in

1980, 32% of rural hospital patients were Medicare beneficiaries, but by 1985, this figure had climbed to 37% (Ermann, 1990).

In an effort to stay viable, rural hospitals have pursued a number of different strategies. One is to diversify, and the movement in this direction has been dramatic. Areas of diversification include outpatient care, home care, and nursing home care. Two of these areas of particular significance to the rural continuum of care are home health and nursing homes. Home health agencies are more likely to be located in rural than in urban hospitals. Hospital-based home health agencies accounted for 32% of those in rural communities, compared to 20% in urban communities. Medicare home health costs are higher in rural communities than in urban communities, owing to increased travel and smaller volume of clients (Hoyer, 1988). In the area of institutional long-term care, there has been a marked increase in the location of nursing home beds in rural hospitals. The "swing bed" provision for rural hospitals under Medicare is reimbursed as skilled nursing facility type care. As of 1985, 447 rural hospitals had skilled nursing units (American Hospital Association, 1987). Rural hospitals have also sought to diversify themselves in the areas of hospice care, urgent care, and specialty clinics.

Community Capacity as a Barrier to Care in Rural Communities

An examination of need for services and of availability of services along the continuum of care leads one to believe that there is substantial variation in both. As shown in North Carolina (Salmon et al., 1991) and elsewhere (Ermann, 1990; Gibbons et al., 1991; Hammond, 1985; Kaiser, Camp, & Gibbons, 1987; Meyer, Lusky, & Wright, 1991; Swan & Benjamin, 1990), rural communities evidence not only different needs for services but markedly different organizational and structural capacities to respond to those needs. In general, it would seem relatively safe to conclude that the development of systems of home and community care in rural communities is heavily influenced by community capacity as evidenced by factors of leadership and availability of providers. Additional factors that seem to influence the development of home and community care services in rural and urban communities are the values and attitudes of both local leaders and older consumers, as well as the consciousness and knowledge of older consumers themselves.

Kaiser et al. (1987) considered the variation in long-term care service provision in rural Kansas communities and conclude that urban bias does not account for all of the differences. They found that rural communities that developed high levels of long-term care services were marked by strong leadership, broad horizontal networking among local constituencies and providers, connections with central decision makers in the larger political environment (usually the state), and values and attitudes that supported the development of such services. These points are supported by other researchers as well. Lapping, Daniels, and Keller (1989) underscore the importance of influential leaders and an involved public, and Lohmann (1982) stresses the importance of organizational and community planning. Planning, in turn, involves the expansion of horizontal networks and the inclusion of older consumers (Ackman, 1988; Bryson, 1989; Nelson, McRae, & Baldwin, 1988; Streets & Nelson, 1990).

Service providers of all sorts, agency-based, professional, and paraprofessional, face real challenges in rural communities. Many home health agencies, hospitals, and nursing homes struggle to attract a sufficient client census to achieve and maintain certain economies of scale, to attract and keep qualified professionals and paraprofessionals, and to obtain adequate reimbursement rates for what are often more expensive services. But some rural communities are able to establish viable long-term care agencies and institutions and attract the necessary doctors, nurses, social workers, allied health professionals, and paraprofessionals to offer a viable continuum of care for older adults in rural communities. These matters are complicated, and the solutions accordingly need to be more creative for the different types of rural communities that exist across the country. In practice, community planning and capacity building in long-term care will mean something different in each rural community, whether it is a frontier community with very low population densities, a rural area adjacent to urban neighbors, or an urbanized area with a number of small cities but distant from any large metropolitan area (Patton, 1989).

Additional factors that may influence local capacity to develop comprehensive long-term care programs in rural communities include community attitudes and values regarding programs for older adults in particular and social welfare programs in general. One may add to this the familiarity with services of older consumers themselves. Program participation rates for older adults are generally believed to be lower in rural compared to urban communities. Kaiser et al. in 1987 and Gibbons et al. in 1991 have argued that rural communities that have developed more comprehensive continuums of long-term care have been marked not only by successful leadership but by community values that support additional formal services and further strengthen informal helping networks. Awareness of and knowledge about services affect service development in rural communities. Joseph and Cloutier (1990) argue that the consumption of health services by rural older Canadians is governed by individual perceptions of (1) health and the consequences of not receiving care, (2) the quality of the local service (including friendly providers), and (3) service accessibility. The perception of accessibility is, in turn, influenced by values and attitudes as well as by more concrete issues such as available transportation.

Kushman and Freeman (1986) argue further that use of services by older adults depends on a general consciousness that particular sorts of services exist as well as more specific knowledge about their availability in the community. Rural residence and educational background were significant negative predictors of both consciousness of and knowledge about a wide range of home and community care services.

Rural Development Strategies for Home and Community Care

Research on home and community care services for older adults in rural communities suggests a number of conclusions. Chief among these is the notion that the development of home and community care systems for older adults is driven as much by the availability of local providers and system capacity as by service needs or the rural nature of the community.

There is an overlap, to be sure, among these three factors. Rurality itself does not unequivocally imply the presence of an underdeveloped system of home and community care. However, the research seems to support the broad assertion that rural communities are marked by a less even development of comprehensive systems of home and community care than are urban ones.

Need for Public Relations and Outreach

Policymakers need to address knowledge and attitudes. The findings on consumer knowledge (Joseph & Cloutier, 1990; Kushman & Freeman, 1986) suggest that outreach and public information may improve participation in existing programs and/or stimulate demand for additional services. However, the findings on rural attitudes (Kaiser et al.,

1987; Osgood, 1977) suggest that special care must be taken in those communities to destigmatize services in the eyes of consumer and polity alike. This may include sensitivity in choosing what to name programs and services, which agencies provide them, and where they are housed.

Need for Collaboration Among Providers

The findings from two decades of research on case-managed home and community care and more recent state efforts to reform long-term care hold a number of implications for rural communities. The first is that many home and community care demonstrations have been marked by an almost confrontational positioning of case-managed programs of care against nursing home or hospital care, a competitive model that may or may not be more suitable to more specialized urban environments. Rural communities, which are often marked by more limited numbers of institutional and noninstitutional providers, are likely to find collaborative models of service provision the more suitable means of insuring choice among older adults for both noninstitutional and institutional care.

The conclusions of Weissert, Cready, and Pawelak (1988) regarding issues of excess capacity and utilization control, the need to couple home and community care programs with nursing home admission, and the need to investigate congregate housing as an efficient site for delivering services seem to support the general appropriateness of collaborative planning and service development models of long-term care in rural communities. Such models are most likely to take root in the context of local efforts to develop the capacity, infrastructure, and leadership necessary to support a comprehensive system of home and community care. Findings from state reform efforts in long-term care (National Governors Association, 1988) point to the importance of both state and local leadership and capacity building for successful reform efforts.

Service Targeting Through Capacity Building

Success in extending long-term care choices, both institutional and non-institutional, to all rural older adults depends on the development of local capacity. If state governments want to facilitate such development, they must be able to identify underserved communities, many but not all of which are rural. Having done this, states should assist them in developing the necessary leadership, infrastructure, and provider and work-force capacity to support a comprehensive system of home and community care. For the most part, funding for long-term care, whether public (e.g., Medicaid and Medicare) or private (e.g., third-party payers or clients' out-of-pocket expense), is not targeted through an allocation of funding streams over which states have direct control. Accordingly, Older Americans Act funds, over which states have more control, may be most effectively used in stimulating community development activities that foster local leadership and other resource capacity necessary to the development of a comprehensive system of care.

Core Services for Rural Communities

Much of the attention to rural communities over the years has focused on their range of service choices available to older adults. State and federal and local efforts in underdeveloped communities all might obtain the best results for older adults by focusing on development of a minimum set of core services. Evidence from demonstrations on home and community care and from state efforts to reform long-term care underscore the importance of such a minimum set of services for home-based care (Kemper, Applebaum, & Harrigan, 1987; Weissert et al., 1988). Services would include chore assistance, personal care, case management, and adult day care or some form of respite. Also included are acute and nursing home care, which, in the case of rural hospitals with swing beds, can be offered in the same facility. Rural communities cannot, and in many cases should not, attempt to support more specialized services, given issues of economy of scale and the limited number of providers available to those in need. Service delivery and professional practice in rural communities are more suited to a generalist rather than a specialist model of service and practice.

Flexible Delivery Systems

Capacity building and establishment of core services in underdeveloped rural communities call for flexible delivery systems. Findings from both case management demonstrations and state long-term care reforms also show the importance of program leadership to the success of such efforts. In keeping with the notion of collaborative planning and model building, appropriate local lead agencies for long-term care services will vary from community to community, depending on the leadership, vision, and capacity of various agencies and coalitions to deliver quality, responsive services (National Governors Association, 1988). In some rural communities, Area Agencies on Aging might be the appropriate choice. In other communities, a department of social services or a health department may be the best candidate. In still other communities, a rural hospital may combine the best talents of leadership and capacity to serve the community. Choice in both quality and variety of services for older adults will also require choice at the local level as to who is best qualified to provide leadership in the community.

Flexible service delivery systems in underdeveloped rural communities must also allow for creative service delivery options. Such options may stress the importance of service diversification as some rural hospitals or nursing homes engage in the provision of home, community, and institutional services. Other options may include extending the range of primary care providers deliver with reimbursement for services, including such formal care providers as physician assistants and nurse practitioners or such informal care providers as volunteers and family members.

Creative Financing

Creative financing is often the essential linchpin to fostering targeted capacity building efforts to develop core services and flexible delivery systems. The provider who made the Freudian slip "We are in the business of meeting people's reimbursable needs" was close to the mark in a system where individuals gain access to services only if providers have found a way to make that access profitable. Creative financing such as supporting swing beds in rural hospitals and promoting service packages in relation to congregate housing, including placing services in domiciliary care facilities, opens up access to services for many rural older adults who might otherwise be excluded. Other financing options available to states include targeting underserved rural communities with Older Americans Act resources for community development and integrating funding streams such as the Older Americans Act, Social Services Block Grant, and state-generated home and community care resources into local block grants that allow increased discretion in the design and funding of local services.

Conclusions

Although recent research has cast serious doubt on the perception that rural counties are universally underserved, there is clear evidence of the need for strategies to bring service equity to older adults in rural counties with service deficits. Such strategies should include the following: attention to public relations and outreach; building collaborative relationships among stakeholders in aging services, including rural hospitals and institutional care providers; developing community capacity through strengthening leadership, planning, and attracting or developing service providers; setting goals that include the provision of a set of core services; allowing delivery systems to be flexible enough to meet the varying capacities of different agencies within any given community; and finding creative funding strategies.

15

Informal Supports Among Older Rural Minorities

VIRA R. KIVETT

Older minorities compose approximately 8% of the population of older rural adults (U.S. Bureau of the Census, 1980) (Table 15.1). Although their proportion is low, their absolute numbers and deprived status make them an important component of the rural population. Little information is available on older minorities living in rural areas. As a result, most information must be extrapolated from the general population of older minorities. Less assimilation of values and traditions might be expected among enclaves or pockets of older minorities located in rural than in urban areas.

Older African Americans

Approximately 1 in 3 Americans 65 years or older in the Unites States is African American (U.S. Bureau of the Census 1980). More material is available on older African Americans than on other ethnic minority groups. African Americans are quite heterogenous as a group, representing Haitian, Jamaican, and Nigerian origins (Wilkinson, 1987). African Americans have settled mainly in the South, with 24% of Southern African Americans residing in rural areas. The National Survey of black Americans, conducted in 1979-1980, has provided a significant body of information on African Americans aged 55 years or older (Inter-University Consortium for Political and Social Research, 1990). Studies using data from this multi-stage probability survey, however, usually have confounded rural and urban differences.

The median income for older African American couples and African American singles is only 60% of that of white couples and 70% of that of white singles (Taylor & Chatters, 1988b). Economic discrepancies continue among older rural adults when education is controlled (Kivett & Scott, 1979). These data confirm the continuity between life-long work opportunities and the resulting economic condition of African Americans in old age.

African Americans, up until the age of approximately 75 years, have a lower life expectancy than corresponding whites (Markides & Mindel, 1987). African American-white morbidity differences (to the disadvantage of African Americans) are found in diseases of the heart, malignant neoplasms, and diabetes (Markides & Mindel, 1987). The higher rates of chronic health problems among older African Americans and older rural adults in general have important implications for support services (Kivett & McCulloch, 1989).

Family Structure, Function, and Support

The majority of African American families have a nuclear family structure but with salient bilateral kin ties (Wilkinson, 1987). However, African American adults of all ages, irrespective of socioeconomic status, are more likely to reside in extended households than corresponding whites (Chatters & Taylor, 1990). African American family structure among lower-class African Americans is dynamic, flexible, and ever-changing, characteristics that meet the needs of its members (Johnson & Barer, 1990; Stack, 1974). Studies show that relatives usually meet emotional needs, but they do not always supply instrumental needs (Johnson & Barer, 1990).

The African-American family is characterized by intimate involvement and a set of unwritten obligations to consanguineal and conjugal relatives regardless of age (Wilkinson, 1987). Important African American family properties include (1) affectional bonds connecting several generations; (2) a central family member who occupies a leadership position, establishes codes of behavior, and participates in the socialization of children; (3) paternal expectations of responsibility in children; (4) an intense communal orientation toward family members;

(5) interdependency of relatives for instrumental and emotional support; (6) an absorption mechanism for taking in those unable to care for themselves; and (7) a mutual aid system (Wilkinson, 1987, p. 194). These qualities are especially pronounced in the southern region (Chatters & Taylor, 1990; Chatters, Taylor, & Jackson, 1985; Taylor, 1985).

Studies on rural and urban African Americans show close family propinquity to immediate family and the receipt of some level of support from extended family members, especially under conditions of low income (Taylor, 1985). Research indicates the importance of proximity to family support. Intergenerational exchanges among rural African Americans have been found to decrease as geographic distance increases (Kivett, 1991). Other findings have shown that older rural African American adults are less likely to have children in close propinquity if the older parents do not own land (Gröger, 1983). That is, children are more likely to remain in the area if parents can share land with them.

Older African Americans (rural and urban) have a larger, more diverse group on whom they can call for support than older whites (Chatters et al., 1985). Older African Americans, however, receive less support from the extended family than younger family members (Chatters & Taylor, 1990). They generally follow a "principle of substitution" in their choices for informal support. The support choices of older African Americans are made with reference to apparent need but within the context of existing interpersonal relationships (Chatters et al., 1985). Daughters are the support of choice among both rural and urban African Americans, followed by sons, and spouses, with choices being closely related to marital status (Chatters, Taylor, & Jackson, 1986). Siblings also figure importantly in the kin support network of older African Americans. Mutual help has been observed to be the most important predictor of sibling associational solidarity for both older rural African American and white adults (Suggs, 1987).

Informal Non-Kin Support

"Para-kin" or "fictive kin" are important components of the African American family and support network (Johnson & Barer, 1990). African American families maintain a practice of fosterage and adoption of children or others who need either permanent or transitional assistance (Martin & Martin, 1978; Stack, 1974). This practice is reflected in the creation of "play" siblings or children. The use of non-kin as support providers is more frequent among older persons who are without spouses and children (Chatters & Taylor, 1990).

Support systems, too, are expanded through involvement in institutions such as the African American church (Taylor & Chatters, 1988a). Church membership and attendance are important in determining the amount of support received. There is some evidence of more nonorganizational religious preoccupation among rural than urban African Americans, for example, religious attitudes, beliefs, private religious activities, and televised religious services (Taylor & Chatters, 1991). High degrees of both organized and nonorganized religious activity have been especially observed among African American women (Chatters & Taylor, 1989). The African American church functions as a "family surrogate" for childless married couples and unmarried persons, filling both social and emotional needs (Taylor & Chatters, 1988a).

The African American church has been likened to the concept of a support convoy (Taylor & Chatters, 1988a). That is, it provides a supportive structure for individuals as they progress through the life cycle. Older rural African Americans, however, are less likely than urban African Americans to rely on the church, family, and friend support networks.

Friends also are important sources of support to older African Americans. Configurations of friends are less well described than family relationships, however (Johnson & Barer, 1990). Older African Americans are viewed as having more interactions with and support from friends, fellow church members, and other associational contacts than older whites.

Older Rural Hispanics

Little information is available on rural Hispanics because of their relatively low number (Table 15.1). The three most common Hispanic groups are Mexican Americans, or Chicanos, located mostly in the Southwest; Puerto Ricans, located mainly in New York; and Cubans, found mostly in Florida, Texas, and New York (Biafora & Longino, 1990). Hispanics vary markedly in their settlement and migration destinations. They also have one of the highest return migration rates of all immigrants. Large numbers of Hispanics are attracted to migrant labor in rural areas (Paz & Applewhite, 1988). Families, including older members, sometimes follow the migrating laborers, traveling in migrant

streams. Standards of living are generally very low, and medical services and social programs are nonexistent. Most Hispanic elders speak
little English, leaning quite heavily on their families for support and as
gatekeepers to additional resources.

Differences have been observed in Mexican Americans according to
urban-rural residence, socioeconomic status, and extent of acculturation
(Mindel, 1983). A strong cultural distinction, however, remains in
Hispanic familism (Becerra, 1983). Incentive to migrate may create
differences in subgroup values and general assimilation into the society. For example, political refugees, such as Cubans, may adapt differently to the new culture than other groups (Biafora & Longino, 1990;
Weinstein-Shr & Henkin, 1991).

Little is known of the health and related problems of older Hispanics
because of difficulties in defining who is Hispanic and in data collection. Information suggests that the life expectancy values of Hispanics
are slightly below those of whites but considerably higher than those of
African Americans (Markides & Mindel, 1987). As with African Americans, the leading cause of death among Hispanics is heart disease
(Markides & Mindel, 1987). Higher death rates are observed from
infective and parasitic diseases and diabetes mellitus than for African
Americans or for whites (Bradshaw & Fonner, 1978).

Data on the mental health status of Hispanics largely center on Mexican Americans. Information shows that Mexican Americans have fewer
mental health disorders than Anglos. This observation has been attributed to the Mexican American kinship structure, which protects and
thus reduces mental disorders among its members (Markides, 1986).
As with other ethnic groups, Mexican American differences on a number of cultural attributes are reduced by socioeconomic controls such as
income and education (Markides, 1986). Older Hispanics are more than
twice as likely to live in poverty as older whites (Layaco, 1984).
Approximately 1 in 3 older Hispanics lives in poverty.

Family Structure, Function, and Support

Hispanics (Latin Americans and Caribbeans, in particular) are more
likely than other groups to express traditional kin values (Litwak, 1985;
Markides, Boldt, & Ray, 1986). Inaccessibility to technological and
other skilled jobs is thought to have encouraged considerable closeness
to and dependency on the family (Litwak & Longino, 1987). Hispanic
families are more distinct in structure and family bonds than other

minorities, however, variation is found within the various subgroups (Wilkinson, 1987). The Hispanic family is seen as a defense mechanism in the adaptation of its members to the mainstream culture.

The Mexican American family operates under the norm of geographical propinquity and strong family bonds. Several characteristics distinguish Mexican American families, including the (1) intergenerational nature of the family in daily living, (2) functional dominance of males, (3) reinforcement of sex-role distinction in childrearing, (4) strong kinship bonds, (5) centrality of children, (6) repression of feminine attributes in males, and (7) precedence for the male as head of household (Wilkinson, 1987, p. 192). The family is usually the primary source of support, with considerable reciprocity among nuclear families (Markides et al., 1986). More frequent interaction has been reported between older Mexican Americans and their families than between whites or African Americans (Becerra, 1983; Dowd & Bengtson, 1978). Furthermore, Mexican Americans have shown more satisfaction with these interactions. Higher developed mutual aid networks also are found among Mexican Americans than among whites and African Americans (Mindel, 1983).

Family participation in Mexican American families is along traditional sex-roles, with greater solidarity among females than other family linkages. Despite sex-role distinctions, males and females provide basic intergenerational links (Wilkinson, 1987). There is some indication that the roles of women grow stronger than those of men with age (Becerra, 1983). Older Hispanics, in general, are thought to continue to play important roles in family decision making, especially among urban families. Maternal aunts also are of particular importance in the linkage and resources of Hispanic families (Wilkinson, 1987).

Other Hispanics also show high family centrality. Older Cuban immigrants tend to live dependently (Biafora & Longino. 1990), a function of marital status and age (Mindel, 1983). Some isolation is observed. The Cuban elderly occupy considerable status in families and the subculture in general through strong roles in ethnic politics and guardianship of group values (Aguirre & Bigelow, 1983). Older Cubans maintain a stronger sense of continuity and outside involvement in their lives than Mexican Americans.

The living arrangements of older Puerto Ricans also suggest some degree of isolation from the general population with many living in "ethnic specific conclaves" (Wilkinson, 1987). Older urban Puerto Ricans have frequent reciprocal exchanges with family and friends and generally perceive their existing support systems as effective (Cruz-Lopez & Pearson, 1985). Although Puerto Ricans are taught respect for older adults from early childhood, negative changes are occurring in Puerto Rican metropolitan areas as a result of acculturation. Some of this change is attributed to frequent social mobility, residential dispersion, and interracial marriage of children (Rogler & Coony, 1991; Wilkinson, 1987).

Informal Non-Kin Support

Information is extremely limited on informal supports for older Hispanics outside of the family. Patterns of family size and interaction suggest little use of outside informal support. Unlike the literature on African Americans, little is written on informal support evolving from older Hispanics' involvement with religious or other groups. In one of the few available studies, Dowd and Bengtson (1978) found lower friend-neighbor contact among older Mexican Americans than among Anglos. It has been suggested that the needs of older Puerto Ricans might be more effectively met if the support of friend networks could be strengthened. Hispanic families have been found to be important links in the service utilization of older members (Biafora & Longino, 1990). There is evidence, however, of considerable under-use of formal supports, especially in the area of mental health (Siddharthan & Sowers-Hoag, 1989; Starrett, Decker, Araujo, & Walters, 1989). Some of this under-use is attributed to cultural attitudes toward illness, roles in the family, and resistance to obtaining help from formal and impersonal Anglo institutions.

Native Americans

Over one-half of American Indians live in rural areas even though they constitute the smallest older rural minority group (Table 15.1). Statistics on Native Americans are scarce and often conflicting (National Indian Council on Aging, 1984; U.S. Bureau of the Census, 1980). American Indians consist of four major groups: reservation Indians, rural Indians, migrant Indians, and urban Indians (Block, 1979). Generalizations from data on Indian and Alaskan Natives, as with other ethnic groups, must be made with caution. For example, there are 206 different Indian tribes, bands, villages, pueblos, and

Table 15.1 Rural Residence According to Total Population of Older Adults, Older Hispanics, Native American, African Americans, and Asian Pacific Islanders

	Total 65+ N	No. Rural Residents 65+ N	Minority Rural 65+ %	Rural Population 65+ %
Hispanic	708,880	79,307	11.1	0.012
Males	305,204	40,103	50.6	
Females	403,676	39,204	49.4	
Native American	74,919	39,989	53.4	0.006
Males	32,977	18,961	47.5	
Females	41,942	21,028	52.5	
African Americans	2,086,858	404,882	19.4	0.062
Males	846,712	180,623	44.6	
Females	1,240,146	224,259	55.4	
Asian Pacific Islanders	211,736	19,430	9.2	0.003
Males	103,924	10,299	53.0	
Females	107,812	9,131	46.9	
Total population 65+ years	25,549,427	6,503,223	8.4	25.453

SOURCE: U.S. Bureau of the Census (1980), *Census of Populations*, Vol. 1, Part 1-B. Washington, DC: U.S. Government Printing Office.

groups spanning 30 states as well as 216 Alaskan communities (Block, 1979).

Native Americans share a history of subordination similar to that of African-heritage Americans (Wilkinson, 1987). They have experienced conquest, dislocation, cultural disintegration, spatial segregation, and, consequently, predictable ethnic identity and family problems (Wilkinson, 1987, p. 191). As with African Americans, the uniqueness of Indian family patterns as well as the composition, life-styles, family interactions, form and type of socialization, and modes of family adaptation have been associated with this subordination. Native Americans are more culturally different from mainstream America than other minority groups, especially in their conceptions of time, world outlook, and cultural values (Markides & Mindel, 1987). In many ways, they are the least assimilated of the ethnic groups.

Native Americans have significant mental and physical problems. About 3 in 4 over the age of 60 are limited in ability to perform activities of daily living (Manson, 1989), especially among reservation Indians (John, 1985). Major health problems that are greater than those of the general American population include tuberculosis, diabetes, liver and kidney disorders, and vision and hearing problems (National Indian Council on Aging, 1984). Most of the information on Native American mental health problems is not empirically based. Conjectures of stress are frequently made as a result of Native Americans' conformation to the pressures of mainstream American values and norms (Markides, 1986). A few available studies have shown alcoholism to be the major mental health problem.

Family Structure, Function, and Support

The family structure of Native Americans, matrilineal in type, is both nuclear and extended (Block, 1979). Although the norm of the extended family is frequently cited, there are few recent data to support this opinion (John, 1985). Tribal distinctions occur in family forms, life course rituals, patterns of linkage, and kin relationships. Differences in family forms and function also are found according to rural or urban residence (Wilkinson, 1987). In addition, there is a movement away from rural areas, with important consequences for families. One such consequence is the decline of family integration that affects the traditional support given to older members (John, 1985). Still, Indian families have shown an under-use of the few services available to them, based largely on a fear and mistrust of the white bureaucratic system (John, 1985).

Informal Non-Kin Support

Data are lacking on the friendship and neighbor supports available to older Native Americans. Limited data show that older rural Indians are more likely than urban Native Americans to call on a friend for support (John, 1985). No information is available on informal supports that emerge as a result of organizational or religious memberships.

The current acute care model of medical facilities does not adequately address the chronic health problems of older Native Americans. As a result, acute care models and a lack of alternatives (skilled and intermediate care facilities) are causing unnecessary dependency on medical systems such as emergency facilities (Manson, 1989). This process, in effect, further reduces the role of the family in the care and support of elders.

Older Asian Americans

Asian Americans, mainly urban dwellers, include Asian and Pacific Islanders and they are the fourth largest group of older rural minorities (Table 15.1). Asian Americans are typically classified into nine groups by the U.S. Census: Asian Indian, Chinese, Filipino, Guamanian, Hawaiian, Japanese, Korean, Vietnamese, and Samoan (Wilkinson, 1987). The young are disproportionately represented. Several major waves of Asian immigration to the United States have occurred since the mid-19th century (Kii, 1984). Each wave has represented different levels of education and skills, resulting in marked distinctions among groups. Most information on Asian Americans has been descriptive rather than analytical.

There has been little systematic documentation of the health of older Asian Americans (Liu, 1986b). Because of the great variability in subgroups, education, and income, it is most likely that health, too, shows considerable variation. There is some evidence that the health profile of Chinese Americans is better than that of white Americans (Liu, 1986b; Yu, 1986). The three leading causes of death for the Chinese are identical to those for the white population: heart disease, cerebrovascular disease, and accidents (Yu, 1986). Within the past few years, however, mortality rates among the Chinese and Japanese have approached those of the general population. Similar to other ethnic groups, the Asian culture plays a significant role in health care (Kii, 1984). Asian Americans, with the exception of Filipinos, use ethnic therapists rather than physicians outside of their ethnic community. This practice suggests the hesitancy of rural Asian Americans to utilize the limited pool of local health practitioners.

Research shows stronger family ties among Koreans than other Asian groups (Kiefer et al., 1985). Traditional Korean values stress the responsibility of sons for parents. Japanese Americans, sometimes referred to as the "model minority," have fared better than other groups economically and, consequently, they have infrequent need for public assistance (Markides & Mindel, 1987). Considerable poverty, however, is found among some Asian groups, such as the Chinese and Filipinos. Two common myths are not supported: (1) Asian families always care for their elderly, and (2) few Asians are poor. The poor sex ratios of some older Asian groups, more men than women as a result of earlier immigration restrictions, also contribute to later life problems (Liu, 1986a).

Family Structure, Function, and Support

Asian Americans place a high value on marriage and the family, displaying strong kin associations (Wilkinson, 1987). Filial piety is a central theme of Confucianism (Osako & Liu, 1986). The socialization of most Asian cultures is contradicted by the American values of independence and emphasis on the "nuclear family" unit. Filial piety in the Chinese family also extends to the parents-in-law of the wife, a sometimes source of intergenerational stress (Kiefer et al., 1985). Although traditional family values are changing as a result of interracial marriage, mobility, and acculturation, most older Asian Americans live with an adult child. Studies show that as many as 75% of older Vietnamese live in this arrangement (Kiefer et al., 1985). It is difficult to determine the intergenerational stress of these arrangements because of traditions that prohibit negative or critical comments about the family (Die & Seelbach, 1988). Disproportional sex ratios (more males than females) are a striking feature of some Asian groups and have important implications for family structure and support (Kii, 1984). The greatest generational differences appear to be among older Japanese Americans (Issei) and their adult children (Nisei) (Markides & Mindel, 1987; Osako & Liu, 1986).

Informal Non-Kin Support

Information is scant on informal supports outside of Asian-American families. Data suggest that among the few Asian Americans located in small towns and cities in the Midwest, friends and neighbors seldom provide emotional or physical support (Liu, 1986a). This is thought to be related to their isolation from other similar ethnic groups to whom they can relate. Japanese and Chinese immigrants frequently form associations on the basis of geographic origins in their native countries as well as kinship affiliations. Little information is available on the social support resulting from these associations.

Information shows that some Asian groups such as the Vietnamese turn to formal supports rather than to informal non-kin supports (Die &

Seelbach, 1988). The church, sometimes serving as sponsors of newly migrated Asians, has been an important component of the informal support network of the Vietnamese in particular (Die & Seelbach, 1988). Older Japanese Americans, especially women, have been found to seldom participate in neighborhood friendships or organizations, including religious services (Montero, 1979). These practices reduce the potential for extending informal networks beyond the family.

Informal Supports of the Ethnic Minority Elderly and the Life Course Perspective

Biological and psychological changes in the later years are universal, irrespective of ethnicity. The family is usually the first line of support in meeting the needs of the aging family member. The family's response, however, is primarily a function of ethnicity, that is, the implicit and explicit expectations of the ethnic group. These norms, in turn, are subject to modification as a result of family members' assimilation into the larger society. Intergenerational discord and stress occur when expectations and actualities of support are discrepant. These observations provide strong support for a life course perspective when examining family relationships and supports within ethnic minority groups.

Rurality has important implications for the informal support system of older ethnic minorities. The lack of critical reference groups in rural areas and services sensitive to ethnic values and needs further impact the quality of lives of older adults. Although small in number, older rural ethnic minorities are a major challenge to those charged with preserving the integrity of the family while providing universal service for all older citizens.

16

The Family Relations of Rural Elders

RAYMOND T. COWARD
GARY R. LEE
JEFFREY W. DWYER

Over the past decade, research in social gerontology has affirmed the critical and far-reaching role of families in determining the quality of life and well-being of elders (Brubaker, 1985, 1990). This research has solidified our understanding and appreciation of several general trends that describe the family relations of older persons. First, American families have not abandoned older family members (Brody, 1985). To the contrary, research has demonstrated repeatedly that most older persons have regular and routine contact and interaction with family members (Lee, 1985; Mancini, 1989). Indeed, despite rising numbers of elders who live alone (U.S. Senate Special Committee on Aging, 1985), the majority of elderly persons in our society continue to live with family members (Coward, Cutler, & Schmidt, 1988). Second, when needed, families are the primary source of aid and assistance for elders. Families often provide help to frail elders who are unable to perform the tasks of daily living by themselves (Stoller & Earl, 1983; Stone, Cafferata, & Sangl, 1987), sometimes make significant financial sacrifices in order to care for dependent older family members (Rimmer, 1983), and are the foundation of the networks of long-term care that

AUTHORS' NOTE: Support for the development of this manuscript was provided under a grant from the National Institute on Aging (No. P20-AG09649).

surround elders with chronic illness (Biegel, Sales, & Schulz, 1991; Litwak, 1985; Soldo & Myllyluoma, 1983).

Yet, despite the widespread applicability and relevance of these generalizations, the family relations of elders do vary among subgroups of the aging population. For example, there is evidence that the family relations of elders who reside in small towns and rural communities are substantively different from their counterparts who live in more urban environments (Coward, 1988; Lee & Cassidy, 1985). In this chapter, we focus on these distinctive features of the family relations of rural elders. First we examine residential differences in the availability of family members among older persons. Then we explore residential variation in several types of interaction between elderly parents and their adult children. Finally, we conclude with a brief review of the research on residential differences in the caregiving patterns of family members.

Residential Differences in the Availability of Family Members

In order for family members to be a positive force in the lives of older persons, they must be available. In this section we examine residential differences in the availability of spouses and adult children, the two principal sources of family support for older family members (Coward, Horne, & Dwyer, 1992). Spouses and adult children represent the primary family members with whom elders live, their central network for socialization and interpersonal interaction, and their principal source of aid and assistance (Cicirelli, 1981; Coward & Cutler, 1991; Hess & Soldo, 1985; Montgomery, 1992; Stoller, 1992).

The Availability of Spouses

Previous research has demonstrated significant residential differences in the marital status of persons 65 years of age and older (Coward, Cutler, & Schmidt, 1988). In these comparisons, elders residing in small towns and rural communities appear to be advantaged in that they are more likely to have a marital partner. Specifically, rural elders who continue to receive income from farming operations, and thus are referred to as "farm" elders, have the highest percentages of elders who are married (69.7%). Rural elders not engaged in farming, "nonfarm" elders, have the second highest rate (59.3%). In contrast, in more urban settings, lower percentages of the elderly are married. Specifically,

56.4% of elders who live in the suburbs of cities are married, 53.4% of elders in communities within the boundaries of an urbanized area, and less than half (47.8%) of those elders who live in the central city of an urbanized area are married.

These residential differences in the availability of marital partners, however, are more pronounced for women than for men and appear to "level" with age. For example, the data in Table 16.1 illustrate that central city males are the least likely to be married at all ages. But, among younger aged elderly males (i.e., those 65-74 and 75-84), residential variation among the four other community types is minimal. Moreover, among the group 85 and older, there are virtually no residential differences in the percentage of males who are married and, therefore, any rural "advantage" no longer exists.

Among females, however, the pattern is quite different. Although there is a leveling effect of age, residential differences among younger groups of female elders are quite pronounced. For example, the percentage of rural farm females aged 65-74 years with a marital partner is two-thirds higher than that of older females living in central cities. Among the next age category (75-84 years), there is a general reduction in the overall percentage of females with marital partners across all residence types; but the gap between females in rural farm areas and those in urban central cities actually widens (there is an 86.5% difference in the percentage married between the two residential groups among those age 75-84). It is not until females who are aged 85 years or more are examined that the variation between residence is reduced to negligible proportions. In this age group, only about 1 in 10 females in all residential settings is married.

Thus, in summary, as a group rural elders appear to be advantaged with regard to having a marital partner in old age. However, on closer examination, this rural advantage is very pronounced only among young-old women and much less so for men of all ages.

The Availability of Adult Children

Although family size is declining in all residential groups, rural families continue to have more children than their urban counterparts (Brown, 1981). This pattern appears to persist among the current cohort of older persons. For example, using data from a nationally representative sample of frail elders, Lee, Dwyer, and Coward (1990) reported

Table 16.1 Marital Status by Residence, Age, and Sex: U.S. Population, 65 Years of Age and Older—1980 (in percent)

	Males					Females				
	Married	Widowed	Divorced/ Separated	Single	(n)	Married	Widowed	Divorced/ Separated	Single	(n)
65-74										
Central city	75.8	10.7	7.4	6.2	(18,969)	42.2	41.1	8.9	7.9	(27,457)
Urban fringe	84.0	8.6	4.0	3.4	(18,837)	50.4	38.2	6.1	5.4	(24,727)
Other urban	83.2	8.2	4.5	4.1	(9,102)	47.7	41.2	6.0	5.2	(12,671)
Rural nonfarm	82.2	8.5	4.9	4.5	(16,723)	55.2	37.3	4.0	3.6	(19,041)
Rural farm	85.0	4.9	2.2	7.9	(2,527)	70.6	24.2	1.3	3.8	(2,224)
75-84										
Central city	67.7	21.3	5.1	5.9	(8,076)	21.5	65.3	5.2	8.0	(15,042)
Urban fringe	74.4	19.5	3.0	3.2	(7,076)	26.0	65.1	3.2	5.8	(12,100)
Other urban	73.3	19.5	3.3	4.0	(3,868)	24.5	65.7	4.0	5.9	(7,082)
Rural nonfarm	72.3	19.5	3.6	4.7	(6,609)	29.6	63.3	2.4	4.7	(8,979)
Rural farm	73.3	17.1	1.5	8.2	(894)	40.1	53.8	1.4	4.7	(922)
85+										
Central city	51.9	39.9	3.6	4.7	(1,720)	8.6	80.6	3.0	7.9	(3,772)
Urban fringe	56.6	37.5	2.7	3.3	(1,395)	11.1	81.2	2.6	5.2	(2,882)
Other urban	54.5	40.0	1.7	3.9	(832)	9.6	82.5	2.0	6.1	(1,654)
Rural nonfarm	53.0	39.6	2.6	4.9	(1,369)	11.6	81.7	1.9	4.9	(2,354)
Rural farm	54.4	38.0	2.2	5.4	(184)	12.9	81.7	0.4	5.0	(241)

SOURCE: U.S. Bureau of the Census, Public-Use Microdata Sample, File C. Reprinted with permission from: Raymond T. Coward, Stephen J. Cutler, & Frederick E. Schmidt (1988), "Residential differences in marital status and household type among the elderly," in Ramona Marotz-Baden, Charles B. Hennon, & Timothy H. Brubaker (Eds.), *Families in rural America: Stress, adaptation and revitalization* (pp. 104-115). St. Paul, MN: National Council on Family Relations.
NOTE: Percentages may not add to 100 because of rounding.

that rural farm and nonfarm elders had a higher mean number of living children (3.57 and 3.66, respectively) than did elders residing in either small or large cities (3.04 and 2.75, respectively).

Notwithstanding this larger number of living children, however, rural elders are not more likely to be living with a child. Using data from the 1980 Census of Population and Housing, Coward, Cutler, and Schmidt (1989) have noted:

> Despite notions that rural farm families are more apt to be living in multigenerational family households, there was actually a remarkable similarity between the different area-of-residence categories. With the exception of the low percentage of elders in the other-urban category that lived in multigenerational households (15.5%), the remaining four residential categories (including rural farm) were almost identical. (p. 820)

Among impaired elders (i.e., those reporting difficulty performing at least one activity of daily living or about 32.7% of all elders residing in community settings), residential differences in coresidence with an adult child have been observed, but rural elders were not found to have the highest rates of coresidence (Lee, Dwyer, & Coward, 1990). Indeed, estimating a multivariate model (with controls introduced for the age, sex, marital status, level of impairment, and number of living children of the older respondents), elderly residents of large cities were found to have higher odds of residing in the same household as a child than small-city, rural nonfarm, or rural farm residents who were 65 years of age or older.

But what about living nearby a child? Do rural elders live in closer proximity to their children? Using data from the National Long-Term Care Survey (NLTCS), Lee, Dwyer, and Coward (1990) also reported that, without making adjustments for population differences, residents of large cities and farm areas were most likely to live within 30 minutes of a child and small-city residents were least likely. When the controls listed in the previous paragraph were entered into a multivariate model, there were no statistically significant differences between elders in large cities and those on rural farms, but both differed significantly from elders in the other two residential categories.

In summary, rural elders appear to have more living children than do elders in other residential categories. However, this fact does not appear to translate into a greater propensity to coreside with a child.

Residential Comparisons of the Interaction of Elderly Parents and Their Adult Children

In this section, we examine the interaction of elderly parents with their adult children. First, we examine residential differences in the degree to which older parents have face-to-face interaction with their children and then explore contact by telephone between older parents and their children. Next, we examine patterns of financial assistance and conclude with a brief review of the impact that interaction with children has on the quality of life of elders.

Face-to-Face Interaction

Any examination of the frequency of face-to-face interaction between older persons and their children must begin by returning to the issue of geographic proximity. Proximity is the single strongest antecedent of the frequency of interaction between parents and their children (Krout, 1988; Lee, 1980); family members who live some distance apart simply cannot interact frequently face-to-face.

Several recent studies have shown that, contrary to prevailing stereotypes, rural nonfarm and small-town elders are less likely to interact with children (Lee, 1988). For example, among a sample of elderly residents of Washington State, Lee and Whitbeck (1987) found a small negative relationship between urban residence and frequency of interaction with adult children. Subsequent analyses of these data, however, demonstrated that this correlation was due entirely to a higher frequency of interaction among farm residents (Lee, 1988). Rural nonfarm residents, who constitute the great majority of the rural population, were less likely than any other residential category of elders, including residents of large cities, to interact frequently with their children.

This pattern is explained largely in terms of geographic proximity and, as mentioned previously, research has indicated that there are residential differences in the degree to which elders live close to their children. Elderly farm residents are likely to have at least one very proximate child, most often a son, who participates in the operation of the farm and will eventually inherit it. Rural nonfarm elders are the least likely of any residential category to have proximate children, because of the fact that these children must often move to more urban areas in pursuit of educational and occupational opportunities. The children of urban elders, in contrast, are more likely to find such opportunities near at hand and thus to remain in the general vicinity of their parents' residences. Because interaction frequency follows the same pattern as geographic proximity (Lee, 1988), this means that interaction frequencies are comparatively high for farm and large-city elders and lower for rural nonfarm and small-town elders.

Krout (1988) reported a small positive effect of community size on frequency of interaction between aging parents and their children when the effects of proximity are controlled. However, this effect was significant for only a few parent-child combinations (e.g., the first child in a two-child family) and was very small in all cases. Proximity, however, explained up to two thirds of the variation in frequency of contact by itself.

In summary, differences in interaction between elderly parents and their children according to residential location are not particularly large (Lee & Cassidy, 1985), and it is clear that rural elders as a category are not advantaged in this regard. It is also clear that the rural category is internally very diverse, with farm elders highest on both proximity to and interaction with children and rural nonfarm elders lowest on both dimensions.

Telephone Contact

Less is known about rural/urban differences in telephone contact between aging parents and their adult children than about differences in face-to-face interaction. Coward, Lee, Dwyer, and Seccombe (1993) found no differences by residence in the frequency of talking with children on the telephone among a sample of elders who lived alone. Just over one third of all elderly parents spoke with a child on the telephone at least once a day, and about 80% did so at least once a week, regardless of residential location. Although telephone contact with children was slightly more frequent for elders who lived alone than for those who lived with others, there is no reason to expect rural/urban differences in such contact among those who live with others.

Geographic proximity is not as much of an obstacle to telephone contact as it is to face-to-face interaction, although the expense of long-distance calls may diminish calling frequency in some cases. However, there is no evidence that elders who live further from their children, and consequently have less face-to-face interaction with them, make up for this by more frequent telephone contact. Although the data are certainly partial at this point, there is no indication that residential location influences frequency of interaction via telephone between elderly parents and their adult children.

Financial Assistance

Accumulating evidence indicates that throughout the life cycle parents are more likely to give financial aid to children than to receive such aid from them (Cheal, 1983; Schulz, 1992). Rural/urban differences in this pattern are less well documented, however. Scott and Roberto (1988) found some small and inconsistent differences in both giving and receiving financial assistance according to residence, with financial exchanges generally more common among rural elders (no distinction was made in this study between rural farm and nonfarm elders). Elderly rural men, in particular, were more likely to give assistance to their children than were their urban counterparts, especially if their children lived nearby (within 50 miles). Among widowed women, rural residents were more likely to assist their children than were urban dwellers. There were no comparable differences among married women.

Coward et al. (1993), in a study of elders living alone, found that rural elders were more than twice as likely to receive regular financial assistance from their children than were urban elders. However, only 5.2% of the rural elders living alone received money from their children on a regular basis. Clearly, this is an uncommon pattern for elders regardless of residence, but rural elders do appear to be slightly more likely to be involved in financial exchanges with children than are their urban counterparts. This is probably not attributable to the generally greater financial need of rural than urban elders (Goudy & Dobson, 1985), because rural elders are also more likely than urban elders to give financial assistance to their children (Scott & Roberto, 1988). However, it may be that financial assistance is more regularly exchanged among the kin networks of poorer people. It is also possible that rural residents feel a stronger sense of obligation to assist kin (Heller, Quesda, Harvey, & Warner, 1981).

Interaction with Children and the Quality of Life of Elders

Relations with adult children are critically important to older persons in a great variety of ways (Mancini & Blieszner, 1989). However, studies have repeatedly shown that frequency of interaction with children is unrelated to measures of psychological well-being among older parents (Lee, 1979; Lee & Ishii-Kuntz, 1987). Frequency of interaction with friends, however, is positively related to psychological well-being (Lee & Ishii-Kuntz, 1987). This may be attributable to the fact that kinship relations are bounded by norms of obligation, whereas friendship is based on mutual and voluntary choice. Close relatives are expected to interact with one another when the opportunity arises, whereas one is chosen as a friend, suggesting that one has qualities others find attractive or desirable.

Scott and Roberto (1988) separately examined morale in samples of rural and urban elders and found no effects of interaction with children on morale for either sample. Lee and Whitbeck (1987) investigated the indirect effect of residence on loneliness via interaction with children and grandchildren. Although rural residents were slightly more likely to interact with family members than were urban residents, this interaction had no effect on loneliness. The most defensible conclusion at this point is that the psychological well-being of older persons does not depend on frequency of interaction with their children, nor is it contingent on residence.

Residential Comparisons of Caregiving by Adult Children

The family is critical to the well-being of elders when illness, physical decline, or frailty reduce the ability of older persons to perform the tasks associated with daily life or jeopardize their ability to remain living independently. In this section, we turn our attention to residential comparisons of the caregiving patterns of adult children. First, we examine residential differences in the rate of participation as caregivers of adult children whose parents live in different community contexts. Next, we explore residential differences in the involvement of families among elders with varying levels of impairment. Finally, we examine residential differences in the stress and burden of family caregivers and close with an examination of residential differences in the evolution of care networks over time.

The Rate of Participation of Adult Children as Caregivers

Previous research has demonstrated that all children do not participate equally in providing parent-care (Dwyer & Coward, 1991). Indeed, certain characteristics of both the care-recipient (e.g., the gender of the elder, their marital status, and the degree of difficulty in performing activities of daily living, ADLs, or instrumental activities of daily living, IADLS) and the caregiver (the gender of the caregiver, their marital status, employment, proximity, and sibling network configuration) increase the odds that a child will be engaged in parent-care.

We wondered whether there was a difference in the participation rate of children whose parents lived in different residential contexts. We used data from the National Long-Term Care Survey to examine this question (U.S. Department of Health and Human Services, 1984). The NLTCS is a nationally representative sample of 6,393 noninstitutionalized disabled elders in the United States. For our purposes here, we examined a subset of elderly parents with living children (4,358 elders with 13,127 children). We divided the sample according to where the elderly parent lived—in a rural area (defined as open country/nonfarm or farm setting of less than 2,500 persons); a small city (city/town/village with more than 2,500 but less than 50,000 persons); or in an urban area (city of 50,000-250,000 persons, the suburb of a large city, or a large city with 250,000 or more persons). Children were counted as providing parent-care if they helped with either ADL or IADL tasks.

In this context, we did discover residential differences in the rate children participated as providers of care to their parents. Overall, about 1 in 4 children was involved in parent-care (3,241 of 13,127 children, or 24.7%). However, among elders living in rural areas, participation rates were smaller (630 of 3,094 children, or 20.2%). Elders who lived in small cities received help from a slightly larger percentage of their children (1,174 of 5,161 children, or 22.7%), and the highest rates of participation were observed among children of elders living in urban places (1,437 of 4,872 children, or 29.5%).

Part of these lower rates of participation among children whose parents live in rural areas may be a combination of the queuing effect of parent-care described by Soldo, Wolf, and Agree (1990)—that is, the tendency for a single child to be providing care while their siblings "wait in the wings" for their turn—combined with the larger sibling networks of rural families (thus, a greater number of children waiting their turn). It could also be a result of the out-migration of younger persons from rural areas (Heaton, Clifford, & Fuguitt, 1984), leaving a smaller proportion of children to provide hands-on help with activities such as ADLs and IADLs. Or, it might be another reflection of the residential differences in proximity discussed earlier. Ultimately, the causes of such differences will only be uncovered by systematically examining the simultaneous effects of a number of variables.

Family Care and Level of Impairment of Elder

Evidence has accumulated that suggests that as the level of impairment of elders increases, the size and composition of their helping network changes (Coward, 1987a; Sauer & Coward, 1985; Stephens & Christianson, 1986). More disabled older persons are apt to be receiving help from a larger number of persons and a greater variety of sources and are most likely to be receiving assistance from a formal health or human service provider.

This trend, however, does vary across areas of residence. For example, Coward, Cutler, and Mullens (1990) reported that severely impaired elders residing in nonmetropolitan communities were less likely than their metropolitan counterparts to be receiving aid from a formal provider and were significantly more likely to be receiving assistance from informal helpers exclusively (see Table 16.2). Using data from the Supplement on Aging to the 1984 National Health Interview Survey, these authors demonstrated that among elders with severe functional limitations (i.e., difficulty performing nine or more ADLs and IADLs), nearly 3 of 4 elders residing in nonmetropolitan places (73.0%) continued to rely exclusively on informal helpers for assistance (primarily family members). In contrast, just over half of the elders with this level of disability who resided in metropolitan communities relied exclusively on informal sources of support (55.2% of residents of central cities and 59.0% of those living in non-central city places that were part of a Standard Metropolitan Statistical Area or SMSA).

The "other side of the coin" of this trend was the greater reliance among metropolitan elders on formal sources of support (either in combination with informal sources or exclusively). For example, Coward, Cutler, and Mullens (1990) indicated that among the severely disabled about 4 of 10 metropolitan elders were receiving care from a formal source (42.7% of central city residents and 39.6% of residents of other parts of SMSAs), whereas about 1 in 4 nonmetropolitan elders (26.3%) with that level of disability was the recipient of care from a formal service provider.

Although the trend for rural elders to be more reliant on informal sources of support than their more urban counterparts appears quite

Table 16.2 Residence Differences in Sources of Assistance by Levels of Impairment (in percentages)

	SMSA Central City[a]	SMSA Not Central City[b]	Non-SMSAc
Difficulty with one task			
No assistance	50.0	48.5	50.4
Informal assistance only	38.8	37.9	37.8
Both informal and formal assistance	1.1	1.2	0.7
Formal assistance only	10.1	12.5	11.1
(n)	(348)	(433)	(561)
	$x^2 = 1.94$, df $= 6$, $p =$ n.s.		
Difficulty with 2 or 3 tasks			
No assistance	25.5	24.0	26.8
Informal assistance only	53.8	58.2	56.2
Both informal and formal assistance	4.4	7.1	4.8
Formal assistance only	16.4	10.8	12.2
(n)	(275)	(325)	(395)
	$x^2 = 7.42$, df $= 6$, $p =$ n.s.		
Difficulty with 4 or 5 tasks			
No assistance	8.9	5.5	9.5
Informal assistance only	68.4	73.1	68.6
Both informal and formal assistance	13.3	11.7	15.2
Formal assistance only	9.5	9.7	6.7
(n)	(158)	(145)	(210)
	$x^2 = 4.18$, df $= 6$, $p =$ n.s.		
Difficulty with 6 to 8 tasks			
No assistance	2.3	1.3	1.3
Informal assistance only	68.2	69.4	73.6
Both informal and formal assistance	19.4	22.5	19.5
Formal assistance only	10.1	6.9	5.7
(n)	(129)	(160)	(159)
	$x^2 = 3.45$, df $= 6$, $p =$ n.s.		
Difficulty with 9 or more tasks			
No assistance	2.1	1.4	0.7
Informal assistance only	55.2	59.0	73.0
Both informal and formal assistance	35.4	34.0	18.4
Formal assistance only	7.3	5.6	7.9
(n)	(96)	(144)	(152)
	$x^2 = 13.87$, df $= 6$, $p = .05$		

[a]For the relationship between sources of assistance and levels of impairment (central city): $x^2 = 293.97$, df $= 12$, $p < .001$.
[b]For the relationship between sources of assistance and levels of impairment (not central city): $x^2 = 357.56$, df $= 12$, $p < .001$.

clear, the explanation of the behavior is not. Coward and Dwyer (1991b) offer three possible interpretations. The first suggests that rural elders are more reluctant than their urban counterparts to accept help from persons outside their kin network. The second interpretation suggests that rural elders are immersed in a family kin network that is stronger and more close-knit and where feelings of filial responsibility and obligation are more durable. Finally, a third explanation suggests that rural elders must rely more on family care simply because they have fewer, and a narrower range of, formal service alternatives available to them. Although there are varying degrees of evidence for all three of these explanations, no one interpretation has received unreserved support. Further research is needed to clarify the relative contribution of each of these factors.

Caregiver Burden and Stress

Only a very few studies have examined residential differences in caregiver burden and stress (Dwyer & Miller, 1990a, 1990b). Using a matched sample of 1,388 noninstitutionalized functionally limited elders and their primary caregivers drawn from the 1982 National Long-Term Care Survey and the National Survey of Informal Caregivers, Dwyer and Miller (1990b) identified no residential differences in the amount of stress reported by caregivers and only one significant difference in the amount of burden (a higher level of burden was reported by urban caregivers compared to their counterparts from rural areas).

These studies did suggest, however, that the underlying factors most predictive of caregiver stress and burden are different across residential categories (Dwyer & Miller, 1990a). Using the NLTCS to estimate multivariate models, Dwyer and Miller (1990a) demonstrated that although the influence of some factors was uniform across residential categories, the effects of other characteristics of the care-receiver or the primary caregiver had differential effects on stress and burden across residential categories. For example, caregiver stress and burden was reduced in all three residential categories when the frail elder was able to reciprocate for the help they received by doing chores, baby-sitting, or providing some other type of assistance for the primary caregiver. In contrast, although caregiver stress was positively associated with the number of ADL tasks performed by the caregiver among the small city and the urban samples, this association was not statistically significant among the rural sample. Collectively, these studies suggest that more research is needed to identify those factors that best predict stress and burden among family caregivers and to clarify more fully the impact of area of residence on these phenomena.

Family Care Over Time

Previous research has documented that families often provide care to elders over extended periods of time (Abel, 1990; Brody, 1985; Doty, 1986). This research has indicated that as the demands of the older person evolve and the circumstances and resources of their caregivers change (physical, emotional, and financial), the composition of their social support network can be altered (Antonucci & Akiyama, 1987). Again, however, there appear to be residential differences in the pattern of these changes over time—not differences in the direction of the evolution (i.e., in all residential settings older and more disabled elders appear to move toward a greater reliance on a diverse helping network that includes both formal and informal helpers), but rather residential differences in the magnitude or the pace of the change that occurs.

For example, Coward and Dwyer (1991b), using data from the longitudinal file of the 1982-1984 National Long-Term Care Survey, examined residential differences in the degree to which elders who were not receiving formal services added formal providers to their helping networks over time. A sample of impaired elders ($N = 2,417$) who lived in noninstitutionalized settings in both 1982 (Time 1) and 1984 (Time 2) and received assistance from only informal sources of support at Time 1 was studied. The analysis indicated that residential differences in network composition did exist at Time 2 for those elders who remained in the community. Whereas small town and urban elders had approximately the same proportion of elders at Time 2 who had added a formal service provider to their network (18.0% and 17.4%, respectively), a considerably smaller proportion of rural elders received support from community-based formal sources at Time 2 (12.2%). In addition, a multivariate model was estimated that included 10 sociodemographic and health-related characteristics of the elder known to influence her or his use of formal services. Residence differences persisted even after the effects of these variables were controlled. Specifically, among persons not receiving formal services at Time 1, urban elders were 1.6 times as likely as rural or small town elders to have added a formal service provider to their helping network by Time 2.

Concluding Comments

In this chapter we have reviewed some of the most recent literature and research describing the family relations of rural elders. Taken as a whole, these works suggest that the family relations of elders residing in small towns and rural communities do differ in important aspects from their older counterparts who live in more urban settings. These differences, however, do not place rural elders in a particularly advantaged position. Rather, the differences may well represent and reflect variation in the population characteristics of older persons by area of residence, in the sociocultural environment in which elders operate, and in the formal health and human service resources associated with different sized communities.

Further research is needed to clarify both the direct and the indirect effects of residing in a small town or rural community on the lives of older persons. The following list represents some of the major areas in which research needs to be completed:

- Research is needed that illuminates the influence of residence on the quality of interactions between older parents and their adult children and explores the consequences of residential differences for the long-term care and quality of life of elders.
- Research is needed to describe more fully differences in family relations among subgroups of older persons who reside in rural America, for example, elders of different racial and ethnic groups, elders living in different household types (alone or in multigenerational households), elders from different regions or socioeconomic classes.
- Research is needed that examines the influence of gender on family interactions and relationships within rural families characterized by more traditional divisions of household labor.
- Research is needed that describes the processes whereby families in different residential contexts make decisions about the long-term care of their older members.
- Research is needed that explores the relationship among and between health and human service providers and family caregivers in residential contexts with varying degrees of formal resources.
- Research is needed that clarifies and illuminates the antecedents and consequences of changes in the patterns of family caregiving that occur over time.

We recognize that family relations are an important element in the lives of older Americans, regardless of their place of residence. However, we also know that the family relations of rural elders have important distinctive characteristics that set them apart from their counterparts in more urban settings. The challenge that confronts scholars in rural gerontology is to illuminate more fully the details and consequences of these differences for the health, well-being, and effective functioning of older persons.

Epilogue

The role of social science research in gerontology is to study, explain, predict, and evaluate changes in specific segments of society. The rapid increase in both the numbers and the proportion of older people living into advanced age in our rural communities is one such change. At the same time, other major changes impacting rural communities have occurred. The most visible in many communities is that of the reduction of jobs, which has led to the out-migration of the young and, as a consequence, a reduction in the level of the tax base. In contrast, in other communities in-migration has led to the expansion of jobs and increases in taxes. There is both expansion and contraction occurring at the same time, thus ensuring that rural America is not a homogeneous set of communities. With the fluctuations in the overall economy, the level of funding available for social services has shifted, which impacts directly on the rural elderly. Especially traumatic has been the continuing reduction of service, both private and public, in the area of health care and long-term care. It is not surprising, therefore, to find that many of the writers in this volume attempt to explain such changes while at the same time seeking to evaluate their impact on the elderly. These researchers also are trying to see how with the limited available resources—private, public, formal, and informal—the elderly can be sustained should they wish to continue to reside in rural America.

In his epilogue to the 1985 book by Coward and Lee (1985), Philip Taietz laments that the gap between what is and what ought to be, both in the area of scientific research and financial support for rural elders, is still apparent even though great strides were made in the 1970s and early 1980s. I am sorry that I must echo a similar refrain—and with the caution that such improvements have if anything been smaller and in many cases reversed in the intervening time period. However, I can say with great pride that more and more sophisticated research on the rural elderly is appearing. The contributions in this volume are only a small part of that trend.

There are some general problems with research on the rural elderly that still need to be solved. First and foremost is the problem of dividing the variable of place of residence into a dichotomy, whether it is urban/rural or metropolitan/nonmetropolitan. What is most disturbing is that there is mounting evidence—best illustrated by the research of Coward and Dwyer (1991b) showing that there are significant differences between farm and nonfarm elders—that there may be greater variation among rural elders than between rural and urban elderly populations. Research must continue to emphasize and show with empirical findings the heterogeneity of rural America. The second problem I wish to bring attention to is that in too many national studies the size of the samples covering the rural elderly are invariably too small. These small sample sizes lead to several problems. First, rural comparisons may be dropped entirely from the analysis. A recent and most frustrating example for me and directly impacting on my present research on the older volunteer is the national study completed in April of 1991 and titled the *Marriott Seniors Volunteerism Study*. With a sample of 962, only data on urban and suburban populations are presented. A second fallout from these small samples is that when urban/rural comparisons *can* be made, that is about as far as we can go. The most important variable of age can often not be used because the number of subjects in each age grouping may be too small. Again we are often forced to deal with another unwanted dichotomy, that of young versus old, yet much of our research tells us that there may be even larger inter-age differences as is well-illustrated with our nominal categories of the *young-old, middle-old*, and *old-old*. The third problem we face is an extension of the second—if we have difficulty in completing even adequate bivariate analysis, how can we even try to explain such findings by introducing a third or fourth control variable? Much rural elderly research suffers from a lack of at least a three-variable analysis. This fact is not to say that all is lost; we can talk about the rural elderly as a single subpopulation as well as compare rural communities with each other. Some of the writers in this book have done just that.

Lucy Rose Fischer has focused in on the oldest-old—a subpopulation that is of growing importance. She specifically is looking at a group of elderly that is poorer and less well educated and has great trouble accessing needed resources. Many more studies looking at these types of populations are needed. Also, community and organizational comparisons are being used. Excellent examples are in this book. Marvin Kaiser and Henry Camp move the focus away from psychological and social psychological variables to the more macro level of community. They show how the rural elderly play a production as well as a consumption role in their local community. In many rural areas the elderly contribute both through their work and service, not to mention their transfer payments and, the authors stress, the various ways that these elderly can and do contribute to both the community policy and community development. Similarly, John McClain and his coauthors look at community structure with the focus on their senior center. Again for these authors, it is the increases and changes in community development that are of importance in their studies. What they are examining is just one way of keeping rural areas from decline and decay. A viable community means adequate services for the elderly and non-elderly alike. A final example in this book is the chapter by Betty Havens and Beverly Kyle, which takes a "systems approach" to the increasing problem of formal long-term care. Through the examination of organizations that play a role as a single locus of responsibility for determining available options along the continuum of health care, they are exploring how a community can provide the correct mix of services that allows the elderly to function at their most independent level.

Another research problem that is far too often neglected is that of longitudinal studies. Many times I find myself asking the question, "Am I seeing a cohort or an aging effect in these data?" In this book regretfully, there is little use of data collected over several points in time. The chapter by Margaret Penning and Neena Chappell looking at health promotion and the chapter by Charles Longino and William Haas looking at the use of census data are two cases in which longitudinal data are used.

I had hoped that this present book would answer some of the major questions that came out of the July 1991 symposium I held in Kansas

City, the papers from which were published by the National Resource Center for Rural Elderly in their monograph titled "The Future of Aging in Rural America: Proceedings of a National Symposium 1991." Regretfully, this has not been the case. However, some progress has been made. First, two areas that were obvious gaps in our knowledge have been covered. The chapter by Eloise Rathbone-McCuan is a start for the subject of rural mental health. Much more empirical research needs to be done here, and with large enough rural samples so that some of the questions raised in McCuan's chapter can be answered. Second, the topic of elder abuse in rural areas is extremely weak when it comes to actual data on which to base any conclusions. Novella Perrin in her chapter begins the task of defining elder abuse, presents some data on the incidence of this behavior, and tries to look at the problems associated with access to the services that could alleviate the problem.

There are, however, other areas that need specific attention and that are missing from this book. First, and most glaring, is the lack of adequate research on rural elderly minorities. This omission is even more startling given that many of the problems faced by the rural elderly are magnified among the African-American population in the rural Southern states. Also, the increasing number of studies on rural Hispanics in the Southwestern states will soon come to fruition and produce some useful information. Finally, research on Native Americans is still sorely missing. All is not gloom and doom in this area, however. The chapter in this book by Vira Kivett has looked at these minority populations with a special emphasis on their informal support systems. Much more is needed and especially good quality quantitative work.

The chapter by Kivett is one of the four that really does start to tackle the debate as to what is, should be, and will be the mix between the formal and informal systems in determining the quality of life and well-being of rural elders. I suspect that it is the clash between the growing numbers of rural elderly and the decrease in the federal and state funds to support formal programs that has brought this debate to the fore. Certainly, as the cost of health care has dramatically risen, as well illustrated by Coward and Dwyer (1991a), it is not surprising that researchers have turned their attention to the family in its primary support role.

With this book as only a stepping stone on which to build future research, what are some of the major areas that still need more work? I feel that there are three. First, resources must be spent to collect sufficient basic information on the rural elderly by completing an annual survey over a minimum of 3 years and preferably over a 10-year period. Only in this way will there be a sufficiently large enough sample from which multivariate analysis could be completed while at the same time allowing for differentiation of cohort versus aging effects. The aging and health care networks have over the last 5 years set up several "centers" or "institutes," each with near or over $1 million budgets. I would suggest that the agencies funding these units request that they set aside resources to complete such a survey or series of surveys. The centers or institutes could either use themselves as the data gathering mechanism or be part of a subcontract with professional national polling organizations such as the Roper Institute or Gallup Incorporated, who run national "omnibus" surveys several times a year.

Second, I have observed that resources for both basic and applied research at the national, state, and community levels are becoming more and more limited. Therefore, it is important that two major actions are taken: an increase in the coordination of and the flexibility of the use of these limited resources. With respect to the term *coordination,* we must go beyond memorandums of agreement (MOGs) to ensure that there is joint funding of important research projects. Also, there is a great need to formalize the communication of basic research information across agency lines. There is some movement in Washington, DC to accomplish this task, as illustrated by the article "Common Beliefs About Rural Elderly: What Do National Data Tell Us?" forthcoming in *Vital and Health Statistics* (1993), the result of many agencies getting together and sharing their national data.

Similarly, but not covered in this book, is the need for agencies to not only identify "model" programs but to ensure prior to expanding the use of such models that rigorous data on outcomes/accountability be collected. Again, interagency communication concerning these evaluated programs needs to be regularized to ensure that the wheel is not reinvented. Similar monitoring of programs produced in the for-profit and not-for-profit sectors must also take place. A program that has been distributed and used in a large number of settings is not necessarily the most efficient and will not necessarily produce the desired outcomes.

The last area I wish to focus on deals with the relationship between the size of the rural community and the availability of services. Although there has been a narrowing of the urban/rural differential in service provision, such a gap still exists. Certainly, increased federal, state, and community funding could continue to narrow this gap. Such funding does not seem likely over the next few years, given the decreases that have occurred in the 1980s. Continued advocacy will be needed at all levels just to ensure that the gap will not again widen. Left unresolved, however, is the major question of just when a rural community is too small to be a part of the total service system. Or to put it another way, should our agencies provide the full range of programs and services to most of rural America? The problem can be handled as the postal, electoral, and telephone services have been. Such coverage can be achieved but at a cost that falls more on the urban areas. At present, I would have to believe that universal coverage is unlikely in rural hamlets, villages, and even small towns. Given this reality, who then is to decide just what services are made available and to what size population centers? Excellent basic research together with rigorous evaluative research is a necessary prerequisite to sound decision making. Will the trends to more regional service centers continue, thus leaving places with less than 500 people with limited or even no services? Also, it will be necessary to look at just which services or programs can be most efficiently run from a regional center and which ones must be more widespread in nature. Similarly, the correct mixture of services provided with tax funds and by the not-for-profit sector must be decided on. It is important that the level of services and programs will differ among communities based on the willingness of a given community to put resources into such endeavors.

The research and summary chapters in this book emphasize the continuing need for greater attention to rural issues. Also, they show the need for greater appreciation of the many difficulties associated with living in a rural community. Still left unanswered is the central question of whether many rural communities can support services as they face changing economic realities, some for the better and some for the worse. There is no perfect model or perfect set of programs that will fit every rural community. What is needed is local innovation and local decision making with these decisions based on the best information available. This book is part of such a process.

References

Abacus Technology. (1989). *Safety, loss control and risk management.* Washington, DC: Department of Transportation, UMTA, Technology Sharing.

Abel, E. K. (1990). Informal care for the disabled elderly: A critique of recent literature. *Research on Aging, 12,* 139-157.

Ackman, A. (1988). *Community based systems of service for older persons.* Reston, VA: SAVANT, Inc.

Aday, R. H., & Miles, L. A. (1982). Long-term impacts of rural migration of the elderly: Implications for research. *The Gerontologist, 22,* 331-336.

Administration on Aging (AoA). (1991). *Community focal points for service delivery: A technical handbook.* Washington, D.C: Author.

Aging and rural economic development: Fitting the pieces together. (1989). Topeka, KS: Kansas Department of Aging.

Aguirre, B. E., & Bigelow, A. (1983). The aged in Hispanic groups: A review. *International Journal of Aging and Human Development, 17*(3), 117-201.

AHA report: Survival of rural hospitals threatened. (1987, 14 December). *American Hospital Association News.*

Ahearn, M. C., & Fryar, M. D. (1985). *Physicians in nonmetro areas during the seventies.* Rural Development Report No. 46. Washington, DC: Department of Agriculture.

Aldwin, C., & Stokols, D. (1988). The effects of environmental change on individuals and groups: Some neglected issues in stress research. *Journal of Environmental Psychology, 8,* 57-75.

American Hospital Association (AHA). (1987). *Environmental assessment for rural hospitals.* Chicago, IL: AHA.

American Hospital Association (AHA). (1989). *Rural hospital closure: Management and community implications.* Chicago, IL: AHA.

Anderson, J. F., Niebuhr, M., Braden, A., & Alderson, S. (1987). Telephone interviews: Cost-effective method for accurate travel surveys. *Transportation Research Record,* No. 1097, 4-6.

Aneshensel, C. S., Frerichs, R. R., & Huba, G. J. (1984). Depression and physical illness: A multiwave, nonrecursive causal model. *Journal of Health and Social Behavior, 25,* 350-371.

Antonucci, T. C., & Akiyama, H. (1987). Social networks in adult life and a preliminary examination of the convoy model. *Journals of Gerontology: Social Sciences, 42,* 519-527.

Atash, F. (1990). *Fiscal conditions in Rhode Island municipalities.* Kingston, RI: University of Rhode Island, Department of Community Planning.

Babchuk, N. (1979). Aging and primary relations. *International Journal of Aging and Human Development, 9,* 137-151.

Bartlett, P. (1990). Qualitative methods in rural studies: Basic principles. *The Rural Sociologist, 10,* 3-14.

Becerra, R. M. (1983). The Mexican-American: Aging in a changing culture. In R. L. McNeely & J. N. Colen (Eds.), *Aging in minority groups* (pp. 108-118). Beverly Hills, CA: Sage.

Behnke, R. (1985). Community Videotex-Parataxi systems. In *Final report: First UMTA and ADA national conference for the elderly and handicapped* (pp. 131-145). Washington, DC: UMTA.

Bell, W. (1987). Mobility and specialized transportation for elderly and for disabled persons. *Transportation Research Record,* No. 1170, 60-68.

Bender, C., & Hart, J. P. (1987). A model for health promotion for the rural elderly. *The Gerontologist, 27*(2), 139-142.

Benjamin, A. E. (1986). Determinants of state variations in home health utilization and expenditures under Medicare. *Medical Care, 24*(6), 535-547.

Bennett, D. G. (1990). *The impact of elderly in-migration on private and public economic development efforts in predominately rural areas along the South Atlantic Coast.* U.S. Department of Commerce, Economic Development Administration Project No. 99-07-13732.

Bergland, B. (1988). Rural mental health: Report of the National Action Commission on the mental health of rural America. *Journal of Rural Community Psychology, 9,* 29-40.

Berkanovic, E., Hurwicz, M., & Lubben, J. E. (1989). Indicators of actions for health promotion among the aged. In S. B. Kar (Ed.), *Health Promotion Indicators and Actions* (pp. 271-291). New York: Springer.

Berkman, L. F., Berkman, C. S., Kasi, S., Freeman, D. H., Jr., Ostfeld, L. A. M., Cornoni-Huntley, J., & Brody, J. (1986). Depressive symptoms in relation to physical health and functioning in the elderly. *American Journal of Epidemiology, 124,* 372-388.

Bernstein, J., Kolimaga, J., & Neuschler, E. (1988). Overview and introduction. In *New alliances for rural America: Background paper submitted to task force on rural development.* Washington, DC: National Governors Association.

Biafora, F. A., & Longino, C. F. (1990). Elderly Hispanic migration in the United States. *Journal of Gerontology, 45*(5), S212-219.

Biegel, D., Sales, E., & Schulz, R. (1991). *Family caregiving in chronic illness.* Newbury Park, CA: Sage.

Biggar, J. C. (1980). Who moved among the elderly, 1965-1970: A comparison of types of older movers. *Research on Aging, 2,* 73-91.

Biggar, J. C., Longino, C.F., Jr., & Flynn, C.B. (1980). Elderly interstate migration: The impact on sending and receiving states, 1965-1970. *Research on Aging, 2,* 217-232.

Blazer, D. G. (1982). Social support and mortality in an elderly population. *American Journal of Epidemiology, 115,* 684-694.

Blazer, D. (1989). The epidemiology of psychiatric disorders in late life. In E. Busse & D. Blazer (Eds.), *Geriatric psychiatry* (pp. 235-262). Washington, DC: American Psychiatric Press.

Blazer, D., Hughes, D. C., & George, L. K. (1987). The epidemiology of depression in an elderly population. *The Gerontologist, 27,* 281-287.

Blieszner, R., McAuley, W. J., Newhouse, J. K., & Mancini, J. A. (1987). Rural-urban differences in service use by older adults. In T. H. Brubaker (Ed.), *Aging, health, and family: Long-term care* (pp. 162-174). Newbury Park, CA: Sage.

Block, M. R. (1979). Exiled Americans: The plight of Indian aged in the United States. In D. E. Gelfand & A. J. Kutzik (Eds.), *Ethnicity and aging: Theory, research, and policy* (pp. 184-192). New York: Springer.

Block, M. R., & Sinnot, J. E. (Eds.). (1979). *The battered elderly syndrome.* College Park, MD: University of Maryland Center on Aging.

Bogue, D. J. (1969). *Principles of demography.* New York: John Wiley.

Bookin, D., & Dunkle, R. E. (1985). Elder abuse: Issues for the practitioner. *Social Casework, 66,* 3-12.

Bould, S., Sanborn, B., & Reif, L. (1989). *Eighty-five plus: The oldest old.* Belmont, CA: Wadsworth.

Bradshaw, B. S., & Fonner, E. (1978). The mortality of Spanish-surnamed persons in Texas: 1969-1971. In F. D. Bean & W. P. Frisbie (Eds.), *The demography of racial and ethnic groups* (pp. 261-282). New York: Academic Press.

Bradsher, J. E., Longino, C. F., Jr., Jackson, D. J., & Zimmerman, R. S. (1992). Health and geographical mobility among the recently widowed. *Journal of Gerontology: Social Sciences, 47*(5), S261-S268.

Bressler, D. S., Loewinsohn, R. J., & Baldwin, L. E. (1984). *Hand in hand: Learning from and caring for older parents.* Washington, DC: American Association of Retired Persons. Page 2.

Brody, E. M. (1985). Parent care as a normative family stress. *The Gerontologist, 25,* 19-25.

Brown, D. L. (1981). A quarter century of trends and changes in the demographic structure of American families. In R. T. Coward & W. M. Smith, Jr. (Eds.), *The family in rural society* (pp. 9-25). Boulder, CO: Westview Press.

Brown, K. (1990). Connected independence: A paradox of rural health. *Journal of Rural Community Psychology, 11,* 51-64.

Brubaker, T. (1985). Health patterns. In E. A. Powers, W. J. Gowdy, & P. M. Keith (Eds.), *Later life transitions: Older males in rural America* (pp. 87-95). Boston: Kluwer-Nijhoff.

Brubaker, T. H. (Ed.). (1985). *Later life families.* Newbury Park, CA: Sage.

Brubaker, T. H. (1990). Families in later life: A burgeoning research area. *Journal of Marriage and the Family, 52,* 959-981.

Bryson, J. M. (1989). *Strategic planning for public and nonprofit organizations.* San Francisco, CA: Jossey-Bass.

Bull, C. N., & Aucoin, J. B. (1975). Voluntary association participation and life satisfaction: A replication note. *Journal of Gerontology, 30,* 73-76.

Bull, C. N., Howard, D. M., & DeCroix Bane, S. (1991). *Challenges and solutions to the provision of programs and services to rural elders.* Kansas City, MO: University of Missouri, National Resource Center for Rural Elderly.

Butler, R. (1969). Age-ism: Another form of bigotry. *The Gerontologist, 9,* 243-246.

Byerts, T. (1982). The Congregate Housing Model: Integrating facilities and services. In R. D. Chellis, J. F. Seagle, Jr., & B. M. Seagle (Eds.), *Congregate housing for older people* (pp. 127-38). Lexington, MA: D. C. Health.

Canfield, A., & Lim, W.-Y. (1983). *Systan's macro-analytic regionwide transportation model: User's guide.* Washington DC: UMTA Office of Technical Assistance.

Carp, F. (1988). *The significance of mobility for the well-being of the elderly.* Transportation Research Board Special Report, No. 218 (pp. 6-8). Washington, DC: Department of Transportation.

Carpiniello, B., Carta, M. G., & Rudas, N. (1989). Depression among elderly people: A psychological study of urban and rural populations. *Acta Psychiatrica Scandinavica, 80,* 445-450.

Chappell, N. L. (1985). Social support and the receipt of home care services. *The Gerontologist, 25,* 47-54.

Chappell, N. L. (1988). Long-term care in Canada. In E. Rathbone-McCuan & B. Havens (Eds.), *North American elders: United States and Canadian perspectives* (pp. 73-88). Westport, CT: Greenwood Press.

Chappell, N. L. (1991). Living arrangements and sources of caregiving. *Journal of Gerontology, 46*(1), S1-S8.

Chappell, N. L., & Havens, B. (1985). Who helps the elderly person: A discussion of informal and formal care. In W. Peterson & J. Quadagno (Eds.), *Social bonds in later life* (pp. 211-227). Newbury Park, CA: Sage.

Chappell, N. L., & Horne, J. (1988). *Study of supportive housing among seniors.* Ottawa, Ontario: Canada Mortgage and Housing Corporation.

Chappell, N. L., Strain, L. A., & Blandford, A. A. (1985). *Aging and health care: A social perspective.* Toronto: Holt, Rinehart & Winston.

Chatters, L. M., & Taylor, R. J. (1989). Age differences in religious participation among black adults. *Journal of Gerontology: Social Sciences, 44*(5), S183-189.

Chatters, L. M., & Taylor, R. J. (1990). Social integration. In Z. Harel, E. A. McKinney, & M. Williams (Eds.), *Black aged: Understanding diversity and service needs* (pp. 82-99). Newbury Park, CA: Sage.

Chatters, L. M., Taylor, R. J., & Jackson, J. S. (1985). Size and composition of the informal helper networks of elderly Blacks. *Journal of Gerontology, 40*(5), 605-614.

Chatters, L. M., Taylor, R. J., & Jackson, J. S. (1986). Aged Blacks' choices for an informal helper network. *Journal of Gerontology, 41*(1), 94-100.

Cheal, D. J. (1983). Intergenerational family transfers. *Journal of Marriage and the Family, 45,* 805-813.

Cicirelli, V. G. (1981). *Helping elderly parents: Role of adult children.* Boston, MA: Auburn House.

Clark, P. G. (1987). Individual autonomy, cooperative empowerment, and planning for long-term care decision making. *Journal of Aging Studies, 1*(1), 65-76.

Clifford, W. B., Heaton, T., & Fuguitt, G. V. (1982). Residential mobility and living arrangements among the elderly: Changing patterns in metropolitan and nonmetropolitan areas. *International Journal of Aging and Human Development, 14*(2), 139-156.

Clifford, W. B., Heaton, T. B., Lichter, D. T., & Fuguitt, G. V. (1983). Components of change in the age composition of nonmetropolitan America. *Rural Sociology, 48*(3), 458-473.

Clifford, W. B., Heaton, T. B., Voss, P. R., & Fuguitt, G. V. (1985). The rural elderly in demographic perspective. In R. T. Coward & G. R. Lee (Eds.), *The elderly in rural society* (pp. 25-56). New York: Springer.

Coates, G. J. (1981). *Rebuilding rural America.* Paper presented at the National Research Conference on Technology and Aging, Racine, WI.

Coe, R. M., Wolinsky, F. D., Miller, D. K., & Prendergast, J. M. (1984). Social network relationships and use of physician services, a reexamination. *Research on Aging, 6*(2), 243-256.

Cohen, G. (1990). Psychopathology and mental health in the mature and elderly adult. In J. Birren & K. Schaie (Eds.), *Handbook of the psychology of aging* (3rd. ed., pp. 359-371). San Diego, CA: Academic Press.

Cohen, S., Mermelstein, R., Kamarek, T., & Hoberman, H. (1985). Measuring the functional components of social support. In I. Sarason & B. Sarason (Eds.), *Social support: Theory, research, and applications* (Chapter 5). Dordrecht, the Netherlands: Martin Nijhoff.

Cohen-Mansfield, J. (1989). Employment and volunteering roles for the elderly: Characteristics, attributions, and strategies. *Journal of Leisure Research, 21*(2), 214-227.

Committee on an Aging Society. (1988). *America's aging: The social and built environment in an older society.* Washington, DC: National Academy Press.

Commonwealth fund survey findings. (1990). *National Council on Aging Newsletter,* p. 9.

Community Council of Greater New York. (1978). *Dependency in the elderly of New York City.* New York: Community Council of Greater New York.

Comptroller General of the United States. (1977). The well-being of older people in Cleveland. Washington, DC: General Accounting Office.

Cook, S. (1989). Riding the silver streak. *Retailing Issues Letter, 2*(4), 1-4.

Coward, R. T. (1979). Planning community services for the rural elderly: Implications for research. *The Gerontologist, 19,* 275-282.

Coward, R. T. (1987a). Factors associated with the configuration of the helping networks of noninstitutionalized elders. *Gerontological Social Work, 10,* 113-132.

Coward, R. T. (1987b). Poverty and aging in rural America. *Human Services in the Rural Environment, 10-11,* 41-47.

Coward, R. T. (1988). Aging in the rural United States. In E. Rathbone-McCuan & B. Havens (Eds.), *North American elders: U.S. and Canadian comparisons* (pp. 161-177). Westport, CT: Greenwood Press.

Coward, R. T., & Cutler, S. J. (1989). Informal and formal health care systems for the rural elderly. *Health Services Research, 23*(6), 785-806.

Coward, R. T., & Cutler, S. J. (1991). The composition of multigenerational households that include elders. *Research on Aging, 13*(1), 55-73.

Coward, R. T., Cutler, S. J., & Mullens, R. A. (1990). Residential differences in the composition of the helping networks of impaired elders. *Family Relations, 39,* 44-50.

Coward, R. T., Cutler, S. J., & Schmidt, F. E. (1988). Residential differences in marital status and household type among the elderly. In R. Marotz-Baden, C. B. Hennon, &

T. H. Brubaker (Eds.), *Families in rural America: Stress, adaptation, and revitalization* (pp. 104-115). St. Paul, MN: The National Council on Family Relations.

Coward, R. T., Cutler, S. J., & Schmidt, F. E. (1989). Differences in the household composition of elders by age, gender, and area of residence. *The Gerontologist, 29*(6), 814-821.

Coward, R. T., & Dwyer, J. W. (1991a). *Health programs and services for elders in rural America.* Kansas City, MO: University of Missouri, National Resource Center for Rural Elderly.

Coward, R. T., & Dwyer, J. W. (1991b). A longitudinal study of residential differences in the composition of the helping networks of impaired elders. *Journal of Aging Studies, 5*(4), 391-407.

Coward, R. T., Horne, C., & Dwyer, J. W. (1992). Demographic perspectives on gender and family caregiving. In J. W. Dwyer & R. T. Coward (Eds.), *Gender, families, and elder care* (pp. 18-33). Newbury Park, CA: Sage.

Coward, R. T., & Lee, G. R. (Eds.). (1985). *The elderly in rural society.* New York: Springer.

Coward, R. T., Lee, G. R., Dwyer, J. W., & Seccombe, K. (1993). *Old and alone in rural America.* Washington, DC: American Association of Retired Persons (AARP), Public Policy Institute.

Coward, R. T., & Rathbone-McCuan, E. (1985). Delivering health and human services to the elderly in rural society. In R. T. Coward & G. R. Lee (Eds.), *The elderly in rural society: Every fourth elder* (pp. 197-222). New York: Springer.

Cowgill, D. O. (1974). Aging and modernization: A revision of the theory. In J. F. Gubrium (Ed.), *Late life* (pp. 123-146). Springfield, IL: Charles C Thomas.

Crane, D. (1972). *Invisible colleges: Diffusion of knowledge in scientific communities.* Chicago: University of Chicago Press.

Cribier, F. (1980). A European assessment of aged migration. *Research on Aging, 2,* 225-270.

Cruz-Lopez, M., & Pearson, R. E. (1985). The support needs and resources of Puerto Rican elders. *The Gerontologist, 25*(5), 483-487.

Cuba, L. J. (1984). Reorientations of self: Residential identification in Anchorage, Alaska. *Studies in Symbolic Interaction, 5,* 219-237.

Cutler, S. J., & Coward, R. T. (1988). Residence differences in the health status of elders. *Journal of Rural Health, 4*(3), 11-34.

Daniels, T. L., & Lapping, M. (1987). Small town triage: A rural settlement policy for the American Midwest. *Journal of Rural Studies, 3*(3), 273-280.

Dean, A., Kolody, B., & Wood, P. (1990). Effects of social support from various sources on depression in elderly persons. *Journal of Health and Social Behavior, 31,* 148-161.

Deimling, G. T., & Harel, Z. (1984). Social integration and mental health of the aged. *Research on Aging, 6,* 515-527.

Die, A. H., & Seelbach, W. C. (1988). Problems, sources of assistance, and knowledge of services among elderly Vietnamese immigrants. *The Gerontologist, 28*(4), 448-452.

Dorwart, R. A. (1990). Managed mental health care: Myths and realities in the 1990's. *Hospital and Community Psychiatry, 41,* 1087-1091.

Doty, P. (1986). Family care of the elderly: The role of public policy. *Milbank Memorial Fund Quarterly, 64,* 34-75.

Doty, P. (1987). Health status and health services use among older women: An international perspsective. *World Health Organization Statistics Quarterly, 3.*

Doty, P., Liu, K., & Weiner, J. (1985). An overview of long-term care. *Health Care Financing Review, 6,* 69-78.

Douglass, R., & Hickey, T. (1983). Domestic neglect and abuse of the elderly: Research findings and a systems perspective for service delivery planning. In J. I. Kosberg (Ed.), *Abuse and maltreatment of the elderly: Causes and interventions* (pp. 115-133). Littleton, MA: John Wright PSG.

Douglass, R. L., Hickey, T., & Noel, C. (1980). *A study of maltreatment of elderly and other vulnerable adults.* Ann Arbor, MI: Institute of Gerontology, University of Michigan.

Dowd, J. J., & Bengston, V. L. (1978). Aging in minority populations: An examination of the double jeopardy hypothesis. *Journal of Gerontology, 33,* 427-436.

Durenberger, D. (1989). Providing mental health care services to Americans. *American Psychologist, 44,* 1293-1297.

Dwyer, J. W., & Coward, R. T. (1991). A multivariate comparison of the involvement of adult sons versus daughters in the care of impaired parents. *Journals of Gerontology: Social Science, 46*(5), S259-269.

Dwyer, J. W., & Miller, M. K. (1990a). Determinants of primary caregiver stress and burden: Area of residence and the caregiving networks of frail elders. *The Journal of Rural Health, 6*(2), 161-184.

Dwyer, J. W., & Miller, M. K. (1990b). Differences in characteristics of the caregiving network by area of residence: Implications for primary caregiver stress and burden. *Family Relations, 39,* 27-37.

Dychtwald, K. (1989). *Age wave: The challenges and opportunities of an aging America.* Los Angeles: J. P. Tarcher.

Ecosometrics. (1981). *Review of reported differences between the rural and urban elderly: Status, needs, services, and service costs.* Washington, DC: Administration on Aging.

Engels, R. A., & Forstall, R. L. (1985, April). Metropolitan areas dominate growth again. *American Demographics,* pp. 22-26.

Epp, J. (1986). *Achieving health for all: A framework for health promotion.* Ottawa: Minister of Supply and Services Canada.

Erickson, R., Gavin, D., & Cordes, S. (1984, April). *The economic impact on Pennsylvania's hospitals.* University Park, PA: Center for Research, College of Business Administration, The Pennsylvania State University.

Ermann, D. A. (1990). Rural health care: The future of the hospital. *Medical Care Review, 47*(1), 33-73.

Estes, C. L. (1986). Institutional versus community health care of the elderly: The delicate balance of social policy, position paper. *Home Health Services Quarterly, 7,* 113-29.

Estes, C. L., Fox, S., & Mahoney, C. W. (1986). Health care and social policy: Health promotion and the elderly. In K. Dychtwald (Ed.), *Wellness and health promotion for the elderly* (pp. 55-69). Rockville, MD: Aspen Publishers.

Executive director's report. (1987, December). *American Association of Retired Person's News Bulletin,* p. 4.

Fagan, M. (1988). *Attracting retirees for economic development.* Jacksonville, AL: Center for Economic Development, Jacksonville State University.

Ficke, S. C., & Kerschner, H. K. (1990). *Senior economic and enterprise development: A blueprint for action.* White Paper No. 10. Washington, DC: The American Association for International Aging.

Fillenbaum, G. G. (1979). Social context and self-assessments of health among the elderly. *Journal of Health and Social Behavior, 20,* 45-51.

Fischer, L. R., & Eustis, N. N. (in press). Care at home: Family caregivers and home care workers. In E. Kahana & D. Biegel (Eds.), *Family caregiving across the lifespan.* Newbury Park, CA: Sage.

Fischer, L. R., Mueller, D. P., Cooper, P. W., & Chase, R. A. (1989). *Older Minnesotans: What do they need? How do they contribute?* St. Paul, MN: Amherst H. Wilder Foundation.

Fischer, L. R., Mueller, D. P., & Cooper, P. W. (1991). Older volunteers: A discussion of the Minnesota Senior Study. *The Gerontologist, 31,* 183-194.

Fischer, L. R., Mueller, D. P., Lossness, S., & Cooper, P. W. (1990). *Sixty plus in Greater Minnesota.* St. Paul, MN: Amherst H. Wilder Foundation.

Fischer, L. R., with Hoffman, C. (1984). Who cares for the elderly: The dilemma of family support. In M. Lewis & J. Miller (Eds.), *Research in social problems and public policies,* vol. 3, (pp. 169-215). Greenwich, CT: JAI.

Flora, J. A., Jackson, C., & Maccoby, N. (1989). Indicators of societal action to promote physical health. In S. B. Kar (Ed.), *Health promotion indicators and actions* (pp. 118-139). New York: Springer.

Freidson, E. (1961). *Patients' views of medical practice.* New York: Russell Sage Foundation.

Frerichs, R. R., Aneshensel, C. S., Yokopenic, P. A., & Clark, V. (1982). Physical health and depression: An epidemiologic survey. *Preventive Medicine, 11,* 639-646.

Fuguitt, G. V., & S. J. Tordella. (1980). Elderly net migration: The new trend of non-metropolitan population change. *Research on Aging, 2,* 191-204.

Galbraith, M. W. (1986). Elder abuse: An overview. In M. W. Galbraith (Ed.), *Elder abuse: Perspectives on an emerging crisis* (pp. 139-167). Kansas City, MO: Mid-America Congress on Aging.

Galbraith, M. W. (1989). A critical examination of the definitional, methodological, and theoretical problems of elder abuse. In R. Filinson & S. R. Ingman (Eds.), *Elder abuse practice and policy* (pp. 35-42). New York: Human Sciences Press.

Gallagher, R. (1978). Taxis and subsidized programs in rural areas. *Transportation Research Record, 696,* 82-87.

Garrett, M. J. (1991). *Stress experience of elite older persons.* Unpublished doctoral dissertation, University of Nebraska.

George, L. K. (1989). Stress, social support, and depression over the life-course. In K. Markides & C. Cooper (Eds.), *Aging, stress, and health* (pp. 241-267). New York: John Wiley.

Gersten, R. (1990, February). Ailing rural health care: Doctor shortage plagues small towns. *Mankato Free Press.*

Gibbons, J. H. (1991, April). *Rural America at the crossroads: Networking for the future.* U.S. Congress, Office of Technology Assessment, OTA-TCT-471. Washington DC: Government Printing Office.

Gibbons, J. E., Camp, H. J., & Kaiser, M. A. (1991). Patterns of long-term care services for the rural elderly: A community approach. *Human Services in the Rural Environment, 14*(3), 6-11.

Gilbert, G. (1977). *Establishing innovative taxi cab services: A guidebook.* Washington, DC: Department of Transportation.

Glaser, B. J., & Strauss, A. L. (1968). *Time for dying.* Chicago: Aldine.

Glasgow, N. (1980). The older metropolitan migrant as a factor in rural population growth. In A. J. Sofranco & J. D. Williams (Eds.), *Rebirth of rural America: Rural migration in the Midwest.* Ames, IA: Iowa State University, North Central Regional Center for Rural Development.

Glasgow, N. (1988). *The nonmetro elderly: Economic and demographic status.* Report No. 70. Washington, DC: Agriculture and Rural Economy Division, Economic Research Service, U.S. Department of Agriculture.

Glasgow, N. (1990). Attracting retirees as a community development option. *Journal of the Community Development Society, 21*(1), 102-114.

Glasgow, N., & Beale, C. L. (1985). Rural elderly in demographic perspective. *Rural Development Perspectives, 2,* 22-26.

Glasgow, N., & Reeder, R. J. (1990). Economic and fiscal implication of nonmetropolitan retirement migration. *Journal of Applied Gerontology, 9*(4), 433-451.

Golant, S. M., Rudzitis, G., & Daiches, S. (1978). Elderly from United States central cities. *Growth and Change, 9,* 30-35.

Goudy, W. J., & Dobson, C. (1985). Work, retirement, and financial situations of the rural elderly. In R. T. Coward & G. R. Lee (Eds.), *The elderly in rural society: Every fourth elder* (pp. 57-77). New York: Springer.

Gove, W. R., Ortega, S. T., & Style, C. B. (1989). The maturational and role perspectives on aging and self through the adult years: An empirical evaluation. *American Journal of Sociology, 94,* 1117-1145.

Greene, V. L. (1984). Premature institutionalization among the rural elderly. In R. T. Coward & S. M. Cordes (Eds.), *Emerging issues in the delivery of rural health services,* No. 38-9970. Washington, DC: Government Printing Office.

Gröger, B. L. (1983). Growing old without it: The meaning of land in a southern rural community. *Research on Aging, 5*(4), 511-526.

Gurian, B. (1982). Mental health outreach and consultation for the elderly. *Hospital and Community Psychiatry, 33,* 142-147.

Gurland, B., Dean, L., Gurland, R., & Cook, D. (1978). *The dependent elderly of New York City.* New York: Community Council of Greater New York, NY.

Haas, W. H. (1990). *The influence of retirement in-migration on local economic development.* Appalachian Regional Commission Contract 89-48 NC-10269-89-I-302-0327.

Haas, W. H., & Crandall, L. A. (1988). Physician's views of retirement migrants' impact on rural medical practice. *The Gerontologist, 28,* 663-666.

Halpert, B. P. (1988). Volunteer information provider program: A strategy to reach and help rural family caregivers. *The Gerontologist, 28*(2), 256-259.

Hammond, J. (1985). Analysis of county-level data concerning the use of Medicare home health benefits. *Public Health Reports, 100*(1), 48-55.

Hanawalt, B. A. (1986). *The ties that bound: Peasant families in medieval England.* New York: Oxford University Press.

Hansell, S., & White, H. R. (1991). Adolescent drug use, psychological distress, and physical symptoms. *Journal of Health and Social Behavior, 32,* 288-301.

Harrington, C., Newcomer, R. J., & Estes, C. L. (Eds.). (1985). *Long-term care of the elderly: Public policy issues.* Newbury Park, CA: Sage.

Harrington, C., Swan, J. H., & Grant, L. A. (1988). Nursing home bed capacity in the States, 1978-86. *Health Care Financing Review, 9*(4), 81-97.

Haug, M. R., Breslau, N., & Folmar, S. (1989). Coping resources and selective survival in mental health of the elderly. *Research on Aging, 11*, 468-491.

Havens, B. (1985). A long-term care system: A Canadian perspective. In R. L. Kane (Ed.), *The feasibility of a long-term care system: Lessons from Canada* (pp. 19-27). Tampa, FL: University of South Florida.

Havens, B. (1986). Boundary crossing: An organizational challenge for community based long-term care service agencies. In A. O. Pelham & W. F. Clarke (Eds.), *Managing home care for the elderly: Lessons from community based agencies* (pp. 77-98). New York: Springer.

Havens, B. (1987). *Introductory remarks.* Presented at the inter-congress meeting of the research committee on aging of the International Sociological Association, Winnipeg, Manitoba.

Havens, B. (1990a). Home care and day care for the elderly. In R. L. Kane, J. G. Evans, & D. Macfadyen (Eds.), *Improving the health of older people: A world view* (pp. 452-472). New York: Oxford University Press (for WHO).

Havens, B. (1990b). Table 20.1, Summary of research on informal care. In R. L. Kane, J. G. Evans, & D. Macfadyen (Eds.), *Improving the health of older people: A world view* (p. 342). New York: Oxford University Press (for WHO).

Havens, B. (1992a). *Community support programs international perspective: Health care: Canada and the U.S.A.* Paper presented at the National Council on Aging Annual Conference. Washington, DC.

Havens, B. (1992b). Making research relevant to policy. *The Gerontologist, 32*, 273.

Heartland Center for Leadership Development. (1990). *Clues to rural community survival.* Research Report No. 1990-6. Lincoln, NE: Author.

Heaton, T. B. (1981). Geographic distribution of the elderly population: Recent trends. In B. B. Hess (Ed.), *Leading edges: Recent research on social and psychological aging.* Washington, DC: Government Printing Office.

Heaton, T. B., Clifford, W. B., & Fuguitt, G. V. (1984). Temporal shifts in the determinants of young and elderly migration in nonmetropolitan areas. *Social Forces, 60*(1), 41-60.

Heintz, K. M. (1976). *Retirement communities: For adults only.* New Brunswick, NJ: The State University Press of New Jersey.

Heller, P. L., Quesda, G. M., Harvey, D. L., & Warner, L. G. (1981). Familism in rural and urban America: Critique and reconceptualization of a construct. *Rural Sociology, 46*, 446-464.

Henton, J., Cate, R., & Emory, B. (1984). The dependent elderly: Targets for abuse. In W. H. Quinn & G. A. Hughston (Eds.), *Independent aging* (pp. 149-162). Rockville, MD: Aspen.

Hess, B., & Soldo, B. (1985). Husband and wife networks. In W. J. Sauer & R. T. Coward (Eds.), *Social support networks and the care of the elderly* (pp. 67-92). New York: Springer.

Hickey, T., & Douglass, R. L. (1981). Neglect and abuse of older family members: Professionals' perspective and case experiences. *The Gerontologist, 21*(2), 171-176.

Hing, E., & Bloom, B. (1990). *Long-term care for the functionally dependent elderly.* National Center for Health Statistics Vital Health Stat. 13, No. 104.

Hochschild, A. (1973). *The unexpected community.* Berkeley, CA: University of California Press.

248   Aging in Rural America

Hooyman, N. R., & Lustbader, W. (1986). *Taking care: Supporting older people and their families*. New York: Free Press.

Housing Assistance Council (HAC). (1992, January). *The FmHA housing program in fiscal year 1991: "A special year"*. Washington, DC: Author.

Housing Assistance Council (HAC). (1992, February). *Not "investing in the future": An analysis of the administration's fiscal year 1993 FmHA, HUD and Indian Housing Budgets*. Washington, DC: Author.

Hoyer, R. (1988). *Urban and rural home health agencies—Some geographic differences.* Unpublished. Washington, DC: National Association for Home Care.

Human, J., & Wasem, C. (1991). Rural mental health in America. *American Psychologist, 46*, 232-239.

Hutner, M., & Windle, C. (1991). NIMH support of rural mental health. *American Psychologist, 46*, 240-243.

Huttman, E. (1987). Continuum of care. In George L. Maddox (Ed.), *The encyclopedia of aging* (pp. 145-147). New York: Springer.

Idler, E. L., & Kasl, S. V. (1991). Health perceptions and survival: Do global evaluations of health status really predict mortality? *Journal of Gerontology: Social Sciences, 46*, S55-65.

Idler, E. L., Kasl, S. V., & Lemke, J. H. (1990). Self-evaluated health and mortality among the elderly in New Haven, Connecticut, and Iowa and Washington Counties, Iowa, 1982-1986. *American Journal of Epidemiology, 131*, 91-103.

Interagency Committee on Support Services to Seniors (1985). *Policy paper on support services to seniors*. Winnipeg, Manitoba: Manitoba Health.

Inter-University Consortium for Political and Social Research (1990). *Catalogue of data collections: National archive of computerized data on aging*. Ann Arbor, MI: Author.

Jackson, D. J., Longino, C. F., Jr., Zimmerman, R. S., & Bradsher, J. E. (1991). Environmental adjustments to declining functional ability: Residential mobility and living arrangements. *Research on Aging, 13*, 289-309.

Jackson, J. S. (1988). Future directions in research on aging black populations. In J. S. Jackson (Ed.), *The black American elderly: Research on physical and psychosocial health* (pp. 369-372). New York: Springer.

John, R. (1985). Service needs and support networks of elderly Native Americans: Family, friends, and social service agencies. In W. A. Peterson & J. Quadano (Eds.), *Social bonds in later life* (pp. 229-247). Newbury Park, CA: Sage.

Johnson, C. L., & Barer, B. M. (1990). Families and networks among older inner-city Blacks. *The Gerontologist, 30*(6), 726-733.

Johnson, D. R., & Ortega S. T. (1992). *Economic decline and psychosocial impairment: Methodology report*. Lincoln, NE: Department of Sociology, University of Nebraska, Lincoln.

Johnson, T. (1986) Critical issues in the definition of elder mistreatment. In K. A. Pillemer & R. S. Wolf (Eds.), *Elder abuse: Conflict in the family* (pp.167-196). Dover, MA: Auburn House.

Johnson, T. P., Hendricks, J., Turner, H. B., Stallones, L., Marx, M. B., & Garrity, T. F. (1988). Social networks and depression among the elderly: Metropolitan/nonmetropolitan comparisons. *Journal of Rural Health, 4*(3), 71-81.

Joseph, A. E., & Cloutier, D. S. (1990). A framework for modeling the consumption of health services by the rural elderly. *Social Science and Medicine, 30*(1), 45-52.

Judd, C. M., & McClelland, G. H. (1989). *Data analysis: A model-comparison approach* (pp. 482-483). Orlando, FL: Harcourt Brace Jovanovich.

Kaiser, M. A., Camp, H. J., & Gibbons, J. (1987). Services for the rural elderly. *Journal of Gerontological Social Work, 11*(1/2), 25-45.

Kane, J. (1990). *Rural America's elderly: January 1979-April 1990.* QB 90-74. Beltsville, MD: Department of Agriculture, National Agricultural Library.

Kane, R. A., & Kane R. L. (1986). *Health care for the elderly in the year 2000: A profile of service needs in the year 2000.* Paper presented at the Health Care for the Elderly in the Year 2000 symposium, Victoria, British Columbia.

Kane, R. L. (1990). Introduction to Part III Health Care. In R. L. Kane, J. G. Evans, & D. Macfadyen (Eds.), *Improving the health of older people: A world view* (pp. 341-45). New York: Oxford University Press (for WHO).

Kansas governor's task force on the future of rural communities. (1988). Topeka, KS: Community Development Division, Kansas Department of Commerce.

Kar, S. B. (1989). Introduction: Health promotion action indicators. In S. B. Kar (Ed.), *Health promotion indicators and actions* (pp. 1-22). New York: Springer.

Kathol, R. G., & Petty, F. (1981). Relationship of depression to medical illness. *Journal of Affective Disorders, 3,* 111-121.

Keller, P., & Murray, J. (1982). *Handbook of rural community mental health.* New York: Human Sciences Press.

Kelman, H. R., & Thoman, C. (1987). *Social support and social policy.* Paper presented at the European Regional Meeting of the International Association on Gerontology, Brighton, UK.

Kempe, C. H., Silverman, F. N., Steele, B. F., Droegemueller, W., & Silver, H. K. (1962). The battered-child syndrome. *Journal of the American Medical Association, 181,* 17-24.

Kemper, P., Applebaum, R., & Harrigan, M. (1987). Community care demonstrations: What have we learned? *Health Care Financing Review, 4,* 87-100.

Kennedy, G., Kelman, H. R., & Thomas, C. (1990). The emergence of depressive symptoms in late life: The importance of declining health and increasing disability. *Journal of Community Health, 5,* 93-104.

Kerschner, H. K. (1991, November). *The incumbent versus the candidate paradigm of productive aging.* Paper presented at the meeting of the Gerontological Society of America, San Francisco, California.

Kerschner, H. K., & Ficke, S. C. (1990). *Senior enterprise development: A strategy for moving aging into the economic mainstream.* White Paper No. 9. Washington, DC: The American Association for International Aging.

Kiefer, C. W., Kim, S., Choi, C., Kim, L., Kim, B. L., Shon, S., & Kim, T. (1985). Adjustment problems of Korean American elderly. *The Gerontologist, 25*(5), 477-482.

Kii, T. (1984). Asians. In E. Palmore (Ed.), *Handbook of the aged in the United States* (pp. 201-217). Westport, CT; Greenwood Press.

Kim, P. K. (1981). The low income elderly: Under-served victims of public inequity. In P. K. Kim & C. Wilson (Eds.), *Toward mental health of the rural elderly.* Washington, DC: University Press of America.

Kivett, V. R. (1990). Older rural women. *Journal of Rural Community Psychology, 11,* 83-102.

Kivett, V. R. (1991). Centrality of the grandfather role among older black and white males. *The Journal of Gerontology: Social Sciences, 46*(5), S250-258.

Kivett, V. R., & McCulloch, B. J. (1989). *Support networks of the very-old: Caregivers and carereceivers.* Final Report, AARP Andrus Foundation. Greensboro, NC: University of North Carolina at Greensboro.

Kivett, V. R., & Scott, J. P. (1979). The rural bypassed elderly: Perspectives on status and needs (The Caswell study). Tech. Bull. No. 260. Greensboro, NC: North Carolina Agricultural Research Service.

Krause, N., & Jay, G. (1991). Stress, social support, and negative interaction in later life. *Research on Aging, 13,* 333-363.

Krishan, I., Drummond, D. C., Naessens, J. M., Nobrega, F. T., & Smoldt, R. K. (1985). Impact of increased physician supply on use of health services: A longitudinal analysis in rural Minnesota. *Public Health Reports, 100,* 379-386.

Krout, J. A. (1983a). *The organization, operation, and programming of senior centers: A national survey.* Final report to the AARP Andrus Foundation. Washington, DC: American Association of Retired Persons (AARP).

Krout, J. A. (1983b). *The rural elderly: An annotated bibliography of social science research.* Westport, CT: Greenwood Press.

Krout, J. A. (1986). *The aged in rural America.* Westport, CT: Greenwood Press.

Krout, J. A. (1987). Rural-urban differences in senior center activities and services. *The Gerontologist, 27,* 92-97.

Krout, J. A. (1988). Rural versus urban differences in elderly parents' contact with their children. *The Gerontologist, 28,* 198-203.

Krout, J. A. (1989). *Senior centers in America.* Westport, CT: Greenwood Press.

Krout, J. A. (1991, March) Rural senior centers in the 1980s. *The Rural Elderly Networker, 3*(2), p. 3-5.

Kushman, J. E., & Freeman, B. K. (1986). Service consciousness and service knowledge among older Americans. *International Journal of Aging and Human Development, 23*(3), 217-37.

Kyle, B (1987a). *Support Services to Seniors program.* Paper presented at the 1987 inter-congress meeting of the research committee on aging of the International Sociological Association, Winnipeg, Manitoba.

Kyle, B. (1987b). *Support Services to Seniors.* Paper presented at Westman Regional Council meeting. Brandon, Manitoba.

Kyle, B. (1991). *The continuum of care.* Paper presented at Housing for Seniors: The challenge in Northern and remote communities, Yellowknife, Northwest Territories.

Largo, A. M., & Burkhardt, J. E. (1980). Predictive models of the demand for public transportation services among the elderly. *Transportation Research Record, 784,* 21-27.

Lapping, M. B., Daniels, T. L., & Keller, J. W. (1989). *Rural planning and development in the United States.* New York: Guilford Press.

Lassey, W. R., & Lassey, M. L. (1985). The physical health status of the rural elderly. In R. T. Coward & G. R. Lee (Eds.), *The elderly in rural society* (pp. 83-104). New York: Springer.

Lau, E. E., & Kosberg, J. E. (1979, September). Abuse of the elderly by informal care providers. *Aging,* pp. 10-15.

Lau, R. R., & Ware, J. (1981). Refinements in the measurement of health-specific locus-of-control beliefs. *Medical Care, 19*(2), 1147-1158.

Lawton, M. P., Moss, M., & Kleban, M. H. (1984). Marital status, living arrangements, and the well-being of older people. *Research on Aging, 6,* 323-345.

Layaco, C. G. (1984). Hispanics. In E. B. Palmore (Ed.), *Handbook on the aged in the United States* (pp. 253-267). Westport, CT: Greenwood Press.

Leanse, J., & Wagner, L. (1975). *Senior centers: A report of senior group programs in America.* Washington, DC: National Council on the Aging.

Lee, G. R. (1979). Children and the elderly: Interaction and morale. *Research on Aging, 1,* 335-360.

Lee, G. R. (1980). Kinship in the seventies: A decade review of research and theory. *Journal of Marriage and the Family, 42,* 923-934.

Lee, G. R. (1985). Kinship and social support of the elderly: The case of the United States. *Aging and Society, 5,* 19-38.

Lee, G. R. (1988). Kinship ties among older people: The residence factor. In R. Marotz-Baden, C. B. Hennon, & T. H. Brubaker (Eds.), *Families in rural America: Stress, adaptation, and revitalization* (pp. 176-182). St. Paul, MN: National Council on Family Relations.

Lee, G. R., & Cassidy, M. L. (1985). Family and kin relations of the rural elderly. In R. T. Coward & G. R. Lee (Eds.), *The elderly in rural society: Every fourth elder* (pp. 151-169). New York: Springer.

Lee, G. R., Dwyer, J. W., & Coward, R. T. (1990). Residential location and proximity to children among impaired elderly parents. *Rural Sociology, 55*(4), 579-589.

Lee, G. R., & Ishii-Kuntz, M. (1987). Social interaction, loneliness, and emotional well-being among the elderly. *Research on Aging, 9,* 459-482.

Lee, G. R., & Whitbeck, L. B. (1987). Residential location and social relations among older persons. *Rural Sociology, 52,* 89-97.

Lichter, D. T., Fuguitt, G. V., Heaton, T. B., & Clifford, W. B. (1981). Components of change in the residential concentrations of the elderly population: 1950-1975. *Journal of Gerontology, 36,* 480-489.

Litwak, E. (1985). *Helping the elderly: The complementary roles of informal networks and formal systems.* New York: Guilford Press.

Litwak, E., & Longino, C. F. (1987). Migration patterns among the elderly: A developmental perspective. *The Gerontologist, 27,* 266-272.

Liu, K., Manton, K., & Liu, B. M. (1985). Home care expenses for the disabled elderly. *Health Care Financing Review, 7,* 51-8.

Liu, K., Manton, K., & Liu, B. M. (1986). Home care expenses for non-institutionalized elderly with activities of daily living and instrumental activities of daily living limitations. *Health Care Financing Review, 8,* 241-5.

Liu, W. T. (1986a). Culture and social support. *Research on Aging, 8*(1), 57-83.

Liu, W. T. (1986b). Health services for Asian elderly. *Research on Aging, 8*(1), 156-175.

Lohmann, R. A. (1982). Comprehensive what? Coordination of whom? Rural AAAs and the planning mandate. *Journal of Applied Gerontology, 1,* 126-140.

Long, L. H., & DeAre, D. (1980). *Migration to nonmetropolitan areas: Appraising the trend and reasons for moving.* Special demographic analyses, CDS-80-2. Washington DC: Bureau of the Census.

Long, L. H., & DeAre, D. (1988). U.S. population redistribution: A perspective on the nonmetropolitan turnaround. *Population and Development Review, 14,* 433-450.

Longino, C. F., Jr. (1979). Going home: Aged return migration in the United States, 1965-1970. *Journal of Gerontology, 34,* 736-745.

Longino, C. F., Jr. (1980). Residential relocation of older people: Metropolitan and non-metropolitan. *Research on Aging, 2,* 205-216.

Longino, C. F., Jr. (1982). Changing aged nonmetropolitan migration patterns, 1955 to 1960 and 1965 to 1970. *Journal of Gerontology, 37*, 228-234.

Longino, C. F., Jr. (1988a). The gray peril mentality and the impact of retirement migration. *The Journal of Applied Gerontology, 7*, 448-455.

Longino, C. F., Jr. (1988b). Who are the oldest-old? *The Gerontologist, 28*, 515-523.

Longino, C. F., Jr. (1990). Geographic mobility and family caregiving in nonmetropolitan America: Three-decade evidence from the U.S. census. *Family Relations, 39*, 38-43.

Longino, C. F., Jr. (1992a). Internal migration. In E. F. Borgatta & M. L. Borgatta (Eds.), *Encyclopedia of sociology*. New York: Macmillan.

Longino, C. F., Jr. (1992b). Where retirees prefer to live. In A. Monk (Ed.), *Columbia handbook on retirement*. New York: Columbia University Press.

Longino, C. F., Jr., & Crown, W. H. (1989). The migration of old money. *American Demographics, 11*, 28-31.

Longino, C. F., Jr., & Crown, W. H. (1990). Retirement migration and interstate income transfers. *The Gerontologist, 30*, 784-789.

Longino, C. F., Jr., Jackson, D. J., Zimmerman, R. S., & Bradsher, J. E. (1991). The second move: Health and geographic mobility. *Journal of Gerontology: Social Sciences, 46*, S218-S224.

Longino, C. F., Jr., & Serow, W. J. (1992). Regional differences in the characteristics of elderly return migrants. *Journal of Gerontology: Social Sciences, 47*, S38-S43.

Longino, C. F., Jr., & Smith, K. J. (1991). Black retirement migration in the United States. *Journal of Gerontology: Social Sciences, 46*, S125-S132.

Longino, C. F., Jr., Wiseman, R. F., Biggar, J. C., & Flynn, C. B. (1984). Aged nonmetropolitan migration patterns over three census decades. *Journal of Gerontology, 39*, 721-729.

Lubben, J. E., Weiler, P. G., Chi, I., & De Jong, F. (1988). Health promotion for the rural elderly. *Journal of Rural Health, 4*(3), 85-96.

Luke, J. S., Ventriss, C., Reed, B. J., & Reed, C. M. (1988). *Managing economic development*. San Francisco: Jossey Bass.

Maclean, U. (1985). Women and health in Europe: The scope and limits of epidemiology. *International Journal of Health Services, 15*, 665-76.

Mancini, J. A. (Ed.). (1989). *Aging parents and adult children*. Lexington, MA: Lexington.

Mancini, J. A., & Blieszner, R. S. (1989). Aging parents and adult children: Research themes in intergenerational relations. *Journal of Marriage and the Family, 51*, 275-290.

Manitoba Health (1992). Quality health for Manitobans—the action plan: A strategy to assure the future of Manitoba's health services system. Winnipeg: Government of Manitoba.

Manitoba Housing. (1991). Public housing—seniors. Winnipeg: Government of Manitoba.

Manson, S. M. (1989). Long-term care in American Indian communities: Issues for planning and research. *The Gerontologist, 29*(1), 38-44.

Markides, K. S. (1986). Minority status, aging, and mental health. *International Journal of Aging and Human Development, 23*(4), 285-300.

Markides, K. S., Boldt, J. S., & Ray, L. A. (1986). Sources of helping and intergenerational solidarity: A three-generations study of Mexican Americans. *Journal of Gerontology, 41*(4), 506-511.

Markides, K. S., & Mindel, C. H. (1987). *Aging and ethnicity.* Newbury Park, CA: Sage.

Marriott Senior Living Services and U.S. Administration on Aging. (1991). *Marriott seniors volunteerism study.* Washington, DC: Marriott Senior Living Services.

Marris, P., & Rein, M. (1973). *Dilemmas of social reform.* Chicago: Aldine.

Martin, E. P., & Martin, J. M. (1978). *The black extended family.* Chicago: University of Chicago Press.

Mattson, G., & Burke, A. T. (1989). Small towns, political culture and policy innovation. *Journal of Planning Literature, 4*(4), 397-412.

Matthews, A. M., & Vanden Heuvel, A. (1986). Conceptual and methodological issues in research on aging in rural areas. *Canadian Journal on Aging, 5*(1), 49-60.

McClain, J. W., Leibowitz, J. M., Lunt, K., Thorson, J., & Foster, B. (1992). *Building a focal point in your rural community: A final report.* Omaha, NE: University of Nebraska for the Nebraska Department on Aging.

McLaughlin, Diane K., & Jensen, Leif. (1991). *Poverty among older Americans: The problem of the nonmetropolitan elderly.* Working Paper No. 1991-22. University Park, PA.: Population Issues Research Center, Pennsylvania State University.

Meddin, J., & Vaux, A. (1988). Subjective well-being among the rural elderly population. *International Journal of Aging & Human Development, 27*(3), 193-205.

Merton, R. K. (1973). Multiple discoveries as strategic research site. In N. W. Storer (Ed.), *Robert K. Merton: The sociology of science: Theoretical and empirical investigations* (pp. 371-382). Chicago: University of Chicago Press.

Metropolitan Life Insurance Company. (1991, July-September). Tuberculosis increases in the United States. *Statistical Bulletin, 72*(3), 10-18.

Meyer, J. W., Lusky, R. A., & Wright, A. (1991). Title III services: Variations in the use within a state. *Journal of Applied Gerontology, 10*(2), 140-56.

Miller, M. K., Stokes, C. S., & Clifford, W. B. (1987). A comparison of the rural-urban mortality differential for deaths from all causes, cardiovascular disease and cancer. *Journal of Rural Health, 3*(2), 23-34.

Mindel, C. H. (1983). The elderly in minority families. In T. H. Brubaker (Ed.), *Family relationships in later life* (pp. 193-208). Beverly Hills, CA: Sage.

Minkler, M. (1985). Building supportive ties and sense of community among inner-city elderly: The Tenderloin Senior Outreach Project. *Health Education Quarterly, 12*(4), 303-314.

Minkler, M., & Checkoway, B. (1988). Ten principles for geriatric health promotion. *Health Promotion, 3*(3), 277-285.

Minkler, M., & Pasick, R. J. (1986). Health promotion and the elderly: A critical perspective on the past and future. In K. Dychtwald (Ed.), *Wellness and health promotion for the elderly* (pp. 39-54). Rockville, MD: Aspen.

Missouri Division of Aging. (1992). *Rural-urban comparisons of hotline calls.* Unpublished data.

Montero, D. (1979). Disengagement and aging among the issei. In D. E. Gelfand & A. J. Kutzik (Eds.), *Ethnicity and aging: Theory, research, and policy* (pp. 193-205). New York: Springer.

Montgomery, R. J. V. (1992). Gender differences in patterns of child-parent caregiving relationships. In J. W. Dwyer & R. T. Coward (Eds.), *Gender, families, and elder care* (pp. 65-83). Newbury Park, CA: Sage.

Mor-Barak, M. E., Miller, L. S., & Syme, L. S. (1991). Social networks, life events, and health of the poor, frail elderly: A longitudinal study of the buffering versus the direct effect. *Family Community Health, 14,* 1-13.

Morginstin, B. (1987, Winter). Long-term care insurance in Israel. *Ageing International,* 10-12.

Morris, J. N., Morris, S., & Sherwood, S. (1984). Assessment of informal and formal support systems in high risk elderly populations. In C. V. Granter & A. E. Gresham (Eds.), *Functional assessment in rehabilitation medicine* (pp. 223-253). Baltimore, MD: Williams & Watkins.

Moschis, G. (1987). *Consumer socialization: A life-cycle perspective.* Lexington, MA: Lexington Book.

Murray, J., & Keller, P. (1991). Psychology and rural America: Current status and future direction. *American Psychologist, 41,* 220-231.

National Center for Health Statistics (1979). *Current estimates from the health interview survey, 1978.* Vital and Health Statistics Series 13, No. 130. Washington, DC: Government Printing Office.

National Center for Policy Analysis (1990). *The elderly: People the supply side forgot.* The National Center for Policy Analysis Report No. 135. Dallas: Author.

National Governors Association (NGA). (1988). *State long-term care reform.* Washington, DC: Center for Policy Research.

National Indian Council on Aging (1984). Indian and Alaskan natives. In E. Palmore (Ed.), *Handbook on the aged in the United States* (pp. 269-276). Westport, CT: Greenwood Press.

Nebraska Department on Aging (NDoA). (1991a). *Building a focal point in your rural community.* Lincoln, NE: Author.

Nebraska Department on Aging (NCoA). (1991b). *Development of rural senior centers as community focal points.* Lincoln, NE: Author.

Nelson, B. O., McRae, J., & Baldwin, G. J. (1988). Using working agreements to promote interorganizational cooperation in rural communities. *Human Services in the Rural Environment, 12*(2), 5-9.

Nelson, G. (1980). Social services to the urban and rural aged: The experiences of area agencies on aging. *The Gerontologist, 20,* 200-207.

New York State Senate. (1980). *Old age and ruralism: A case of double jeopardy. Report on the rural elderly.* Albany, NY: New York State Senate.

Newcomer, R. J., Lawton, M. P., & Byerts, T. O. (1986). *Housing an aging society.* New York: Van Nostrand Reinhold.

Newhouse, J., & McCauley, W. J. (1987). Use of informal care by rural elders. *Family Relations, 36*(4), 456-460.

Noack, H. (1987). Concepts of health and health promotion. In T. Abelin, Z. J. Brzezinski, & V. D. L. Carstairs (Eds.), *Measurement in health promotion and protection* (pp. 5-28). WHO Regional Publications, European Series No. 22. Copenhagen: WHO Regional Office for Europe.

Nyman, J. A., Sen, A., Chan, B. Y., & Commins, P. P. (1991). Urban/rural differences in home health patients and services. *The Gerontologist, 31,* 457-466.

O'Malley, H., Bergman, J., Segars, H., Perex, R., Mitchell V., & Kruepfel, G. (1979). *Elder abuse in Massachusetts: A survey of professionals and paraprofessionals.* Boston: Legal Research and Services for the Elderly.

Ontario Advisory Council on Senior Citizens (OACSC). (1980). *Toward an understanding of the rural elderly.* Toronto, Ontario: Queen's Printer.

Oregon Senior Services Division (in press). *Residential care facilities assisted living.* Administrative Rule No. 4.

Ortega, S. T., & Johnson, D. R. (1990). *Urban/rural differences in the structure and consequences of social support.* Paper presented at the International Sociological Association meetings, Madrid, Spain.

Osako, M. M., & Liu, W. T. (1986). Intergenerational relations and the aged among Japanese Americans. *Research on Aging, 8*(1), 128-155.

Osgood, M. H. (1977). Rural and urban attitudes toward welfare. *Social Work, 22,* 41-47.

Palmore, E. B. (Ed.). (1984). *Handbook on the aged in the United States.* Westport, CT: Greenwood Press.

Parks, A. G. (1988). *Black elderly in rural America: A comprehensive study.* Bristol, IN: Wyndham Hall.

Passuth, P. M., & Bengtson, V. L. (1988). Sociological theories of aging: Current perspectives and future directions. In J. E. Birren & V. L Bengtson (Eds.), *Emergent theories of aging* (pp. 333-355). New York: Springer.

Patton, L. (1989). Setting the rural health services research agenda: The congressional perspective. *Health Services Research, 23*(6), 1005-1051.

Payne, B., & Bull, C. N. (1977). *Critical issues in volunteer satisfaction.* Paper presented at the Gerontological Society Meeting, San Francisco.

Paz, J., & Applewhite, S. R. (1988). Empowerment: Strengthening the natural support network of the Hispanic rural elderly. In S. R. Applewhite (Ed.), *Hispanic elderly in transition: Theory, research, policy and practice* (pp. 143-155). Westport, CT: Greenwood Press.

Pearlin, L., Lieberman, M., Menaghan, E., & Mullen, J. (1981). The stress process. *Journal of Health and Social Behavior, 22,* 543-552.

Pedrick-Cornell, C., & Gelles, R. J. (1982, July). Elderly abuse: The status of current knowledge. *Family Relations, 31,* 457-465.

Penning, M. J., Blandford, A. A., & Chappell, N. L. (1991). *Outcome evaluation of the Discover Choices Community Program.* Winnipeg, Manitoba: Centre on Aging, University of Manitoba.

Petchers, M. K., & Milligan, S. E. (1988). Access to health care in a black urban elderly population. *The Gerontologist, 28,* 213-217.

Peterson, W. (1975). *Population.* New York: Macmillan.

Phillips, L. R. (1989). Issues involved in identifying and intervening in elder abuse. In R. Filinson & S. R. Ingman (Eds.), *Elder abuse practice and policy* (pp. 86-93). New York: Human Sciences Press.

Piazza, J. (1989). Toward health: A staff learns to use mentally ill clients, families and communities as advisors. *Clinical Social Work Journal, 17,* 259-270.

Pifer, A. (1986). The public policy response. In A. Pifer & L. Bronte (Eds.), *Our aging society: Paradox and promise* (pp. 391-413). New York: W. W. Norton.

Pifer, A., & Bronte, L. (Eds.). (1986). *Our aging society: Paradox and promise.* New York: W. W. Norton.

Pitts, R., & Woodside, A. (1984). *Personal values and consumer psychology.* Lexington, MA: Lexington Books.

Popper, D. E., & Popper, F. (1987). The great plains from dust to dust. *Planning, 55*(12), 572-577.

Powell, F. C., & Thorson, J. A. (1989). *Elderly blacks on Omaha's Near North Side: Their health status, utilization of services, and attitudes.* A technical report prepared for the Eastern Nebraska Office on Aging and the Charles Drew Health Foundation. Omaha, NE: Department of Gerontology, University of Nebraska at Omaha.

Powell, F. C., & Thorson, J. A. (1991). *Incidence of functionally impaired elderly: Comparing ENOA samples with a rural sample.* A technical report prepared for the Eastern Nebraska Office on Aging and the University of Nebraska Center for Public Affairs Research. Omaha, NE: Department of Gerontology, University of Nebraska at Omaha.

Prehn, J. W. (1986). Migration. In *The encyclopedic dictionary of sociology* (3rd ed.). Guilford, CT: Dushkin.

President's National Advisory Commission on Rural Poverty. (1967, September). *The people left behind.* Washington, DC: Author.

Public transportation coalition building. (1989, March). Draft: A Multi-State Technical Assistance Project, American Association of State Highway and Transportation Officials.

Quinn, M. J., & Tomita, S. K. (1986). *Elder abuse and neglect—Causes, diagnoses, and intervention strategies.* New York: Springer.

Rakowski, W. (1992). Disease prevention and health promotion with older adults. In M. G. Ory, R. P. Abeles, & P. D. Lipman (Eds.), *Aging, health, and behavior* (pp. 239-275). Newbury Park, CA: Sage.

Rappaport, J. (1981). In praise of paradox: A social policy of empowerment over prevention. *American Journal of Community Psychology, 9*(1), 1-25.

Rappaport, J. (1987). Terms of empowerment/exemplars of prevention: Toward a theory for community psychology. *American Journal of Community Psychology, 15*(2), 121-148.

Raskind, M. A. (1989). Organic mental disorders, In E. Busse & D. Blazer (Eds.), *Geriatric psychiatry* (pp. 313-368). Washington, DC: American Psychiatric Press.

Rathbone-McCuan, E. (1980). Elderly victims of family violence and neglect. *Social Casework, 61,* 296-304.

Rathbone-McCuan, E. (1981). A step toward integrated health and mental health planning for the rural elderly. In C. P. Wilson & P. K. Kim (Eds.), *Toward mental health of rural elderly* (pp. 257-273). Washington, DC: University Press of America.

Rathbone-McCuan, E., & Bricker-Jenkins, M. (1992). A general framework for elder self-neglect. In E. Rathbone-McCuan & D. Fabian (Eds.), *Self-neglecting elders: A clinical dilemma* (pp. 13-24). New York: Auburn House.

Rathbone-McCuan, E., & Fabian, D. (1992). *Self-neglecting elders: A clinical dilemma.* New York: Auburn House.

Rathbone-McCuan, E., & Hashimi, J. (1982). *Isolated elders: Health and social intervention.* Rockville, MD: Aspen.

Redfoot, D., & Gaberlavage, G. (1991, Summer-Fall). Housing for older Americans: Sustaining the dream. *Generations,* pp. 35-38.

Reed, B. J., & Paulsen, L. (1990). Small towns lack capacity for successful development efforts.*Rural Development Perspectives, 6*(3), 26-30.

Regnier, V. (1976). Neighborhoods as service systems. In M. P. Lawton, R. J. Newcomer, & T. O. Byerts (Eds.), *Community planning for an aging society: Designing services and facilities* (pp. 240-257). Stroudsburg, PA: Dowden, Hutchinson and Ross.

Reitzes, D. C., Mutran, E., & Pope, H. (1991). Location and well-being among retired men. *Journal of Gerontology, 46,* 195-203.

Ries, P., & Brown, S. (1991, 21 May). *Disability and health: Characteristics of persons by limitation of activity and assessed health status, 1984-88.* National Center for Health Statistics Advance Data, No. 197.

Rimmer, L. (1983). The economics of work and caring. In J. Finch & D. Groves (Eds.), *A labour of love: Women, work, and caring* (pp. 131-147). London: Routledge & Kegan Paul.

Robinson, R., & Lovelock, C. (1979). *Marketing public transportation.* Chicago: American Marketing Association.

Rogers, A. (1990). Return migration to region of birth among retirement-age persons in the United States. *Journal of Gerontology: Social Sciences, 45,* S128-S134.

Rogers, A., & Watkins, J. F. (1987). General versus elderly interstate migration and population redistribution in the United States. *Research on Aging, 9,* 483-529.

Rogler, L. H., & Coony, R. S. (1991). Puerto Rican families in New York City: Intergenerational processes. *Marriage and Family Review, 16*(3 & 4), 331-349.

Rosenberg, M. (1965). *Society and the adolescent self-image.* Princeton, NJ: Princeton University Press.

Rosenbloom, S. (1988). The mobility needs of the elderly. In *Transportation Research Board Special Report, No. 218* (pp. 21-71). Washington, DC: Department of Transportation.

Rosow, I. (1967). *Social integration of the aged.* New York: Free Press.

Rowland, D., & Lyons, B. (1989). Triple jeopardy: Rural, poor and uninsured. *Health Services Research, 23*(6), 975-1004.

Rowles, G. (1990). Place attachment among the small town elderly. *Journal of Rural Community Psychology, 11,* 103-120.

Rowles, G. D. (1983). Between worlds: A relocation dilemma for the Appalachian elderly. *International Journal of Aging and Human Development, 17,* 301-314.

Rowles, G. D., & Watkins, J. F. (1991). *Change in the mountains: Elderly migration and population dynamics in Appalachia.* Lexington, KY: Sanders-Brown Center on Aging.

Rubin, S. S. (1986). *Family caregivers: The invisible network of long-term care.* New York: Unitarian Universalist Service Committee.

Rundall, T. G., & Evashwick, C. (1982). Social networks and help-seeking among the elderly. *Research on Aging, 4,* 205-225.

Rural conditions and trends. (1990). Economic Research Service. Washington, DC: Department of Agriculture, *1*(1).

Salmon, M. A., Nelson, G. M., & Gralen-Rous, S. (1991, November). *The continuum of care revisited: A rural perspective.* Paper presented at the National Gerontological Society of America Conference, San Francisco.

Sauer, W. J., & Coward, R. T. (Eds.). *Social support networks and the care of the elderly: Theory, research, and practice.* New York: Springer.

Scheidt, R., & Norris-Baker, C. (1990). A transactional approach to environmental stress among older residents of rural communities: Introduction to a special issue. *Journal of Rural Community Psychology, 11,* 5-30.

Schneider, M. J., Chapman, D. D., & Voth, D. E. (1985). Senior center participation: A two-stage approach to impact evaluation. *The Gerontologist, 25*(2), 194-199.

Schooler, K. K. (1975). A comparison of rural and non-rural elderly on selected variables. In R. C. Atchley & T. O. Byert (Eds.), *Rural environments and aging* (pp. 27-42). Washington DC: Gerontological Society.

Schulz, J. H. (1992). *The economics of aging* (5th ed). Dover, MA: Auburn House.

Schwab, J. J., Bell, R. A., Warheit, G., & Schwab, R. B. (1979). *Social order and mental health.* New York: Brunner/Mazel.

Schweitzer, S. O. (1989). *UCLA Passport to Health: UCLA Medicare, health promotion and disease prevention demonstration.* UCLA School of Public Health, Los Angeles.

Scott, J. P., & Roberto, K. (1987). Informal supports of older adults: A rural-urban comparison. *Family Relations, 36*(4), 444-449.

Scott, J. P., & Roberto, K. (1988). Informal supports of older adults: A rural-urban comparison. In R. Marotz-Baden, C. B. Hennon, & T. H. Brubaker (Eds.), *Families in rural America: Stress, adaptation, and revitalization* (pp. 183-191). St. Paul, MN: National Council on Family Relations.

Seeman, T. E., Kaplan, G. A., Knudsen, L., Cohen, R., & Guralnik, J. (1987). Social network ties and mortality among the elderly in the Alameda County Study. *American Journal of Epidemiology, 126,* 714-723.

Segall, A. (1983). *Interview schedule, 1983 Winnipeg area study.* Winnipeg: Department of Sociology, University of Manitoba.

Select Committee on Aging, U.S. House of Representatives. (1981). *Elder abuse: An examination of a hidden problem.* Washington, DC: Government Printing Office.

Senate Special Committee on Aging with American Association of Retired Persons (1987-8). *Aging America: Trends and projections.* Washington, DC: Senate Special Committee on Aging.

Sengstock, M. C., & Hwalek, M. (1985). *Comprehensive index of elder abuse.* Detroit, MI: Wayne State University.

Sengstock, M., Hwalek, M., & Moshier, S. (1986). A comprehensive index for assessing abuse and neglect of the elderly. In M. W. Galbraith (Ed.), *Elder abuse: Perspectives on an emerging crisis* (pp. 41-74). Kansas City, MO: Mid-America Congress on Aging.

Serow, W. J. (1978). Return migration of the elderly in the USA: 1955-1960 and 1965-1970. *Journal of Gerontology, 33,* 288-295.

Serow, W. J., & Charity, D. A. (1988). Return migration of the elderly in the United States: Recent trends. *Research on Aging, 10,* 155-168.

Serow, W. J., Charity, D. A., Fournier, G. M., & Rasmussen, D. W. (1986). Cost of living differentials and elderly interstate migration. *Research on Aging, 8,* 317-328.

Serow, W. J., & Haas, W. H. (1992). Measuring the economic impact of retirement migration: The case of Western North Carolina. *Journal of Applied Gerontology, 11*(2), 200-215.

Serow, W. J., & Sly, D. F. (1988). The demography of current and future aging cohorts. In Committee on an Aging Society (Ed.), *America's aging: The social and built environment in the older society* (pp. 42-102). Washington, DC: National Academy Press.

Severinghaus, J. (1989). *Economic expansion using retiree income: A workbook for rural Washington communities.* Pullman, WA: Rural Economic Assistance Program, Washington State University.

Shanas, E. (1979). The family as a social support system in old age. *The Gerontologist, 19*, 169-74.

Shanas, E. (1980). Older people and their families: The new pioneers. *Journal of Marriage and the Family, 42*, 9-18.

Shanas, E., & Maddox, G. L. (1985). Health, health resources, and the utilization of care. In R. H. Binstock & E. Shanas (Eds.), *Handbook of aging and the social sciences* (2nd ed.) (pp. 697-726). New York: Van Nostrand Reinhold.

Shane, P. (1987). Linkages between the mental health and aging systems from the perspective of the aging network. In E. Lurie & J. Swan (Eds.) *Serving the mentally ill elderly* (pp. 179-200). Lexington, MA: Lexington Books.

Shapiro, E. (1986). Patterns and predictors of home care use of the elderly when need is the sole basis for admission. *Home Health Care Services Quarterly, 7*, 29-44.

Shapiro, E. (1987). *Multidisciplinary health assessment of the elderly in Manitoba, Canada.* Paper presented at International Work Group meetings on multidisciplinary health assessment of the elderly. Goteborg, Sweden.

Shapiro, E., & Roos, L. L. (1984). Using health care: Rural/urban differences among the Manitoba Elderly. *The Gerontologist, 24*(3), 270-274.

Sherbourne, C. D., & Hays, R. D. (1990). Marital status, social support, and health transitions in chronic disease patients. *Journal of Health and Social Behavior, 31*, 328-343.

Siddharthan, K., & Sowers-Hoag, K. (1989). Elders' attributes and access to health care: A comparison of Cuban immigrants and native-born Americans. *Journal of Applied Gerontology, 8*(1), 86-96.

Skoglund, J. (1979). Work after retirement. *Aging and Work: A Journal of Aging, Work and Retirement, 2*(2), 103-112.

Sofranko, A. J., Fliegel, F. C., & Glasgow, N. (1983). Older urban migrants in rural settings: Problems and prospects. *International Journal of Aging and Human Development, 16*, 297-309.

Soldo, B. (1983). *The elderly home care population: national prevalence rates, selected characteristics and alternative sources of assistance.* Working Paper No. 1466-9. Washington, DC: The Urban Institute.

Soldo, B., & Myllyluoma, J. (1983). Caregivers who live with dependent elderly. *The Gerontologist, 23*, 605-611.

Soldo, B. J., Wolf, D. A., & Agree, E. M. (1990). Family, households, and care arrangements of frail older women: A structural analysis. *Journal of Gerontology: Social Sciences, 45*(6), S238-249.

Solomon, K. (1990). Mental health and the elderly. In A. Monk (Ed.), *Handbook of gerontological services* (2nd. ed., pp. 228-267). New York: Columbia University Press.

Sotomayor, M. (1981). The rural elderly. In P. K. H. Kim & C. P. Wilson (Eds.), *Toward mental health of the rural elderly* (pp. 31-51). Washington DC: University Press of America.

Speake, D. L., Cowart, M. E., & Stephens, R. (1991). Health life-style practices of rural and urban elderly. *Health Values, 15*, 45-51.

Stack, C. (1974). *All our kin.* New York: Harper & Row.

Starrett, R. A., Decker, J. T., Araujo, A., & Walters, G. (1989). The Cuban elderly and their service use. *Journal of Applied Gerontology, 8*(1), 69-85.

Steinhauer, M. B. (1980). Obstacles to the mobilization and provision of services to the rural elderly. *Educational Gerontology, 5,* 399-407.

Steinmetz, S. (1977). *The cycle of violence.* New York: Praeger.

Steinmetz, S. (1978). Battered parents. *Society, 15*(5), 54-55.

Stephens, S. A., & Christianson, J. B. (1986). *Informal care of the elderly.* Lexington, MA: Lexington Books.

Stoller, E. P. (1984). Self-assessments of health by the elderly: The impact of informal assistance. *Journal of Health and Social Behavior, 25,* 260-270.

Stoller, E. P. (1992). Gender differences in the experiences of caregiving spouses. In J. W. Dwyer & R. T. Coward (Eds.), *Gender, families, and elder care* (pp. 49-64). Newbury Park, CA: Sage.

Stoller, E. P., & Earl, L. L. (1983). Help with activities of everyday life: Sources of support for the noninstitutionalized elderly. *The Gerontologist, 23,* 64-70.

Stone, R., Cafferata, G. L., & Sangl, J. (1987). Caregivers of the frail elderly: A national profile. *The Gerontologist, 27,* 616-626.

Stone, J., Cafferata, G. L., & Sangl, J. (no date). Caregivers of the frail elderly: A national profile. Washington, DC: DHHS, U.S. Public Health Service.

Storer, N. W. (1973). *Robert K. Merton: The sociology of science: Theoretical and empirical investigations.* Chicago: University of Chicago Press.

Strain, L. A. (1991). Use of health services in later life: The influence of health beliefs. *Journal of Gerontology: Social Sciences, 46,* S143-150.

Strauss, M. A., Gelles, R. J., & Steinmetz, S. K. (1980). *Behind closed doors: Violence in the American family.* Garden City, NY: Anchor Press/Doubleday.

Streeter, C., & Franklin, C. (1992). Defining and measuring social support: Guidelines for social work practitioners. *Research on Social Work Practice, 2,* 81-98.

Streets, D. W., & Nelson, G. M. (1990). *Strategic planning for population aging in North Carolina.* Unpublished. Chapel Hill, NC: Center for Aging Research and Educational Services.

Streib, G. F. (1965). Intergenerational relations: Perspectives of two generations on the older parents. *Journal of Marriage and the Family, 27,* 469-476.

Streib, G. F. (1985). Social stratification and aging. In R. H. Binstock & E. Shanas (Eds.), *Handbook of aging and the social sciences* (pp. 339-368). New York: Van Nostrand Reinhold.

Subcommittee on Health and Long-Term Care of the Select Committee on Aging, House of Representatives. (1985). *Elder abuse: A national disgrace.* Washington, DC: Government Printing Office.

Suggs, P. K. (1987). *Predictors of association among older siblings: A black/white comparison.* Paper presented at the annual scientific meeting of the Gerontological Society of America, Washington, DC.

Swan, J. H., & Benjamin, A. E. (1990). Medicare home health utilization as a function of nursing home market factors. *Health Services Research, 23,* 479-500.

Taietz, P. (1973). Structural complexity of New York State communities: Health and welfare. *Search, 2,* 1-6.

Taietz, P., & Milton, S. (1979). Rural-urban differences in the structure of services for the elderly in upstate New York counties. *Journal of Gerontology, 34* 429-437.

Taylor, R. J. (1985). The extended family as a source of support to elderly Blacks. *The Gerontologist, 25*(5), 488-495.

Taylor, R. J., & Chatters, L. M. (1988a). Church members as a source of informal social support. *Review of Religious Research, 30*(2), 193-203.

Taylor, R. J., & Chatters, L. M. (1988b). Correlates of education, income, and poverty among black aged. *The Gerontologist, 28*(4), 435-441.

Taylor, R. J., & Chatters, L. M. (1991). Nonorganizational religious participation among elderly black adults. *Journal of Gerontology: Social Sciences, 46*(2), S103-111.

Tennstedt, S. L., Sullivan, L. M., McKinley, J. B., & D'Agnostino, R. B. (1990). How important is functional status as a predictor of service use by older people? *Journal of Aging and Health, 2*(4), 439-461.

Thompson, E. B., & Sidor, J. (1991). *State housing initiatives: The 1990 compendium.* Washington, DC: Council of State Community Affairs Agencies.

Thorson, J. A., & Powell, F. C. (1992). Rural and urban elderly construe health differently. *The Journal of Psychology, 126*, 251-260.

Tobin, S. S., & Kulys, R. (1980). The family and services. *Annual Review of Gerontology and Geriatrics, 1*, 370-99.

Townsend, P. (1981). The structured dependency of the elderly: A creation of social policy in the twentieth century. *Aging and Society: The Journal of the Centre for Policy on Aging and The British Society of Gerontology, 1*(1), 5-28. New York: Cambridge University Press.

Traxler, A. J. (1986). Elder abuse laws: A survey of state statutes. In M. W. Galbraith (Ed.), *Elder abuse: Perspectives on an emerging crisis* (pp. 139-167). Kansas City, MO: Mid-America Congress on Aging.

Turner, R. J. (1983). Direct, indirect and moderating effects of social support on psychological distress and associated conditions. In H. G. Kaplan (Ed.), *Psychological stress: Trends in theory and research* (pp. 105-155). New York: Academic Press.

Turner, R. J., & Noh, S. (1988). Physical disability and depression: A longitudinal analysis. *Journal of Health and Social Behavior, 29*, 23-37.

U.S. Bureau of the Census (1980). *Census of population*, vol. 1, part 1-B. Washington, DC: Government Printing Office.

U.S. Bureau of the Census. (1983). *America in transition: An aging society.* Current Population Report No. 128. Washington, DC: Government Printing Office.

U.S. Bureau of the Census. (1991). Urban population tops 75% mark for first time. *U.S. Department of Commerce News,* Economics and Statistics Administration. CB91-334:1-3.

U.S. Congress. House. Subcommittee on Housing and Consumer Interests, Select Committee on Aging. (1987). *Dignity, independence and cost effectiveness: The success of the Congregate Housing Services Program.* Publication No. 100-650. Washington, DC: Government Printing Office.

U.S. Department of Commerce, Bureau of the Census. (1991, August). *Poverty in the United States: 1990.* Curr. Pop. Repts., Series P-6O, No. 175.

U.S. Department of Commerce, Bureau of the Census, and U.S. Department of Housing and Urban Development. (1991, July). *American housing survey for the United States in 1989.* Curr. Hous. Repts., H150/89.

U.S. Department of Health and Human Services. (1984). *1982 national long-term care survey/National survey of informal caregivers: Methods and procedures.* Washington, DC: Government Printing Office.

U.S. Department of Housing and Urban Development. (1984, December). *Technical assistance handbook for the Congregate Housing Services Program.* HUD Technical Handbook 4640.1.

U.S. Health Care Resources Administration. (1977). *The future of long-term care in the United States: The report of the task force.* Washington, DC: Government Printing Office.

U.S. National Office of Vital Statistics. (1957) *Mortality from selected causes by age, race, and sex, U.S. 1955.* Vital Statistics Special Reports National Summary No. 46, p. 5.

U.S. Senate Special Committee on Aging. (1985). *How older Americans live: An analysis of census data.* Serial No. 99-D. Washington, DC: Government Printing Office.

Vaughan, E., & Elliot, C. (1978). *Fundamentals of insurance.* New York: John Wiley.

Vienna International Plan of Action on Ageing. (1982). *Proceedings of the World Assembly on Aging, 1982.* Vienna, Austria: United Nations Center for Social Development and Humanitarian Affairs.

Wagenfeld, M. (1990). Mental health and rural America: A decade review. *Journal of Rural Health, 6,* 507-522.

Wallston, B. S., Wallston, K. A., Kaplan, G. D., & Maides, S. A. (1976). Development and validation of the health locus of control scale. *Journal of Consulting and Clinical Psychology, 44*(4), 580-585.

Wan, T. T. H., & Arling, G. (1983). Differential use of health services among disabled elderly. *Research on Aging, 5,* 411-431.

Wechsler, R., & Minkler, M. (1986) A community-oriented approach to health promotion: The Tenderloin Senior Outreach project. In K. Dychtwald (Ed.), *Wellness and health promotion for the elderly* (pp. 301-311). Rockville, MD: Aspen.

Weiler, P. G., Lubben, J. E., & Chi, I. (1987) *Evaluation of the Preventive Health Care for the Aging program.* Davis, CA: Center for Aging and Health, Department of Community Health, University of California, Davis.

Weiner, J. M. (1987). Policy issues. In J. M. Weiner (Ed.), *Swing beds: Assessing flexible health care in rural communities* (pp. 13-23). Washington, DC: The Brookings Institute.

Weinstein-Shr, G., & Henkin, N. Z. (1991). Continuity and change: Intergenerational relations in southeast Asian refugee families. *Marriage and Family Review, 16*(3 & 4), 351-367.

Weissert, W., Cready, C. M., & Pawelak, J. E. (1988). The past and future of home and community based long-term care. *Milbank Quarterly, 66*(2), 366.

Wilkinson, D. (1987). Ethnicity. In M. B. Sussman & S. K. Steinmetz (Eds.), *Handbook of marriage and the family* (pp. 183-210). New York: Plenum Press.

Wilson, L.. (1985). Jaunt, Inc. A consolidated system that works. In *Final report of the first UMTA and AOA National Conference on Transportation for the Elderly and Handicapped* (pp. 105-120). Washington, DC: UMTA, 1985.

Wilson, W. R., & Battino, R. (1987). *Long-term care alternatives: A project to develop informal caregivers for the elderly in the community.* Paper presented at the American Public Health Association meeting, New Orleans.

Wiseman, R. F. (1980). Why older people move: Theoretical issues. *Research on Aging, 2,* 141-154.

Wiseman R. F., & Roseman, C. C. (1979). A typology of elderly migration based on the decision-making process. *Economic Geography, 55,* 324-337.

Wiseman, R. F., & Virden, M. (1977). Spatial and social dimensions of intra-urban elderly migration. *Economic Geography, 53,* 1-13.

Woehrer, C. E. (1978). Cultural pluralism in American families: The influence of ethnicity on social aspects of aging. *Family Coordinator, 27,* 329-338.

Wolf, R. S., & Pillemer, K. A. (1984). *Working with abused elders: Assessment, advocacy, and intervention.* Worcester, MA: University of Massachusetts Medical Center.

Wolinsky, F. D. (1990). *Health and health behavior among elderly Americans: An age-stratification perspective.* New York: Springer.

Workers over 50: Old myths, new realities. (1985). Washington, D.C: American Association of Retired Persons.

World Health Organization. (1984). Health promotion: A World Health Organization discussion document on the concept and principles. *Canadian Public Health Association Digest, 8*(6), 101-102.

Wright, J. S., & Jablonski, A. R. (1987). The rural-urban distinction of health professionals in Georgia. *Journal of Rural Health, 3,* 53-70.

Yin, P. (1985). *Victimization and the aged.* Springfield, IL: Charles C Thomas.

Yu, E. S. H. (1986). Health of the Chinese elderly in America. *Research on Aging, 8*(1), 84-109.

Zopf, P. E., Jr. (1986). *America's older population.* Houston, TX: Cap and Gown Press.

Zuckerman, H., & Merton, R. K. (1973). Age, aging and age structure in science. In N. W. Storer (Ed.), *Robert Merton: The sociology of science: Theoretical and empirical investigations* (pp. 496-559). Chicago: University of Chicago Press.

Index

About the Contributors

Joseph N. Belden is Deputy Executive Director of the Housing Assistance Council (HAC), a Washington, DC-based nonprofit working to create more affordable rural housing. Previously at HAC, he served as Associate Director for Program Development and Senior Research Specialist. He also has worked on Capitol Hill and for the Social Policy, the National Center for Economic Alternatives, the Office of Technology Assessment, the National Conference of State Legislatures, and other agencies and groups. He is principal author of *Dirt Rich, Dirt Poor: America's Food and Farm Crisis* and also is author of a number of articles and reports on housing, poverty, aging, agriculture, welfare policy, and rural issues. He holds a B.A. degree from the University of Texas and a J.D. from the Baylor University Law School, and he is a member of the District of Columbia and Texas bar associations.

C. Neil Bull graduated from the University of Oregon in 1971 with a Ph.D. in sociology and immediately joined the faculty in the Sociology Department at the University of Missouri–Kansas City. In 1976 he was promoted to Associate Professor and took over as chair of the department for the next 6 years, and he was promoted to Full Professor in 1992. In May 1992 he became Associate Dean of the College of Arts and Sciences. His area of research interest is that of social gerontology, with specific focus on the rural elderly and the role of the older volunteer in our modern society. At the Center of Aging Studies he spent 3 years as Co-Director of a Kellogg Foundation grant, where he helped in the coordination of the Center on Rural Elderly. Also, through a second grant from the Administration on Aging, he directed, as principal investigator, a second center—The National Resource Center for Rural Elderly. From these experiences he has been able to write or edit several books—among them, *The Older Volunteer: An Annotated Bibliography* and a co-edited book, *Health Services for Rural Elderly*, both scheduled to appear in 1993.

Henry J. Camp serves as Professor and Head of the Department of Sociology and Criminal Justice at the University of Northern Florida, Jacksonville. He received his M.A. and Ph.D. degrees in sociology from the University of Nebraska-Lincoln and taught in the Department of Sociology, Anthropology, and Social Work at Kansas State University from 1971 through 1991. He has authored several articles and book chapters on rural development and rural aging issues. He has also been the recipient of several research and service grants focusing on rural community development and community service.

Neena L. Chappell has a Ph.D. in sociology and was founding Director of the Research Center on Aging at the University of Manitoba, now in its 10th year. She has published extensively in the gerontology area, including three books and over 100 articles in refereed journals, chapters in books, and governmental and agency reports. The focus of her research is in the area of informal support, health care, and social policy for seniors. She is particularly successful in attracting funds and receives numerous speaking invitations. She has received many awards, both for her research and for her outreach to ensure that research is applied. She is Director of the Center on Aging at the University of Victoria.

William B. Clifford, Professor of Sociology and Associate Head of the Department of Sociology and Anthropology at North Carolina State University, received his undergraduate education at Grove City College and his Ph.D. from the University of Kentucky. His specialties are in applied sociology, demography, and human ecology. He has published articles on fertility behavior, ecological variations in cause-specific mortality, and the demography of the elderly in such journals as *Rural*

Sociology, Demography, Social Biology, Journal of Rural Health, Social Science and Medicine, Journal of Gerontology, Research on Aging, and *Journal of Aging and Human Development.* He is currently involved in research on population trends in North Carolina and the sociology of natural resources and the environment.

Raymond T. Coward, M.S.W., Ph.D., is Professor of Medicine and Affiliate Professor of Sociology at the University of Florida, where he is also Director of the Center on Rural Health and Aging and Associate Director of the Institute for Health Policy Research. He was the founding editor of *The Journal of Rural Health* and currently serves on the editorial boards of *The Gerontologist* and *The Journal of Applied Gerontology.* In 1991, he was named a "Distinguished Alumni" of Purdue University and in that same year received the "President's Award" from the National Rural Health Association. He is co-editor of *The Family in Rural Society* (with William M. Smith, Jr.), *Family Services: Issues and Opportunities in Contemporary Rural America* (with William M. Smith, Jr.), *The Elderly in Rural Society: Every Fourth Elder* (with Gary R. Lee), and *Emerging Issues in the Delivery of Rural Health Services* (with Sam M. Cordes).

Jeffrey W. Dwyer, Ph.D., is Associate Professor in the College of Nursing and Associate Research Scientist in the Institute for Health Policy Research and the Center on Rural Health and Aging at the University of Florida. In 1992 he was named a Brookdale National Fellow. In 1990 and 1991, he was selected as the "Graduate Faculty Teacher of the Year" in the UF College of Nursing. Currently, his research is concentrated in the areas of family caregiving, health and aging, the impact of social structure on health outcomes, health policy, and the education of health professionals.

In 1990, Dwyer was guest editor (with Raymond T. Coward and Michael K. Miller) of the "decade review" issue of *The Journal of Rural Health.* He is also co-editor (with Raymond T. Coward) of *Gender, Families, and Elder Care.*

Lucy Rose Fischer, Ph.D., was Senior Research Scientist at Wilder Research Center. Her most recent book is *Older Volunteers: A Guide to Research and Practice* (Sage, 1993). She is also the author of *Linked Lives: Adult Daughters and Their Mothers* (translated into German,

1991) and *Older Minnesotans: What Do They Need? How Do They Contribute?* and has written numerous professional articles and research reports on intergenerational family relationships, informal caregiving, paid home care, and volunteering. She has been on the faculties of the University of Minnesota and St. Olaf College and is a Fellow of the Gerontological Society of America. She is now with Group Health Foundation of Minneapolis.

William H. Haas III, received his Ph.D. in 1980 from the University of Florida. He was granted a certificate in gerontology the same year from the Center for Gerontological Studies at the same university. He is Associate Professor in the Department of Sociology, was director of the Gerontology Program, and was one of the charter faculty members of the Center for Creative Retirement at the University of North Carolina at Asheville. His gerontology research has centered largely on the impact of retirement migration on local economy and health care in rural communities. In 1990 he edited a special issue of the *Journal of Applied Gerontology* on this and related topics. For 4 years in the mid-1980s he was Research Assistant Professor of Family Medicine in the College of Medicine at the University of North Carolina at Chapel Hill. His research in medical sociology has focused primarily on the relationship between physicians and physician assistants; it is published in *The New England Journal of Medicine*.

Betty Havens was appointed Provincial Gerontologist of Manitoba in 1982 and Acting Assistant Deputy Minister of Community Health Services Division in 1990. In 1991, she was named Assistant Deputy Minister of the Continuing Care Programs Division of the Department of Health. Prior to these appointments, for 10 years, she was Director of Research and Planning for the Manitoba Department of Health. Her contribution to the field of health care and aging encompasses her work as a civil servant, a researcher, and a teacher. Her most important contribution to research has been the development and maintenance of the Aging in Manitoba data sets. This longitudinal data base was begun in 1971 and now contains interview data on over 9,000 older Manitobans. It is widely recognized as one of the most comprehensive social-psychological sources of data on aging and the health of aging persons. In recognition of her understanding of health care and aging issues, Havens has been invited to serve as a consultant and/or expert by the United Nations, World Health Organization, PAHO, International Institute on Aging, and various universities and governments in Canada, the United States, and Europe.

David R. Johnson is Professor of Sociology at the University of Nebraska-Lincoln. He received his Ph.D. in sociology from Vanderbilt University in 1972. He has authored or co-authored more than 40 articles and chapters in books and has been investigator on a number of federal research grants. His recent research interests include the methodology of panel analysis, marital instability over the life course, the impact of economics on mental health, and rural mental health.

Marvin A. Kaiser serves as Associate Dean of the College of Arts and Sciences, Director of the Kansas Center for Rural Initiatives, and Professor in the Department of Sociology, Anthropology and Social Work at Kansas State University, Manhattan. He received his Ph.D. in sociology from the University of Nebraska-Lincoln. He has served as a staff consultant to the House Select Committee on Aging, the U.S. House of Representatives, the U.S. Agency for International Development, and the United Nations Office at Vienna, Center for Social Development and Humanitarian Affairs. He is the author of articles, book chapters, and monographs on rural and international aging. He has worked with the United Nations to prepare background papers for the development of the Banyan Fund, the Second Review, and Appraisal of the Vienna International Plan of Action on Ageing and the Setting of Global Targets and National Priorities for Target Setting for the Decade 1992-2001. He serves as a consultant to a United Nations-sponsored research project on the developmental implications of population aging in least developed countries.

Mary R. Kihl is currently Professor of Community and Regional Planning and Associate Director of the Design Research Institute of Iowa State University. Prior to coming to Iowa State in 1980, she taught at the University of Nebraska and at the University of Pittsburgh at Johnstown where she also directed the Center for Appalachian Regional Studies. She received her AB degree from Juniata College, Huntingdon, Pennsylvania in 1963, an M.A. degree from the University of Michigan in 1964, a Ph.D. from Pennsylvania State University in 1968, and an MURP degree from the University of Pittsburgh in 1977. She serves on several committees of the Transportation Research Board of the National Academy of Sciences, including the Committee on Rural and

Intercity Bus, Economic and Social Factors and Land Use and Transportation, and is a member of the Transportation Division of the American Planning Association. She has written extensively on subjects related to rural transportation for the *Transportation Research Record* and the *Transportation Quarterly* and is joint author of a book entitled *Impacts of Deregulation on Small Communities*. Her current research, sponsored by the Midwest Transportation Research Center based at Iowa State University, includes a study of the impact of the Americans with Disabilities Act on coordinated public transit.

Vira R. Kivett is Professor in the Department of Human Development and Family Studies, School of Human Environmental Sciences, the University of North Carolina at Greensboro. She holds a joint appointment with the North Carolina Agricultural Research Service, North Carolina State University, Raleigh. Her research has focused on the kin relations and supports of older rural adults, and she has studied select groups of the rural elderly—such as widows, African Americans, men, fathers, affinal kin, grandmothers, grandfathers, and the very-old. Her teaching is in the areas of families of later life, research methodology, and family analyses. She has conducted both longitudinal and cross-sectional studies of older rural adults. Other than kin structure and function, this research also has focused on the characteristics and needs of adults aging in largely rural, underserved areas. These data have served as background support for policy and programs at the local, regional, and national levels. Her current research focuses on the kin relations and support of older adults relocating away from family in retirement and the implications for individuals, families, and local service providers.

Beverly Kyle is Director of the Gerontology Branch, Manitoba Health. Prior to joining Manitoba Health in 1984, she was a Senior Center Director for 7 years with Age and Opportunity, a citywide nonprofit agency delivering services to the well-elderly. In 1984, she became Program Coordinator for the Support Services to Seniors Program, a new initiative to work with communities to develop a range of services aimed at maintaining the independence of seniors living in the community. The program now funds 160 projects throughout Manitoba. In her capacity as Director of the Gerontology Branch, she has responsibility for providing program and policy consultation on issues related to maintaining the health and independent functioning of seniors in the community. Her involvement in the community includes teaching in the Advanced Certificate in Gerontology through the University of Manitoba as well as sitting on the boards or advisory committees for the Center on Aging at the University of Manitoba, Winnipeg Municipal Hospital, Community Therapy Services, and Tache Nursing Home.

Gary R. Lee received his Ph.D. from the University of Minnesota in 1973. He is currently Professor of Sociology at the University of Florida and Research Scientist with the Center on Rural Health and Aging. His research interests involve both family sociology and the sociology of aging and concentrate particularly on the intersection of those two fields. His recent research has involved marital happiness in later life and rural-urban differences in the availability of adult children as caregivers for the frail elderly. He is the author of *Family Structure and Interaction: A Comparative Analysis* and *Family Systems in America* (with Ira L. Reiss). He is also co-editor (with Raymond T. Coward) of *The Elderly in Rural Society: Every Fourth Elder.*

J. Michael Leibowitz did his undergraduate work at New York University and his graduate work at the University of Maryland, receiving his master's degree in general psychology in 1972 and a Ph.D. in clinical psychology in 1974. He worked at the Johns Hopkins School of Medicine at the Kennedy Institute for 6 years before coming to Nebraska in 1974. He came to the Meyer Rehabilitation Institute of the University of Nebraska Medical Center as Director of Psychology and to the Department of Pediatrics as Director of Pediatric Psychology and Assistant Professor of Medical Psychology. He is currently Deputy Director of MRI and Associate Professor of Medical Psychology, Department of Pediatrics. He is also Section Chief for Rehabilitation Medicine in the Department of Pediatrics.

Stephen C. Lilley attended Louisiana Tech and received graduate degrees in sociology and demography from the University of Georgia. Prior to coming to North Carolina, he was Assistant Professor in the Department of Agricultural Economics and Rural Sociology at Clemson University. Currently he is Associate Professor and Extension Specialist in North Carolina State University's Department of Sociology and Anthropology. He has extension responsibilities in the areas of applied demography, needs assessment, and program evaluation. Working with other agencies and organizations across the state, he helped establish the Business/Industry Data Center in North Carolina and is currently affiliated with the North Carolina State Data Center, a consortium of county and municipal governments, universities, and chambers of commerce focused on providing demographic data and analyses. His research work has been centered on the demography of North Carolina, rural development, and social changes in agriculture. He has been co-director of the NC Farm and Rural Life Study and is currently working on an assessment of rural labor markets and economic development in North Carolina.

Charles F. Longino, Jr. became Wake Forest Distinguished Professor of Sociology and Public Health Sciences at Wake Forest University in 1991. He is Associate Director of the J. Paul Sticht Center on Aging at the Bowman Gray School of Medicine and Director of the Reynolda Gerontology Program. For the previous 14 years he taught sociology at the University of Miami and served first as Director of the Center for Social Research in Aging and then as Associate Director of the Center on Adult Development and Aging. He has also taught at the Universities of Kansas, Virginia, and North Carolina earlier in his career. He received his Ph.D. from the University of North Carolina in Chapel Hill in 1967 and in the mid-1970s he was a postdoctoral fellow in the Midwest Council for Social Research in Aging. He has authored or co-authored 93 journal articles and chapters and 10 books, monographs or compendia. Since 1975, his research has been continuously funded by either the National Institute on Aging, the Social Security Administration, or the AARP-Andrus Foundation. He is currently North American Chair of the International Association of Gerontology and serves on the editorial boards of several gerontology journals.

Karin S. Lunt is presently working in Madison, Wisconsin. Prior to this, she was Project Coordinator for the Meyer Rehabilitation Institute evaluation team (University of Nebraska Medical Center) in the project "Transitioning Rural Senior Centers into Community Focal Points." In addition, she has served as Project Assistant for the Nebraska Center for Rural Health and Research, also based at the University of Nebraska Medical Center. She holds a BS degree in the social sciences from the University of Wyoming.

John W. McClain, Jr., is Associate Professor of Pediatrics and Director of Social Work at Meyer Rehabilitation Institute of the University of Nebraska Medical Center in Omaha. He is also a member of the faculty of the Gerontology Department at the University of Nebraska at Omaha. Prior to this, McClain was Associate Director of the Southeastern New England Long-Term Care Gerontology Center administered by the Brown University Program in Medicine in Providence, Rhode Island. He holds a BA from Colby College, an M.A. (sociology) from Brown University, an MSW from Boston College, and a Ph.D. from Brandeis University. Among his present accomplishments, McClain is a co-author of the Nebraska State Plan for Aging Individuals with Developmental Disabilities.

Martha J. Metroka is a doctoral student at the University of Nebraska-Lincoln. She received her master's degree from the University of Nebraska-Lincoln in 1992. Her research interests are marriage and the family, sex and gender, mental health, and social psychology.

Gary M. Nelson received his D.S.W. from the University of California at Berkeley, where his emphasis was in aging, social policy, and planning. He has taught at the University of Hawaii at Manoa and currently is Associate Professor and Director of the Center for Aging Research and Educational Services (CARES) at the School of Social Work, University of North Carolina at Chapel Hill. His research interests are in the areas of aging policy and planning, long-term care, and rural aging.

Suzanne T. Ortega is Associate Professor of Sociology at the University of Nebraska-Lincoln. Her most recent research has focused on the social psychological consequences of aging, social support and minority aging, and mental health issues among rural, older, and economically disadvantaged populations. In addition to papers appearing in edited collections, her work has been published in journals such as *American Journal of Sociology*, *Social Science Quarterly*, *Criminology*, and *Journal of Family Issues*.

Margaret J. Penning has completed her Ph.D. in sociology. She is also Research Associate at the Center on Aging, University of Manitoba, Winnipeg. Her research interests and activities are in the areas of self-care and preventive health behavior among older adults, health promotion, and the roles of both informal and formal networks for the provision of support to older adults.

Novella Perrin is Professor of Sociology and Director of the CMSU Gerontology Institute at Central Missouri State University in Warrensburg. She earned her doctorate in sociology from the University of Kansas. A member of many national, regional, and state professional organizations, she has most recently served as Chair of the Research Committee on Rural Aging for the American Sociological Association, Member of the National Eldercare Institute on Human Resources Advisory Board, Regional Representative for the American Society on Aging, Board Member of the Mid-America Congress on Aging, and Chair of the Minority Scholars Committee of the Midwest Sociological Society. She has also served as a consultant to long-term care facilities and is a frequent workshop presenter in the areas of elder abuse, quality of life issues, psychosocial aspects of aging, and long-term care problems and solutions. Her publications include articles in professional journals and several books covering a wide range of topics. For the past 4 years, she has served as Executive Director of Sigma Phi Omega (the national honor society in gerontology) and recently has assumed the position of Executive Officer for the Sociological Practice Association.

Stephen B. Plumer received his Ph.D. from Syracuse University, his M.S. from Columbia University, and his B.A. from Brooklyn College. He has had extensive experience in the development of client-centered delivery systems for human service organizations. During the past several years he has developed market-driven, customer-centered, quality services for older people. At the present time, he is working with B'nai B'rith to develop a national program of products and services for older people and their adult children.

F. C. (Chuck) Powell, Ph.D., is Senior Community Services Associate and Associate Professor, Department of Gerontology, University of Nebraska at Omaha, and Fellow of the Graduate College of the University of Nebraska. A political scientist, he has conducted numerous studies of health status among the aged, perceptions of health well-being, satisfaction with services, and voting behavior of the elderly. He has served as a consultant to the National Resource Center for Rural Elderly and the U.S. Administration on Aging.

Eloise Rathbone-McCuan, Ph.D., is Associate Chief of Social Work Service for Research at the Colmery-O'Neil V.A. Medical Center in Topeka, Kansas. She has adjunct appointments as Professor of Social

Welfare at the University of Kansas and Professor of Family Studies at Kansas State University. As a consultant to the National Resource Center for Rural Elderly, she has written in the area of rural mental health service development. Her publications in the field of aging and mental health cover topics such as the mental health of older women, intergenerational family counseling, integration of rural health and mental health services, and self-neglect among elderly protective-service cases. Rathbone-McCuan is a Fellow of the Geriatric Society of America and currently serves on the Aging Subcommittee of the National Association of Social Workers.

Mary Anne P. Salmon received her Ph.D. in sociology from the University of North Carolina at Chapel Hill, where her emphasis was in aging/demography. Since that time she has worked in applied social research at her alma mater. After gaining experience with national survey research as coordinator of two major smoking-cessation projects with Health Services Research Center—where she was also active in the research group for aging, disablement, and long-term care—she came to the Center for Aging Research and Educational Services (CARES) at its inception. At CARES, her research foci have been the human services work force serving older adults, rural services, and service-equity issues.

James A. Thorson, EdD, is Jakob Isaacson Professor and Chairman, Department of Gerontology, University of Nebraska at Omaha. He is also Professor of Vocational and Adult Education, University of Nebraska-Lincoln, and a Fellow of the Gerontological Society of America. His publications have been in the areas of educational gerontology, attitudes toward aging and attitudes toward death, meanings of death and religiosity, humor, and lethal behaviors. He has served as a consultant to the U.S. Administration of Aging, the National Council on Aging, and the National Resource Center for Rural Elderly.